Foreword

The *Hidden Places* is a collection of easy to use travel guides taking you in this instance on a relaxed but informative tour of Lancashire, Cheshire and the Isle of Man . **Lancashire** is a county, which has lakes, woods, rolling hills, a sandy coastline and many picturesque towns and villages. **Cheshire** is a county of scenic contrasts. To the east are high moorlands and crags, to the west are the soft red sandstone plains of the Mersey and Dee, whilst to the south may be found a rich, pastoral landscape. Visitors to both counties will certainly find evidence of the significant contributions they have made to England's industrial, political, social and cultural heritage. **The Isle of Man** is blessed with beautiful scenery, sandy beaches, a very intersesting heritage and lively seaside resorts. Lancashire, Cheshire and the Isle of Man are definitely worth a visit!

The covers and pages of the *Hidden Places* series have been comprehensively redesigned and this edition of *The Hidden Places of Lancashire & Cheshire including the Isle of Man* is the first title to be published in the new format. All *Hidden Places* titles will now be published in this new style which ensures that readers can properly appreciate the attractive scenery and impressive places of interest in Lancashire, Cheshire and the Isle of Man and, of course, throughout the rest of the British Isles.

Our books contain a wealth of interesting information on the history, the countryside, the towns and villages and the more established places of interest. But they also promote the more secluded and little known visitor attractions and places to stay, eat and drink many of which are easy to miss unless you know exactly where you are going.

We include hotels, inns, restaurants, public houses, teashops, various types of accommodation, historic houses, museums, gardens and many other attractions throughout the area, all of which are comprehensively indexed. Most places are accompanied by an attractive photograph and are easily located by using the map at the beginning of each chapter. We do not award merit marks or rankings but concentrate on describing the more interesting, unusual or unique features of each place with the aim of making the reader's stay in the local area an enjoyable and stimulating experience.

Whether you are visiting the area for business or pleasure or in fact are living in the counties we do hope that you enjoy reading and using this book. We are always interested in what readers think of places covered (or not covered) in our guides so please do not hesitate to use the reader reaction forms provided to give us your considered comments. We also welcome any general comments which will help us improve the guides themselves. Finally if you are planning to visit any other corner of the British Isles we would like to refer you to the list of other Travel Publishing titles to be found at the rear of the book and to the Travel Publishing website at www.travelpublishing.co.uk.

Travel Publishing

D0302181

Contents

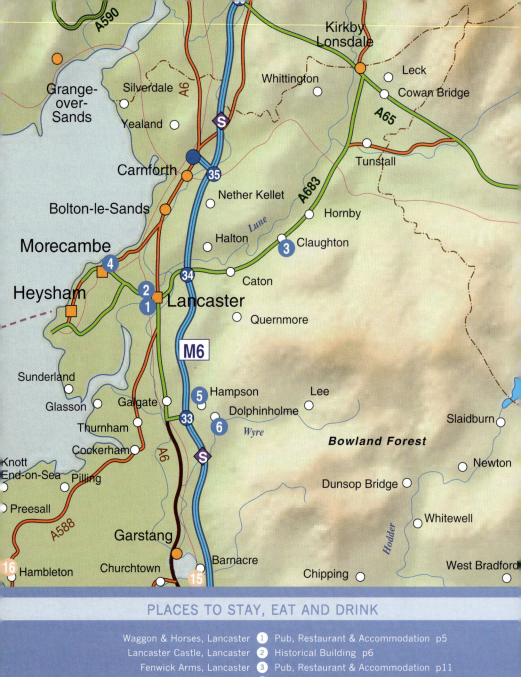

PLACES TO STAY, EAT AND DRINK

⬤ Denotes entries in other chapters

1 North Lancashire & Forest of Bowland

As the well-known Lancashire comedian, Les Dawson, commented in his book on the county, it is "many things to many people" with "vast smoky grey blocks of heavy industry" but also a countryside of "lakes and woods and rolling hills". It is also a place of great history: the Wars of the Roses; the old Catholic families and their support of Charles I during the Civil War; the trials of the Pendle Witches; and the innovators that started the Industrial Revolution in the textile industry.

The county of Lancashire is known to many people but, perhaps, more than any other area in the country it has suffered from cliché images of its landscape and people: the harsh life of the mill towns and the brashness of Blackpool. Before the reorganization of the county boundaries in 1974, this large area also included Liverpool and Manchester in the south and the Furness Peninsula to the north. Though each, with their own distinctive character, were lost, the "Red Rose" county, which has put many a king on the throne of England, has much more besides.

The ancient county town of Lancaster, in the north, is an excellent place to start any journey of discovery. With a variety of museums and a wealth of interesting buildings, the life of Lancastrians through the ages is mapped out for any visitor to explore. Small and compact, it has the added advantage of having been off the general tourist routes which can make its larger, "White Rose" equivalent, somewhat hard going

Bleadale, Lancashire

in the height of the season.

To the northeast lies Leck Fell, just south of Kirkby Lonsdale and Cumbria. It is easy for the visitor to mistake this for the Yorkshire Dales as there is a typical craggy limestone gorge along the little valley of Leck Beck, as well as one of the most extensive cave systems in the British Isles for the experienced potholer to explore. A natural route from Kirkby Lonsdale back to the county town is marked by the River Lune. For those who like walking, the best way to enjoy this wonderful green and hilly area of Lancashire is to follow the **Lune Valley Ramble** which travels the valley's intimate pastoral setting, through woodland, meadows, and along the riverside itself.

To the west of Lancashire lies Morecambe Bay, a treacherous place where, over the centuries, many walkers have lost their lives in an attempt to make the journey to the Furness Peninsula in Cumbria considerably shorter. Walks across the sands, at low tide, should only be undertaken with the aid of one of the highly knowledgeable and experienced guides. However, despite its grim history, the bay offers superb views, including glorious sunsets, as well as being an important habitat for a wide variety of birds.

Extending across much of the north of the county is the Forest of Bowland, an ancient royal hunting ground that is dotted with small, isolated villages. With no major roads passing through the area, it has remained little changed and,

with so many splendid walks and fine countryside, it is also relatively quiet even during the busiest summer weeks.

Lancaster

An architecturally pleasing city, Lancaster is one of the most appealing of English county capitals. Most of the county's administrative offices are now based in Preston so Lancaster enjoys all the prestige of being the capital without the burden of housing the accompanying bureaucrats. (The city also takes pride in the fact that the Duke of Lancaster is the only duke in the kingdom who is a woman – no less a personage than H.M. the Queen for whom the dukedom is one of many subsidiary titles).

Lancaster's story begins some 2000 years ago when the Romans built a fort on a hill overlooking a sweep of the River Lune, a site now occupied by the unspoiled 15th century **Priory Church of St Mary.** Right up until the Industrial Revolution, Lancashire was one of the poorest counties in England, lacking the wealth to endow glorious cathedrals or magnificent parish churches. St Mary's is a notable exception, the finest medieval church in the county. It stands on the site of Lancashire's first monastery which was closed not, like most others, by Henry VIII, but by Henry V in 1413. Henry was at war with France, the monastery's mother abbey was at Sées in Normandy, so the 'alien priory' in Lancaster had to be dissolved. The

Wagon & Horses

27 St George's Quay, Lancaster,
Lancashire LA1 1RD
Tel: 01524 846094
e-mail:
davehorner@42oxfordstreet.freeserve.co.uk

Ideally located on St George's Quay, right by the riverbank and with outside seating on the Embankment where you can watch the river traffic passing by, the **Wagon & Horses** is a real gem of a pub and guest house. Much of the inn's success is due to its owners, Dave Horner, a great extrovert with a wonderful sense of humour, and his charming wife, Natalie. Regular

Another major attraction is the excellent

food on offer, appetising fare prepared from only the very best and freshest produce. At present, the restaurant serves only lunch but there are plans to extend the building and the new restaurant will be serving food throughout the day. On the bar side, there's a full range of local and imported beers, spirits and wines, along with a choice of hand-pulled ales. The new building will also extend the accommodation available which at present offers a mix of family and double rooms, all with en suite facilities.

Regular entertainment includes Jazz and Blues evenings. St George's Quay is a fascinating part of the city. The great stone warehouses were once busy with cargoes of mahogany, tobacco, rum and sugar from the West Indies, taxes on which were paid at the imposing Custom House which is now an award-winning maritime museum.

present church contains treasures rescued from the closed priory such as the sumptuously carved wooden choir stalls from around 1345.

Each stall is covered by a superb canopy, lavishly carved with around a hundred small heads and faces surrounded by abundant foliage. Also of note are the fragments of Anglo-Saxon crosses and some very fine needlework. The **Priory Tower**, also on the hilltop, was rebuilt in 1759 as a landmark for ships navigating their way into the River Lune. Nearby is one of Lancaster's links with its Roman past – the remains of a bath house which also served soldiers as an inn.

Close by is **Lancaster Castle,** one of the best-preserved Norman fortresses in the country. Dating back to 1200 and with a massive gatehouse flanked by sturdy twin towers, the castle dominates the centre of the city. For centuries, the castle served as a prison, only relinquishing that function as recently as 1996. At the back of the castle, the **Shire Hall** is still in use as a Crown Court and one of its more macabre attractions is the Drop Room where prisoners were prepared for the gallows. The Court's long history has been blemished by two shocking major miscarriages of justice. The first was in 1612 when the Pendle "witches" (see Chapter 4) were convicted of sorcery and executed; the second in 1975 when the "Birmingham Six" were found guilty of an IRA bombing and spent 15 years in prison before their

LANCASTER CASTLE

c/o P O Box 26, County Hall,
Preston PR1 8RE
Tel: 01524 64998 Fax: 01524 847914
website: www.lancashire.gov.uk/resources/
ps/castle/index.htm

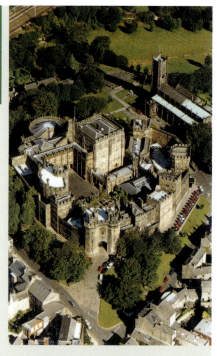

Lancaster Castle is owned by Her Majesty the Queen in right of her Duchy of Lancaster. For most of its history the castle has been the centre of law and order for the county, and this magnificent building is still in use as a prison and a crown court.

The castle has dominated the town for almost 1000 years, ever since it was first established in 1093. But the hill on which it stands has a history which goes back a thousand years further, almost to the birth of Christ. The Romans built the first of at least three military forts on the site in AD79.

Little is known about Lancaster until 1093 when the Norman Baron, Roger of Poitou, built a small motte and bailey castle which was replaced 50 years later by a large stone Keep which still stands today as the oldest part of the Castle.

Throughout its long history it has witnessed many trials, including that of the were condemned to die; the beautiful Gillow furniture in the Grand Jury Room; the dungeons and 'Drop Room' from where the condemned went to their deaths; the Crown Court from where thousands were transported to Australia; 'Hanging Corner' the site of public hangings and the magnificent Shire Hall with its display of heraldic shields.

Criminals and convicts,

Lancashire Witches of 1612, which resulted in the execution of ten people.

Although still a working building, guided tours of the castle include where the witches monarchs and majesty, dungeons and death, treason and transportation, witches and martyrs, all have their place in the history of this most fascinating building.

names were cleared.

A short walk from the castle leads into the largely pedestrianised city centre, full of shops, the market, and much besides. The **City Museum** (free) in the Market Place occupies the Old Town Hall, built between 1781-3 by Major Jarrett and Thomas Harrison. As well as the city's art collection and an area of changing exhibitions, there are displays and collections of material illustrating aspects of the city's industrial and social history. Also here is the **Museum of the King's Own Royal Regiment**, a regiment which was based in Lancaster from 1880 onwards.

Lancaster grew up along the banks of the River Lune which is navigable as far as Skerton Bridge so there has always been a strong association between the town and its watery highway. Documents from 1297 make reference to the town's small-scale maritime trade, but it was not until the late 1600s and early 1700s that Lancaster's character as a port fully emerged. The splendid buildings of the 18th century Golden Age were born out of the port wealth, and the layout and appearance of the town was much altered by this building bonanza. Lancaster's importance as a port steadily declined throughout the 19th century so that many buildings originally intended for maritime purposes were taken over for other uses.

Lancaster enjoyed its era of greatest prosperity during the 18th century when its quays were busy servicing a thriving trade with the West Indies in rum, sugar,

cotton – and slaves. The city's rich maritime history is celebrated at St George's Quay which, with its great stone warehouses and superb Custom House, is now an award-winning **Maritime Museum**. Visitors today are given a vivid insight into the life of the mariners and quayside workers with opportunities for knot-tying and the practising of other maritime skills. Every year, over the four days of the Easter weekend, St George's Quay is home to the Lancaster Maritime Festival with a programme that involves boisterous "smugglers", sea songs, and shanties.

Fire destroyed most of Tudor and Jacobean Lancaster, but one notable survivor is the **Judge's Lodging** in Church Street, a charming Jacobean house built in the 1620s and now a museum: two museums in fact. There's the **Museum of Childhood** which includes the Barry Elder Doll collection, and the **Gillow and Town House Museum** containing many examples of the fine workmanship produced by the famous Lancaster cabinet-makers, Gillows. It was a scion of this family, Richard Gillow who designed the city's Maritime Museum.

Close by is the **Cottage Museum** in a house, built in 1739, that was divided into two dwellings in the 19th century. Furnished in the style of an artisan's house of the early to mid-19th century, the museum is open from Easter to the end of September. Just around a corner or two, in Sun Street, is the **Music Room**, an exquisite early Georgian building originally designed as a pavilion in the long vanished garden of Oliver Marton. It is notable for some superb decorative plasterwork.

Lancaster's most prominent landmark, visible for miles around, is the extravagant, temple-like Ashton Memorial – "the grandest monument in England" according to Nikolaus Pevsner. Erected in 1907 as a memorial to his wife by the local MP and millionaire lino manufacturer Lord Ashton, it stands on the highest point in Lancaster, set within a beautifully landscaped park and enjoying sweeping views of the Cumbrian hills and across Morecambe Bay. The building now houses exhibitions and multi-screen presentations about the life and times of Lord Ashton and the Edwardian period.

Williamson Park was Lord Ashton's own personal project as a means of providing work for local people during the cotton famine crisis in the textile industry during the American Civil War in the 1860s. Constructed on the site of old quarries, which gives the park its undulating contours, the park was opened in 1896. As well as the magnificent Ashton Memorial there is also a delightful Butterfly House in the now restored Edwardian Palm House and a Conservation Garden and Wildlife Pool, which opened in 1991.

Another place the whole family can enjoy is **Lancaster Leisure Park** on Wyresdale Road. Set in 42 acres of landscaped parkland, the site includes a mini marina, a Wild West adventure playground, a miniature railway, a rare breeds unit, a children's farmyard, pony rides, a gift shop, a tea garden, and a pottery shop.

North of Lancaster

Halton
3 miles NE of Lancaster off the A683

The high mound, **Castle Hill**, which rises above this ancient village on the River Lune was firstly the site of a Roman camp and later a Saxon castle. The village's parish **Church of St Wilfrid** was founded in the 7th century and although nothing survives of that original foundation there are some stone crosses, both inside the building and out, that date from the 9th century. One of them, unusually, bears both pagan and Christian symbols. Roman remains, in the form of a votive altar (where offerings were made before a military operation began), were found on the site in the late 18th century. Around the same time, a labourer tilling his allotment on Halton Moor unearthed more than 1000 coins from the reign of King Cnut (1017-35) and a gold necklace. This treasure trove is now in the British Museum.

Nether Kellet
4 miles N of Lancaster off the B6254

This farming village has a traditional village green which as well as being the central focus of the community also features several old wells and pumps. This is appropriate since the Old Norse word *chellet*, now Kellet, means "a spring". Local brewers of home ale still use the spring water because of its purity and absence of chemicals. Quarrying has taken place here for many centuries and lime burning has been an important local industry. Its remains, in the form of lime kilns, can still be seen around the village and the local pub is named the Lime Burners Arms.

The village also has its own cave, Dunold Mill, through which flows a large stream that dives underground to appear 2 miles further north at Carnforth. During the mid 1800s the cave was occupied by a hermit who lived there until his death at the age of 100. His descendants still live in the village.

Carnforth

5 miles N of Lancaster on the A6

The town lies around what was once a major crossroads on the A6 but it is, perhaps, its fame as a busy railway junction town - whose station was used as the setting for the 1940s film classic *Brief Encounter* - by which most people know Carnforth. Though the station has declined in importance – it is now an unstaffed halt – the old engine sheds and sidings are occupied by **Steamtown**, one of the

largest steam railway centres in the north of England. Visitors are likely to see such giants of the Age of Steam as the *Flying Scotsman* or an A4 Pacific being stabled here, together with a permanent collection of over 30 British and Continental steam locomotives. There are steam rides in the summer months on both standard gauge and miniature lines.

Yealand

8 miles N of Lancaster off the A6

To the south of the village lies **Leighton Hall** – a fine early 19th century house which is open to the public. During the Middle Ages the land on which it stands, together with much of the surrounding area, was owned by the d'Avranches family. Over the centuries, the house and the land passed through many hands before becoming the property of the Gillows family of Lancaster. Now in the hands of the Reynolds family, a branch of the Gillows, the fine furniture seen in the

Leighton Hall, Yealand

hall reflects the trade that made the family fortune.

As with many estates in Lancashire, Leighton Hall was a Catholic house and one owner, Sir George Middleton, was fined heavily by Cromwell after the Civil War for his loyalty to Charles I and to his religion. Later, another owner of the hall, Albert Hodgson, suffered for his loyalty to Catholicism and the Stuart claim on the throne of England. Taking part in the Jacobite rebellion of 1715, Hodgson was captured at Preston and the Government troops inflicted such damage on the hall that little remained of the Tudor structure.

The hall, today, dates from 1800 when it was built out of pale, local sandstone to the Gothic designs of Harrison, a Chester architect. One of the finest houses in the county, the views from the extensive grounds are magnificent and take in the nearby Leighton Moss Bird Reserve.

Silverdale

8 miles N of Lancaster off the A6

The village lies at the northwesternmost corner of the county and has the Lakeland hills as a backdrop as well as superb views over Morecambe Bay. The latter half of the 19th century saw Silverdale develop as a quiet seaside resort where those so inclined could take medicinal baths of fresh sea water in one of the many small villas situated along the coast. One frequent visitor was Elizabeth Gaskell who is said to have written some of her books whilst holidaying here.

However, Silverdale's history goes back well beyond the days of a genteel Victorian resort. Its name comes from a Viking family that settled here and which signifies that this was Sigward's or Soevers' valley. Fishing, naturally, was the key provider of local income but in the 18th century a copper smelting works was built here. All, however, that remains of the foundry is the chimney near **Jenny Brown's Point**, said to be named after an old woman who lived here in the 1700s.

Essentially, now a small residential village, Silverdale is well worth visiting for the network of footpaths from here that pass through the limestone woodlands that are such a joy for the botanist, being rich in wild flowers in spring – primroses, violets, orchids, bird's eye primroses, rockroses, and eglantines abound.

Leighton Moss near Silverdale is a nationally known RSPB bird sanctuary. The reed beds are the most important part of the reserve because they have become a northern stronghold of the rare bearded tit and are also the major British breeding centre for the bittern.

The Lune Valley

Caton

3 miles NE of Lancaster on the A683

Caton climbs up the hillside from the leafy glades of the Crook o'Lune, subject of one of Turner's paintings, to heather

Littledale, Lancashire

on the northern edges of the Forest of Bowland, is **Littledale**, one of Lancashire's most hidden gems. Chiefly wooded, a walk through the dale alongside Artle Beck to Littledale Hall is well worthwhile and provides a view of Lancashire that is not normally seen.

moorlands commanding a panoramic view of Morecambe Bay. A popular commuter town nowadays, in the 19th century Caton was a busy place with no fewer than eight cotton and wood-turning bobbin mills. Just to the south of the village, tucked away among the hills

Claughton
6 miles NE of Lancaster on the A683

The Old Toll House Garage on the road into this village (which is pronounced Clafton), is famous for a rather curious reason. In the 1920s the garage owner

FENWICK ARMS

Lancaster Road, Claughton, Lancaster, Lancashire LA2 GLA
Tel: 01254 221250
e-mail: steven.williams57@btopenworld.com

Conveniently located about 4 miles from Junction 34 of the M6, the **Fenwick Arms** is an attractive black and white building in the half-timbered style and well worth seeking out.

Dawn and Steven Williams bought the pub in June 2002 and set to work completely refurbishing the bars, restaurant and accommodation. Dawn is a Lancashire lass; Steven hails from Birmingham but now considers himself a naturalised Lancastrian! Together they have made the Fenwick Arms a popular social centre for the village with good cooking being one of the inn's major attractions.

Food is served all day and the menu offers between 60 and 70 different items which must be one of the largest choices available in any British pub. On top of that, there are daily and seasonal specials. All dishes are prepared from the freshest and choicest ingredients, freshly prepared to order and attractively presented. Staff seem to have been chosen for their friendly personalities and the service is both prompt and efficient.

The inn is a free house so there's a wide choice of beverages on offer – local and international beers, a regularly changing selection of guest ales and a full range of spirits, wines and soft drinks.

This is definitely a pub you'll want to return to time and time again.

painted the first white lines on the road at the nearby corner because of the many accidents that had occurred there. After much debate their value was recognised by the government of the day and from then onwards the use of white lines became accepted as a means of road marking, eventually spreading world-wide.

Hornby

9 miles NE of Lancaster on the A683

Immortalised in paint by J.M.W. Turner, the ruins of **Hornby Castle** (private) were incorporated into a picturesque mock medieval Hall in the 19th century. Perched atop a hill, the castle dominates the attractive village of Hornby. Sadly, it isn't open to the public but it's visible for miles around and there's a particularly photogenic view of it from the bridge over the River Wemming at the southern edge of the village.

The situation of this attractive village, by a bluff overlooking the valley of the River Lune, not only gives Hornby panoramic views of the surrounding countryside but also makes this a strategic position that has been utilised over the centuries. Just to the north of the village is the attractive stone-built **Loyn Bridge**, which takes the road over the River Lune and on to Gressington. Constructed in 1684, it replaced a ford. Beside the bridge is **Castle Stede**, the best example of a Norman motte and bailey castle in Lancashire.

The graceful **Church of St Margaret**

of **Antioch** dates from around 1300 when it was built as a chapel of ease to the parish church at Melling. Its unusual and impressive octagonal tower was ordered by Sir Edward Stanley, Lord Mounteagle, who made a vow before the Battle of Flodden Field in 1513 that if he returned victorious he would construct the tower in honour of his patron saint, St Margaret.

Tunstall

11 miles NE of Lancaster on the A683

The village is famous for its fine 15th century **Church of St John the Baptist**, that was known to the Brontë sisters and which is referred to in *Jane Eyre* as "Brocklebridge church". When the sisters were attending the Clergy Daughters' School at Cowan Bridge they walked the 6 mile round trip to the church each morning. After attending service, they had their mid-day meal in the room above the church porch.

Cowan Bridge

13 miles NE of Lancaster on the A65

In 1823, the Rev. William Carus Wilson, vicar of neighbouring Tunstall, opened his Clergy Daughters' School at Cowan Bridge. Amongst his early pupils were 4 daughters of the Rev Patrick Brontë of Howarth – Maria, Elizabeth, Charlotte and Emily. Charlotte immortalised the school and its austere regime in *Jane Eyre* where it appears as "Lowood". It can still be seen, though it is now part of a row of terraced cottages just north of the bridge on the A65. The school moved to Casterton in 1833.

Leck

13 miles NE of Lancaster off the A65

Over the A65 from Cowan Bridge lies the small village of Leck. To the northeast of this village lies **Green Hill**, surrounded by moorland and the highest point, at 2,060 feet, in the county. At just over three feet higher than the top of the neighbouring fell, Gragarth, it was only a recent, more accurate survey, that distinguished Green Hill as the higher. This is the most northerly part of Lancashire and from the summit there are superb views of both Cumbria and North Yorkshire, as well, of course, as Lancashire.

Whittington

12 miles NE of Lancaster on the B6254

This delightful village, in the green and sheltered valley of the River Lune, is well worth a visit. It was Wordsworth, in his *Guide to the Lakes*, who recommended that Kendal be approached via the Vale of Lune and it remains a popular place today.

West of Lancaster

Morecambe

3 miles NW of Lancaster on the A589

Featuring prominently on the Lancashire coastline, Morecambe has long been one of the most successful and popular seaside resorts in the North, and it can truly be said to enjoy one of the finest views from its promenade of any resort in England – a magnificent sweep of coastline and bay, looking across to the Lakeland mountains.

Morecambe Bay, a vast wide, flat tidal plain situated between Lancashire and Cumbria, is the home of many forms of marine life as well as being a very popular and important habitat for birds. The Rivers Lune, Kent, Keer, Leven, and Crayke create the gulleys, mud, and sandbanks that make this not only one of the most important ornithological sites in Europe but also a great source of mussels and shrimps.

The largest estuary in Britain, Morecambe Bay is noted for its rich marine and bird life, for its vast expanse of sands and mudflats – and for their treacherous nature. Over the years, many have lost their lives in the Bay's ever-shifting quicksands while attempting to make the apparently straightforward crossing from Morecambe to Grange-over-Sands on the Cumbrian coast. In medieval times, this perilous track formed part of the main west coast route from Scotland to England and at one time the monks of the Furness peninsula acted as guides to those wishing to make their way to Cumbria without taking the long overland route. Today, you can join one of the **Cross Bay Walks** led by the Queen's Guide to the Sands, Cedric Robinson who has been guiding walkers

THE TERN BAY HOTEL

43/45 Heysham Road, Morecambe LA3 1DA
Tel: 01524 421209 Fax: 01524 831925
e-mail: reservations@ternbayhotel.co.uk
website: www.ternbayhotel.co.uk

Situated only 25 yards from the sea front and Morecambe's splendidly regenerated Promenade, **The Tern Bay Hotel** is a relaxed private licensed hotel which has been comprehensively refurbished while retaining its Victorian charm. The hotel is owned and run by David Morris, Richard Higgins and Kate Hancock who between them have many years experience in the hotel industry. It was while they were working together at a hotel in Wales that they decided to buy a small hotel of their own where they could put into practice their principle of providing quality accommodation, good food and service all at reasonable prices.

The Tern Bay has 20 well-appointed bedrooms, all with en suite facilities, TV, radio and hospitality tray. At breakfast time there's a good choice that ranges from Continental to full English or vegetarian options. Evening meals are also available if ordered beforehand and consist of a 3-course table d'hôte meal prepared from the very best of local seasonal produce. Guests can relax in the well-stocked bar with its extensive range of beers, wines and spirits, or settle down in the residents dry lounge with a coffee. The hotel offers attractive rates for group bookings and is also experienced in

arranging special interest weekends. If you are arriving by ferry, the hotel is located on the main road to Heysham Port and will happily cater for late arrivals if forewarned. A secure off-road compound for motor-cycles, scooters and bikes is available and there's unrestricted parking in the immediate area.

across the Bay since 1963. Cedric is the 25th appointed guide to the sands since the original appointment in 1536. More details and times of walks can be obtained from the Tourist Information Centre (015395 34026).

Modern Morecambe is a relatively recent town that grew up as a direct result of the expansion of the railways to the north Lancashire coast. There were originally three villages, Bare, Poulton, and Torrisholme that were quiet fishing communities. In 1848 all this changed as the railways brought visitors from the textile towns of Lancashire and, especially, Yorkshire to what was jokingly called "Bradford-by-the-Sea". Hotels and boarding houses were built as well as the usual seaside amenities such as parks and promenades and soon the villages were absorbed into one thriving resort.

A lively resort, well-provided with every kind of traditional and modern holiday amusement, Morecambe has always vied with its much larger competitor to the south, Blackpool, in offering varied entertainment for its visitors. During the late 1800s, the town spent lavishly, building two grand piers, an elegant **Winter Garden**, sumptuous theatres and hotels, but the town's attempt to build a tower to rival Blackpool's was not a success. However, Morecambe did manage to introduce its Autumn Illuminations several years before Blackpool caught on to the idea.

Of the many buildings dating from Morecambe's heyday as a holiday destination, one in particular, the **Midland Hotel** stands out. Situated on the seafront, at the southern end of the promenade, the hotel, which was built in the early 1930s to designs by Oliver Hill, is concave towards the sea and convex facing inland. The elegant, sweeping balconies of the luxurious rooms remain a superb feature of the hotel and, whilst filming *Brief Encounter* at nearby Carnforth both Celia Johnson and Trevor Howard made their home here along with others working on the film.

Like other resorts, Morecambe has changed with the times and major new attractions include the multi-million pound Bubbles Leisure Park and Superdome, as well as a Wild West Theme Park. WOMAD, Morecambe's annual world music festival, attracts visitors from around the globe. There are also popular seafront illuminations in late summer, together with all the usual lively shops and variety of entertainment associated with a busy seaside resort.

But perhaps the town's most popular attraction is the **Eric Morecambe Statue** near the Stone Jetty. Few can resist the opportunity of posing in suitably one-legged fashion beside sculptor Graham Ibbeson's life-size statue. Lyrics from Eric's best-known song, *Bring Me Sunshine*, are carved into the granite steps leading up to the statue which is surrounded by flower beds and flashing lights that bring this "stage" to life even after dark.

Heysham
5 miles W of Lancaster on the A683

Southwards along the coast, Morecambe merges imperceptibly into Heysham, an ancient settlement with a quaint old main street that winds down to the shore. The town is notable for the tiny **St Patrick's Chapel** which is reckoned to be the oldest religious building in Lancashire. According to tradition, St Patrick himself built the now ruined chapel as a thanks-offering to God after surviving a shipwreck on the rocks below. Historians aren't too sure about the veracity of that legend, but there's no doubting the interest of the chapel graveyard. Hewn out of the rock are six body-shaped coffins with an incised space above them in the shape of a cross. These 8th or 9th century coffins

St Patrick's Chapel, Heysham

were originally covered by a similarly shaped slab of stone and would have been created as the final resting place for Saxon notables.

The little **Church of St Peter** on the headland below the chapel is equally interesting. It dates back to Saxon and Norman times, with an Anglo-Saxon cross on which the Madonna and other figures have been crudely carved by 9th century masons and there is a rare Viking hog-back gravestone. It is one of the oldest churches in western Europe to have been in continuous use.

Alongside these antiquities is the modern port of Heysham with regular car ferry sailings to the Isle of Man and to Northern Ireland and, of course, the two modern nuclear power stations, Heysham A and Heysham B.

Sunderland
6 miles SW of Lancaster off the A683

This is, unbelievably, an old port and seaside resort which flourished until larger-berthed ships, silting channels, and the growth in the 19th century of rail-served Morecambe caused it to decline. A little wharf, quiet cottages, some with faded and evocative elegance, a sandy shore where sea thrift flourishes among the pebbles, are all that remains. The River Lune estuary is now a Site of Special Scientific Interest because of its wildlife value – visitors are likely to see such birds as redshank feeding on the rich supplies of worms, shellfish, and shrimps on the salt marshes, while a

variety of wildfowl such as shell duck, widgeon, and mallard, are to be seen in autumn.

A particularly sad story acts as a reminder of Sunderland's time as a port. Sambo was a sea captain's servant at the time of the slave trade into Lancaster. Sambo fell ill of a fever just before the captain was setting off to the West Indies and was left in the care of an innkeeper. Sambo, believing himself abandoned, willed himself to die. Because he was not a baptised Christian, Sambo was not allowed to be buried in consecrated ground. In later years, his death and grave, marked by a simple cross and stone, became a potent local symbol of the anti-slavery cause.

His grave can be still seen, in a field at the west side of Sunderland Point. It can be reached by walking along The Lane from the village foreshore, past Upsteps Cottage, where Sambo died, and turning left at the shore then over a stile on the left which gives access to the simple gravestone. Fresh flowers are usually to be seen here, anonymously placed on the grave.

South of Lancaster

Glasson
4 miles SW of Lancaster on the B5290

A few miles south of Heysham, the river Lune pours into Morecambe Bay. On its south bank lies **Glasson Dock**, once an important commercial port for larger boats unable to negotiate the tricky river as far upstream as Lancaster. The dock was built in 1791 and the tiny lighthouse erected at the same time is still in place. The dock could accommodate 25 sea-going ships and traded extensively in slaves, rum, tobacco, sugar, and cotton. Glasson Dock today is a busy, colourful marina, serving both sea-going craft and boats arriving at the western terminus of the Lancaster Canal. Constructed in 1797, the Lancaster Canal is one of the earliest engineering marvels of the Industrial Age. *"The Lanky"*, as it's known, is a favourite with canal travellers since there's not a single lock in the whole of its 41 mile length, thanks to the ingenuity of the canal's designer, John Rennie. He accomplished his engineering tour de force by linking the level stretches with six elegant aqueducts, the most impressive of them the 5 arched **Lune Aqueduct** near Lancaster which has attracted a stream of admiring visitors ever since it was first opened in 1797.

The canal was supplemented by the arrival of a railway line in 1883. This railway, long dismantled, is now the footpath and cycle-way to Lancaster's St George's Quay.

From Glasson there is a footpath along the coast to Plover Scar, where a lighthouse guards the River Lune estuary, and further along lie the ruins of **Cockersand Abbey**. The abbey was founded in 1190 by the Premonstratensian Order on the site of a hospital that had been the home of a hermit, Hugh Garth, before becoming a colony for lepers and the infirm. The 13th century Chapter House of the abbey remains since it was a burial chapel for the Dalton family of nearby Thurnham, descendants of Sir Thomas More.

Thurnham

5 miles S of Lancaster on the A588

Just outside the village and at the end of a sweeping drive lies **Thurnham Hall**, which has been built, over the years, around a 14th century pele tower. The home of the Dalton family for 400 years, they were responsible for the Elizabethan

extensions and a fine Jacobean staircase. Still in private hands and not open to the public, although the hall has been divided up into flats, much of its original character has been retained.

Galgate

4 miles S of Lancaster on the A6

The village of Galgate wa originally located on the banks of the River Conder, which, for about half a mile, forms part of the Lancaster Canal. The village still contains some of its original mills, though they have now been put to other uses. One of them, a silk mill, was reputed to be the oldest working mill in the country, dating back to 1760, closed down in the 1960s. Galgate has a craft centre, a marina for around 100 boats

and there's a well maintained pathway that leads from the village through locks to Glasson Dock.

Dolphinholme

6 miles S of Lancaster off the A6

This small village of around 600 souls sits in the foothills of the Pennines at the edge of the Forest of Bowland. Dolphinholme was one of the first villages with a main street lit by gas. This was around 1806 and remains of the old gas holder can still be seen. A single street lamp has survived and is now fuelled by bottle gas.

Cockerham

6 miles S of Lancaster on the A588

This sleepy little village lies on the

THE FLEECE INN

Dolphinholme, on the Forest of Bowland, nr Lancaster LA2 9AQ
Tel: 01524 791233 Fax: 01524 791509
e-mail: thefleeceinn@talk21.com
website: www.thefleece.org.uk

Only a couple of miles from Junction 33 of the M6, **The Fleece Inn** is a handsome stone building dating back to the late 1700s. Originally a farmhouse, this appealing country inn stands at the crossroads of two old drovers roads, close to the Wyre Valley and the scenic Forest of Bowland. Mine hosts, Kim and John, took over here in December 2001 and very quickly made the inn a popular place for dining out. John is in charge of the kitchen and the menu reflects his aim to provide fresh locally produced food at affordable prices.

The speciality of the house is Bowland Forest Meat, lamb and beef, but you'll also find starters such as Japanese Prawns, Chicken Tikka Bites and Deep Fried Brie. Main meals offer a good choice of fish,

chicken and meat dishes and the regular menu is supplemented by daily specials. Food is served Tuesday to Sunday from noon until 2pm, and from 5pm to 8.45pm. (On Mondays, food is only served if it's a Bank Holiday). Booking for the non-smoking dining room is strongly advised on weekends and Wednesday evening which is Steak Night. To

quench your thirst, the inn stocks an extensive range of beverages that includes 4 real ales – Boddington's and Black Sheep Bitter plus 2 rotating guest ales. Quiz fans should try to arrive on Tuesday evening around 9.30pm.

shore of Morecambe Bay between the estuaries of the Lune and the Wyre. Cockerham once boasted a windmill but it was in such an exposed position that a gale in 1802 sent the sails spinning and the friction set fire to the mill. **Cockerham Hall,** (private) is a fine and rare example of a medieval timber-framed building that dates from the late 15th century. It is now a farmhouse.

East of Lancaster

Quernmore
3 miles E of Lancaster off the A683

Lying at the head of the Conder Valley, this peaceful farming village had a pottery industry as well as slate quarrying in the 17th century. The word "quern" refers to a particularly ancient form of hand-mill that was hewn from the rocks found on the nearby moorside and, indeed, corn milling continued here until World War II.

To the east of the village lies **Clougha Pike**, on the western edges of the Forest of Bowland, an Area of Outstanding Natural Beauty and one of the few places in the area that is accessible to walkers. Although it is not the highest peak in the forest – it rises to just over 1300 feet – the walk up Clougha Pike is very pleasant and offers

splendid views from the summit, not only of the Lakeland Fells but also of Morecambe Bay and, on a clear day, Blackpool Tower.

Lee
7 miles SE of Lancaster off the A6

To the northwest of this typical Bowland village soars the highest summit in the forest, **Ward's Stone**. Dotted with outcrops of gritstone boulders, the top of the fell is marked by two triangulation pillars: one of which is just over three feet higher than the other though, on first inspection, they look the same height. The panoramic views from this point are magnificent and, to the north and east, the Three Peaks of Yorkshire can be seen whilst the Lakeland fells roll away to the northwest.

Forest of Bowland
8 miles SE of Lancaster

Designated an Area of Outstanding Natural Beauty in February 1964, this large scenic area is a veritable paradise

Newton Fells, Forest of Bowland

Celtic Cross, Trough of Bowland

by marriage, they came into the hands of the Earls of Lancaster and in 1399, when the then Duke of Lancaster ascended the throne as Henry IV, Bowland finally became one of nearly a hundred royal hunting forests.

The remains of a Roman road can be clearly seen traversing the land and many of the village's names in this area date back to the Saxon period. Perhaps the most celebrated of the many routes across Bowland is the minor road from Lancaster to Clitheroe which crosses **Abbeydale Moor** and the **Trough of Bowland** before descending into the lovely Hodder Valley around Dunsop Bridge. This is a popular route in the summer months, with most lay-bys and parking places filled as people pause to take in the breathtaking moorland views.

for walkers and country lovers and is dotted with picturesque villages. The 11th largest of such designated areas, the Forest of Bowland is something of a misnomer, the term 'forest' is derived from the Latin 'foris' which was formerly used to denote a royal hunting ground, an unenclosed tract of land, rather than a distinct wooded area. In fact, even this description is not entirely correct. Throughout the 11th century the area was a "chase" – a private rather than a royal hunting ground. Before 1066, the broad acres of Bowland were the personal property of Earl Tostig of Northumbria, a brother of King Harold. Banished from his earldom, Tostig, with the help of the King of Norway, attempted to regain his lands and both he and the Norwegian king were killed at Stamford Bridge, just weeks before the fateful Battle of Hastings.

Following the Norman Conquest, Bowland became part of the Honour of Clitheroe and the vast estates that belonged to the de Lacy family. In time,

Slaidburn
15 miles SE of Lancaster on the B6478

This pretty village of stone cottages and cobbled pavements lies in the heart of the Forest of Bowland. The village's focal point is the 13th century public house **Hark to Bounty**. The inn was originally named The Dog but one day in 1875 the local Hunt gathered here. A visiting Squire, listening to the hounds giving voice outside, clearly distinguished the tones of his own favourite hound rising above the others. His exclamation of delight, "Hark to Bounty!" was so whole-hearted that the landlord changed the name of his pub on the spot.

The inn also contains an old courtroom, with its original oak furnishings, where from around 1250 the Chief Court of Bowland, or Halmote, was held. The only courtroom between York and Lancaster, it was used by visiting justices from the 14th century onwards, is said to have also been used by Oliver Cromwell when he was in the area, and continued in use right up until 1937.

From the village, a network of beautiful, little used lanes radiate westwards up into the fell country with some of the best walking that Lancashire has to offer. One walk in particular that offers solitude as well as excellent views of the Bowland landscape, leads to the lonely valley of the River Whitendale, northwest of the village. To the northeast of Slaidburn lies Stocks Reservoir, another popular walker's destination. Beneath its waters lie the remains of 20-odd dwellings that made up the hamlet of Stocks-in-Bolland. They were submerged in 1925 but in very dry summers the remains of the old Chapel bridge can be seen where it crosses the original Hodder river, along with the foundations of houses.

Bolton by Bowland
21 miles SE of Lancaster off the

A59

Lying alongside a "bow", or bend, in the River Ribble this tranquil village with its two ancient green, stone cross and old stocks, lies on the southern edge of the forest area. Part of the Bolton Hall estate, the village has been protected from insensitive development – the most recent dwelling to be built is already more than a hundred years old. The 15th century village Church of St Peter & St Paul is home to the famous **Pudsey Tomb** with its engraved figure of Sir Ralph Pudsey in full armour alongside figures of his three wives and their 25 children. In the folds of each lady's gown is inscribed with a Roman numeral indicating how many children she bore – respectively six, two and 17.

Newton
15 miles SE of Lancaster on the B6478

Little more than a hamlet, Newton lies on the main route between Clitheroe and Lancaster and so, in their time, both John Paslew, the last abbot of Whalley, and the Pendle witches passed through on their way to trial in Lancaster. Here also is a **Quaker Meeting House** that was founded in 1767: the associated Quaker school, where the 19th century reformer John Bright was a pupil, has long since gone. Regarded with great suspicion by the Church of England, and by other nonconformists, because of their unorthodox views and their informality, the Quakers sought to settle

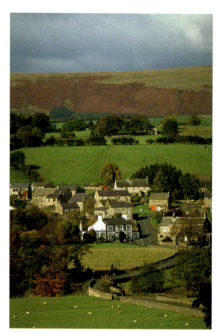

Newton Village

Ordnance Survey, lies near Whitendale Hanging Stones and, to confirm the claim, the explorer Sir Ranolph Fiennes unveiled a commemorative plaque here. British Telecommunications have also offered the village a unique honour by putting their 100,000th phone box here.

St Hubert's Roman Catholic Church on Lancaster Road has an unusual provenance. It was built by the Towneley family when their racehorse Kettledrum won the 1861 Derby. The family spent a further £1000 on the huge white angel that stands in the graveyard and commemorates Richard Henry Towneley.

Whitewell

15 miles SE of Lancaster off the B6478

Little more than a hamlet in the heart of the Forest of Bowland, Whitewell consists of a small church, built in the early 19th century on the site of a medieval chapel, and an inn, built on the site of the old manor house.

in out of the way villages. Newton is typical of the places where they built their meeting houses and successfully lived according to their beliefs.

Dunsop Bridge

14 miles SE of Lancaster off the B6478

Often known as the *'Gateway to the Trough of Bowland'* and located in a designated Area of Natural Beauty, Dunsop Bridge is, despite its remote location, the centre of the British Isles. The actual centre point, worked out by the

Browsholme Hall, Whitewell

Just to the southeast lies **Browsholme Hall,** a Tudor mansion dating from 1507 that has the rare distinction of being occupied by the same family ever since. From the 16th century onwards, the owners, the Parker family, were also bowbearers, or warders, of the Forest of Bowland – the king's agent and upholders of the law in the forest. Though much of the original Tudor house can still be seen, there have been many additions over the centuries but it remains a homely building perhaps due to the continuous occupation by the same family and as a result of its remote location. The house is not open to the public.

Chipping

15 miles SE of Lancaster off the B6243

This picturesque village overlooking the River Loud is now a conservation area and it is also home to a post office, built in 1668, which claims to be Britain's oldest shop. Very much at the heart of the local agricultural communities, the annual village show is one of the best in Lancashire and its very name comes from the old English word for a market place - *chepyn.* In medieval times there were no fewer than five watermills along the banks of Chipping Beck and, later, one of the mills, Tweedies Mill, made ships' portholes which were used on the clipper ships bringing tea back from the east.

There are a number of attractive inns here and one of them, the Sun Inn, is associated with a melancholy tale. The story of Lizzie Dean whose ghost is said to haunt the inn is poignant, sad – and true. In 1835, Lizzie was 18 years old and a serving wench at the inn. She had fallen in love with a local man and a date had been set for their wedding at the church just across the road from the inn. Lizzie lodged at the inn and on the morning of her wedding she heard the church bells ringing. Looking out of her window she saw her intended bridegroom leaving the church with another maiden on his arm.

Sunset at Chipping

Humiliated and distraught, Lizzie crept up into the inn's attic and hanged herself. She left a note requesting that she should be buried beneath the path leading to the church porch so that her faithless lover would have to step across her body every Sunday on his way to divine service.

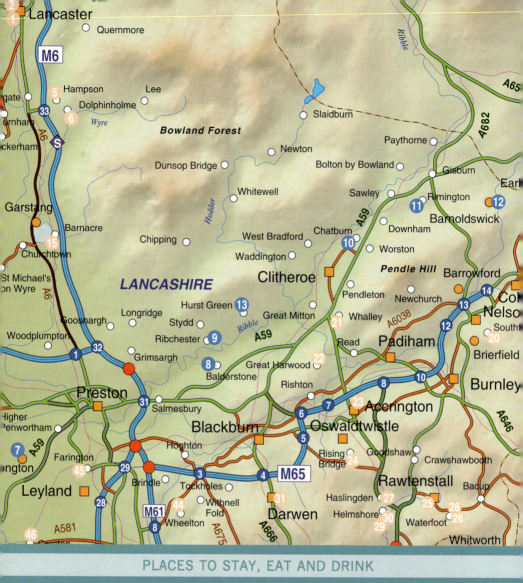

PLACES TO STAY, EAT AND DRINK

The Red Lion, Longton, Preston	7	Pub with Restaurant p30
The Myerscough, Balderstone, Blackburn	8	Pub with Food p31
The Stonebridge Bistro & Ribchester Arms Country Inn, Ribchester	9	Pub, Bistro, Restaurant & Accommodation p32
The Brown Cow, Chatburn, Clitheroe	10	Pub with Food p34
Raikes Barn, Rimington, Clitheroe	11	Self Catering p37
The Monks House, Barnoldswick	12	Guest House p38
The Shireburn Arms, Hurst Green, nr Clitheroe	13	Pub, Restaurant & Accommodation p40

● Denotes entries in other chapters

2 The Ribble Valley

A dramatic contrast of stark fellsides flecked with woolly sheep, and valleys green with woodland and lush pastures grazed by obviously contented sheep. It's not the conventional image of Lancashire as half-Blackpool, half wall-to-wall grimy chimneys. That's because the Ribble Valley is the county's best-kept secret – 150 square miles of peaceful countryside, almost two-thirds of it designated as Areas of Outstanding Natural Beauty.

The best overview of this beautiful area can be enjoyed by walking or driving along **Longridge Fell**. Within the space of a few miles, huge vistas unfold, not just of the Ribble Valley from Pendle Hill to Preston but also of the Fylde Plain, the Loud and Hodder valleys, and the Forest of Bowland. This is captivating countryside so it's no wonder that, according to one of her biographers, the Queen herself has divulged that she would like to retire to this region of rural Lancashire.

Flowing between the Forest of Bowland in the

north and the hill country of Pendle in the south, the River Ribble cuts a pleasant and green course along a narrow valley. The **Ribble Way** middle-distance footpath follows the full 70 miles of the river, from its source at Ribblehead in North Yorkshire to the flat, tidal marshes of its estuary west of Preston.

A beautiful, unspoilt yet small area, the Ribble Valley has long been a favourite with the people of Lancashire. Not only is it easily accessible but there are numerous gentle walks in the sheltered valley and a wealth of wildlife is supported by the lush countryside. It is also a place of pretty villages which, even in the 21st century, remain

Whalley Abbey, Ribble Valley

almost unscathed.

The central point of the valley is Clitheroe, a typical ancient Lancashire market town that clusters around one of the smallest Norman castles in the country. The Normans were not the only invaders to built a fortification in the valley: further down stream lies Ribchester and the Roman fort of Bremetannacum. Up river from Clitheroe lies Sawley and another interesting ruin. The Cistercian monks of Fountains Abbey founded the religious house here in the 13th century and their influence in the area of agriculture can still be seen in the surrounding fields.

The valley is also home to two great houses. The first, Stonyhurst, was originally the home of the Shireburn family and is now the world famous Roman Catholic public school. The second, on the outskirts of Preston, is Salmesbury Hall, a wonderful 14th century house that is now a Mecca for antiques collectors.

Finally, at the mouth of the river lies Preston, the county's administrative centre and a town with more to offer than first appearances would suggest. Best known to some as the home of the UK Snooker and World Indoor Bowls Championships, this ancient town also saw one of the key battles of the Civil War and it still continues the tradition of the Guild Celebrations. Dating back to medieval times and occurring once every 20 years, this week-long festival is well worth seeing. Our exploration of the Ribble Valley begins at its estuary near Preston and travels upstream through a fertile and versatile valley to the river's remote source in the bleak Pennine Hills.

Preston

"Proud Preston" is the largest town in the county and its administrative centre. It's 'Proud' because it was the first town in the county to receive a borough charter, (in 1179), the first borough in which every male over 21 had a vote in parliamentary elections (1798), the first town outside London to light its streets with gas lamps (1816), and in 1958 the Preston bypass was the first stretch of motorway to be built in Britain. Civic pride was fostered even more by Preston's elevation in 2002 to the status of a city, one of only six in the UK so honoured to mark the Queen's diamond Jubilee. Around the same time, multi-million pound plans were announced to redevelop the City Centre.

During the 19th century, Preston became a 'town of spires' as the evenly-split Protestant and Roman Catholic communities vied to build the most splendid churches. The palm is usually awarded to the Catholic St Walburge's Church whose slender 300ft steeple is the third tallest in England.

In Victorian times, Preston was a major cotton-weaving centre. The mill owners' ruthless exploitation of the cotton workers provoked a major strike in 1854 and the bitter confrontation attracted the attention of Charles

Dickens. He had already started to write a novel highlighting the degrading conditions and pitiful wages imposed on industrial workers by outrageously wealthy mill owners. He came to Preston, staying at the Bull and Royal Hotel in Church

School of Art, Preston

Street, and his first-hand observations of the unacceptable face of Victorian capitalism displayed in that conflict were embodied in the grimmest novel he ever wrote, *Hard Times*. Many of Preston's old red-brick mills still stand, although now converted to a variety of imaginative uses.

Lancaster may enjoy the distinction of being the elegant county town, but Preston revels in its macho role as Lancashire's administrative centre – always busy, enterprising, forward-looking but still proud of a historical legacy that stretches back to Roman times. The port activity may have declined but the dockland area, now called Riversway, has become an area of regeneration with a marina catering for pleasure craft, yachts, and windsurfers. The complex forms part of the recently opened **Millennium Ribble Link** which forms a 3-mile-long linear waterpark providing opportunities for walking, angling, cycling and boating as well as a newly commissioned sculpture trail.

Also in Riversway and due to open in 2003 is the new **Ribble Steam Railway Museum.**

Though the town has both a Roman and a medieval past nothing of this is visible today. However, the lasting legacy of those days is reflected in the famous **Guilds Celebrations** which have been taking place every 20 years since 1500. The Royal Charter establishing the rights to hold a Guild Merchant was granted by Henry II in 1179. These medieval guilds were unions of tradesmen who came together in the pursuit of fair dealing and with the intention of preventing cheats from offering a second rate service. Each guild operated from what amounted to their own weights and measures office, the guild hall. As the guilds grew they also became insurance companies, looking after any member who was taken ill and unable to work. In order to ensure that the high standards within a given trade were maintained the apprentice system was started and any member found to be cheating or offering substandard workmanship was expelled from the guild. The last Guild Celebration took place in 1992 and, already, preparations are being made for the next in 2012.

A popular annual event is the Easter Egg Rolling event held in **Avenham Park**, one of the city's two splendid Victorian parks: the other is the adjacent **Miller Park,** noted for its impressive floral displays and an elaborately designed fountain.

Preston featured in the *Domesday Book* although at that time it was known as Priest-town and, in the 1260s, the Greyfriars settled here. The Catholic traditions of Preston continued, as they did elsewhere in the county, and this has, along with the associated loyalty to the crown, had a great part to play in the town's history. During the Civil War it was the Battle of Preston in 1648 which confirmed the eventual defeat of the supporters of Charles I. Later, at the time of the 1745 Jacobite rebellion, Preston played host to Prince Charles Edward, Bonnie Prince Charlie.

The many public buildings of Preston all reflect the prosperity of the town during the Victorian age. This wealth was built upon the textile industry helped by the general location of the town: midway between London and Glasgow, on a major railway route, and with extensive docks. Though the town's prosperity was built on cotton, textiles were not new to Preston as linen had been produced here from as far back as Tudor times. Preston was also the place

where, in 1768, the single most important machine of the textile industry was invented: Richard Arkwright's water-frame cotton spinning machine. Almost overnight, the cottage industries of spinning and handloom weaving were moved from the workers' homes into factories and the entrepreneurs of Preston were quicker than most to catch on. One gentleman in particular, John Horrocks, saw the potential of combining the spinning and weaving operations under the same roof and so he was able to take raw cotton in and produce the finished article on delivery. His firm became the largest of its kind in the world, further adding to the town's prosperity, but it did not do Horrocks himself much good as, by the age of 36, he was dead.

Although the great days of the textile industry are long gone in Preston, as elsewhere in Britain, the cotton workers of the town are remembered in a statue which stands outside the old Corn Exchange.

Looking at the town now it is hard to imagine those hectic days and may be even hard to believe that when the docks were completed here in 1892, Preston was the second largest container handling port in Britain. In 1900, 1,285 vessels carrying nearly half a million tons of cargo entered and left the port. Unfortunately, the battle of keeping the channel open and free of silt became too expensive, particularly as trade was lost to other, non-tidal ports, and the docks eventually closed.

One of the best places to start any exploration of the town is the **Harris Museum and Art Gallery**. Housed in a magnificent neoclassical building which dominates the Market Square, the museum and art gallery were opened in 1893. Funded by a successful local businessman and reminiscent of the British Museum, as well as the fine collection of paintings and watercolours by major 19th century British artists, there is an excellent exhibition of the story of Preston. The two other museums in the town are regimental. Housed in the former county court building, and with limited opening times, the **County and Regimental Museum**, which is guarded by a giant Howitzer gun, has galleries dedicated to three regiments: the 14th/20th Kings Hussars, the Duke of Lancaster's Own Yeomanry, and the Queen's Lancashire Regiment. There is also an interesting and very informative display on the history of Lancashire. The Fulwood Barracks, which were built in 1848 of Longridge stone, are home to the **Loyal Regiment (North Lancashire) Museum**. With a rich history that covers many campaigns, the exhibits here are numerous and include the famous silver mounted Maida Tortoise, items connected with General Wolfe, souvenirs from the Crimea War, and artefacts from the Defence of Kimberley, the diamond town in South Africa which the 1st Battalion the Loyals defended without assistance from any other troops.

Preston's Guild Hall, built in 1972 to celebrate that year's Guild, is known, or at least its interior is, to many snooker and bowls fans since it is the venue for the UK Snooker and the World Indoor Bowls Championships. Another building, less well-known but still a distinctive landmark is **Preston Prison**. Built in 1789, it replaced the town's first House of Correction. In an interesting move to provide the inmates with work, during the 19th century looms were installed in the prison and the prisoners were paid for their labour. Industrial unrest in the area soon followed and, in 1837, it was only the threat of a cannon which saved the prison from invasion by an angry mob intent on destroying the machines. Although the prison was closed in 1931, it re-opened in 1948 and remains so.

As might be expected for a town on the banks of a river, there are many bridges but two crossings are particularly worthy of note. **Penwortham Old Bridge** is perhaps the most attractive in Lancashire; slightly hump-backed and built of a mixture of stone. Constructed chiefly of buff gritstone and pink sandstone in 1756, it replaced a bridge that had collapsed. By 1912 traffic had increased to such an extent that its use by motor cars and heavy carts was prohibited. For over 150 years, the bridge was the lowest crossing of the River Ribble. By contrast, the **Ribble Viaduct** is a completely different structure. One of the oldest works of railway engineering in the area and a construction of great elegance and

THE RED LION

138 Liverpool Road, Longton, Preston,
Lancashire PR4 5AU
Tel: 01772 612168
e-mail: annmariej_uk@yahoo.co.uk

A sturdy mid-Victorian building in redbrick and stone, **The Red Lion** was taken over in August 2002 by Annmarie Jackson and her son Adam who have completely refurbished the pub in traditional style with quality furnishings throughout. Open all day, every day, the pub serves appetising food every lunchtime (noon to 2.30pm) and evening (5pm to 8.30pm). Children are welcome and the dining room is non-smoking when food is being served. Two real ales are always on tap along with a wide selection of all the familiar brews. On Thursday evenings the inn hosts a quiz, with a free mini-buffet, and on Saturday evenings there's live entertainment. A popular amenity is the rear patio garden with its children's adventure playground.

dignity, it was built in 1838 and brought the railway from Wigan to the centre of Preston.

Located on the northern outskirts of the city is Preston's latest visitor attraction to open, **The National Football Museum**. Containing the world's most significant football collections, including the official FIFA collection, the museum offers more than 1000 objects, photographs, more than 90 minutes of film and a number of lively interactive displays.

Around Preston

Higher Penwortham
8 miles NW of Chorley on the A59

Situated on Penwortham hill and overlooking the River Ribble, **St Mary's Church** has a 14th century chancel and a splendid tower. It stands on the site where the Romans are known to have had a building – probably a fort protecting the river crossing. A charming old bridge of 1755, complete with its cobblestones, still stands but is now only open to pedestrians.

Salmesbury
4 miles E of Preston on the A59

To the east of the village, close to the busy A59, lies **Salmesbury Hall**, built by the Southworth family. The hall seen today, an attractive black and white timbered manor house, is actually the second house they built since their original hall was burned to the ground by Robert the Bruce in the early 14th century. Thinking that the original position, close to a crossing of the River Ribble was too vulnerable to attack, the family built their subsequent home in what was then an isolated location.

More peaceful times followed and the hall, surrounded by a moat and with a drawbridge, was a reflection of the family's wealth. A staunchly Catholic family, their 15th century chapel contains a mullioned Gothic window that was rescued from Whalley Abbey after the Dissolution in the 1530s.

THE MYERSCOUGH

Whalley Road, Balderstone, nr Blackburn,
Lancashire BB2 7LE
Tel: 01254 812222

A charming old inn, **The Myerscough** dates back to the late 1700s but was a private residence until 1830 when it became an inn with a smithy attached. It stands on the A59, directly opposite British Aerospace. In good weather, customers can take advantage of the peaceful beer garden at the rear and enjoy the excellent fare provided by landlord Ian Lord-Riddoch. A speciality of the house is a tasty

Steak & Kidney Pudding which, rather mystifyingly, is known to locals as "The Baby's Head". Real ale lovers have a choice of 4 brews – Robinson's Best, Hatter's Mild, and 2 rotating guest ales. The Myerescough has a non-smoking snug and on Wednesday evenings hosts a Quiz, with proceeds going to charity.

However, it was the loyalty to their faith that finally saw the demise of the Southworth family. Their continued practice of Catholicism saw Sir John Southworth imprisoned in Manchester in the late 16th century and, by the time of his death a few years later, the family, having kept their faith, had seen their fortune dwindle away.

The hall was sold to the Braddyll family who, having a house near Ulverston, simply stripped Salmesbury Hall of its assets. Somehow the hall survived but by the 1870s it was in a shocking state of repair. First, Joseph Harrison stepped in and began a

successful restoration programme, to the point where he was able to entertain the likes of Charles Dickens. However, the building work took all his money and, facing ruin, Harrison committed suicide. By 1925, the hall was once again in a dilapidated condition and was only saved from demolition by a timber merchant by the efforts of the Salmesbury Hall Trust, a group that is still managing the property today. The hall's unusual history is only equalled by the unconventional manner in which it, quite literally, earns its keep. With no assets left, after being stripped by the Braddylls, the hall is once again full of antiques but these are all for sale. As salerooms go, this has to be one of the most atmospheric.

Salmesbury Hall

Ribchester
8 miles NE of Preston on the B5269

Situated on the banks of the River Ribble, the village is famous for its **Roman Fort,**

THE STONEBRIDGE BISTRO & RIBCHESTER ARMS COUNTRY INN

Blackburn Road, Ribchester, Lancashire
PR3 3ZQ
Bistro : Tel: 01254 878664
Fax: 01254 820397
Ribchester Arms: Tel: 01254 820888
Fax: 01254 820397

Standing on opposite sides of the road on the main street of this historic village, The **Stonebridge Bistro and Ribchester Arms Country Inn** between them offer a superb choice of food, drink and accommodation. The Bistro is housed in what were originally four farm workers cottages and has been owned and run by Maria and Stephen Joyson for the past 10 years. The couple have plenty

of experience in the hospitality business · Maria's father opened the first Greek restaurant in Lancashire. The bistro is beautifully decorated throughout and furnished to a high standard but, although it seats 60 comfortably, booking is necessary at weekends to avoid disappointment. Stephen is the chef and his varied and extensive menu offers a wide choice of dishes, all freshly prepared from prime ingredients. Fresh fish and traditional dishes are the speciality of the house but there's also a good selection of vegetarian dishes such as Broccoli & Blue Cheese Bake or Stir Fried Oriental vegetables and noodles. In addition to the regular menu, daily specials are also on offer. Children are welcome and have their own menu. The Bistro is open Wednesday to Saturday evenings from 6.30pm until late; on Sundays, when the Sunday roast is

supplemented by special dishes of the day, opening hours are from noon until 8pm.

Stephen and Maria's son Leon is the licensee of the Ribchester Arms, a stylish modern building with a wide range of amenities. Although Leon only took over in October 2001, the establishment is already renowned for its excellent food. The menu is different from the bistro and includes a wide range of starters (home made pâté, for example); main courses such as steaks, chargrilled chicken, bangers and mash with locally produced sausages, fish and vegetarian dishes, and salads. Also available are ploughman's lunches, sandwiches or an honest-to-goodness Lancashire cheese with pickle, and a selection of dishes for young diners. Meals are served either in the bars or in the 45-seater non-smoking restaurant and are available Monday to Saturday at lunchtime (noon to 3pm) and evening (5.30pm to 9pm); on Sunday from noon until 7pm.

If you are planning to stay in this scenic corner of the county, the Ribchester Arms has 4 superb en suite rooms, all attractively furnished and decorated. Other amenities at the inn include private function rooms available for meetings and all kinds of celebrations.

Bremetannacum, on the northern river bank. It was the Roman governor, Gnaeus Julius Agricola, in AD 79, who first established a fort here at the junction of the two important roads between Manchester and Carlisle, and York and the west coast. Although little of the fort's walls remain, the granary or storehouse, with its hypocaust (underfloor heating), has been excavated and has revealed some interesting coins, pottery, sculptures, and inscriptions.

The fort's **Roman Museum** is designed to transport visitors back to the days of the Roman occupation and it offers an excellent insight into those times. Unfortunately, the finest artefact found on the site, an ornate helmet, is not on display here (though they do have a replica) – the original can be seen in the British Museum in London.

Back in the village proper, the discovery of some pre Norman Conquest crosses in and around **St Wilfrid's Church** would suggest that this 13th century building occupies the site of a Saxon church. The church is named after the first Bishop of Ripon, who in the 7th century took a prominent role in the Synod of Whitby. This would seem to confirm the earlier buildings existence in the absence of any direct evidence. A great place for tourists during the summer months, Ribchester not only has these two sights to offer but also several excellent pubs, restaurant, and cafés.

Perhaps the most appealing little market town in Lancashire, Clitheroe nestles around its miniature Norman castle. The town has a reputation for high quality specialist shops acclaimed for their individuality, some of which have gained international recognition: establishments such as Cowman's Sausage Shop in Castle Street which offers 58 different varieties of sausage, amongst them Welsh pork & leek, venison and wild boar. Fifty-nine varieties if you count his special Christmas sausage, only available during the festive season and containing exotic ingredients such as port, juniper berries and ground almonds. As with the French, traditional Lancashire meat cuisine wastes no part of the animal. Black Pudding, tripe and onions, chitterlings, lamb's fry and sweetbreads are still popular dishes here although rarely seen in southern England. Interestingly, there's an annual

Clitheroe Castle

The Ribble Valley

THE BROWN COW

19 Bridge Street, Chatburn, Clitheroe,
Lancs BB7 4AW
Tel: 01200 441272 Mobile: 07734 232600

Located in the quiet village of Chatburn, **The Brown Cow** is a smart black and white building dating back to the mid-1800s. Mine hosts are Peter and Mary Hodgkinson, a friendly and welcoming couple who have been in the hospitality business for some 35 years. Peter is well known in the area as the chairman of the Ribble Valley Licensed Victuallers and treasurer for various local sports leagues. The Brown Cow has a well-established reputation for outstanding food, served every lunchtime and evening, and for quality ales, including 2 real ales – Boddingtons and Tiger. On Sunday evenings a general knowledge quiz alternates with karaoke or live entertainment.

competition between French and Lancashire butchers to see who makes the best Black Pudding.

In King Street there's Byrne's Wine Merchants which stocks more than 1,550 wines and 100 malt whiskies. *Which? Wine Guide* judged the shop to be the best wine merchant in the country. Also well worth visiting is the Platform Gallery, housed in a refurbished railway station of 1870. The Gallery presents a regularly changing programme of visual art exhibitions – paintings and prints, textiles, glassware, ceramics, jewellery, papier maché and baskets, with the majority of the work on show produced by regionally based artists.

Clitheroe is Lancashire's second oldest borough, after Wigan, receiving its first charter in 1147 and since then the town has served the surrounding villages of the Ribble Valley as their market town. Like Lancaster, it too is dominated by an 800-year-old **Castle** standing on a 100ft high limestone crag high above the town. Today only the Keep remains, the second smallest in England and one of

the oldest stone structures in Lancashire. According to local legend, the large hole in the keep's east wall was the work of the Devil who threw a large boulder from the summit of nearby Pendle Hill. Boring historians say it was Oliver Cromwell's troops who inflicted the damage. Modern day visitors can stand within the keep as hidden voices recount the castle's history, complete with appropriate sound effects.

Standing on another prominent limestone mound, close to the castle, is **Clitheroe Castle Museum**, home to many exhibits and displays reflecting the history and geology of the Ribble Valley area. Archaeological finds illustrate life in the valley from the earliest days and in this section too can be seen the famous Hacking ferryboat now restored to its former glory. Closer to the present day is the re-creation of an Edwardian kitchen, complete with its unique sound system that brings this turn of the century room to life.

As well as the local history displays the museum also has a fine collection relating to the geology of the area. Here, the appearance of the valley is explained in a series of unusual and interesting formats whilst the history of Salthill quarry is also explained. Now a nature reserve and place of special scientific interest, the quarry is famous for the fossils, which have been found there.

A short walk from the Castle Museum stands the parish **Church of St Mary Magdalen** which, though it was rebuilt by the Victorians, was founded in the 13th century. At that

Edisford Bridge, Clitheroe

time the town also had a school; however, the present Royal Grammar School was not established until 1554. The school's official charter, granted by Mary Tudor but lost for many years, was eventually found in the vaults of a local solicitor's office in 1990.

The town's narrow, winding streets are full of character and charm and amidst the ancient buildings is the rather incongruous **Civic Hall Cinema**. Built in the 1920s, this unspoilt monument to the golden days of the silver screen is still lined with plush velvet, has retained its grand piano that was used to accompany the silent films, and remains the town's cinema.

Just outside the town can be found **Edisford Picnic Area**, a popular place for family outings that stands on the site of a battle ground where the Scots fought the Normans. Also near Clitheroe, at **Brungerley**, are a set of stepping stones across the river that are said to be haunted. Apparently the evil spirit living in the water drags a traveller to his watery death every seven years.

There are few grand houses in the Ribble Valley open to the public, but **Browsholme Hall** near Clitheroe is open at certain times in the summer. Dating back to the early 1500s, the Hall has been the family home of the Parkers for 600 years and there's a special pleasure in being shown around the house by a member of the family. The Parkers took their name from the family's hereditary role in medieval times as keepers of the deer park in the royal hunting ground of the Forest of Bowland.

North of Clitheroe

West Bradford

1 mile N of Clitheroe off the B6478

This tucked away village, just south of the Forest of Bowland, was mentioned in the *Domesday Book* and there are records of some villagers paying the first poll tax levied by Richard II in 1379. The old part of the village is set around a green bordering the River Ribble. It's a pleasant spot with a stream running alongside the road through the bottom half of West Bradford and access to the houses bordering the beck is made by crossing a quaint stone bridge.

Worston

1 mile NE of Clitheroe off the A59

This tucked away village, down a lane off the main road, has remained unchanged over the years and can certainly be described as unspoilt. Keen-eyed visitors may even recognize the surrounding countryside as this was one of the locations used during the filming of *Whistle Down the Wind*. Behind the village inn, where the amusing and bizarre ritual of the village's Mock Corporation was revived in 1989, can still be seen the bull ring. Set into a stone, this was where the beast was tethered and baited with specially trained dogs in the belief that the 'sport' tenderized the meat.

Downham

3 miles NE of Clitheroe off the A59

Some 40-odd villages are sprinkled along the banks of the Ribble Valley, all of them built in the appealing local stone. One of the prettiest is Downham, renowned as the setting for the cinema classic *Whistle Down the Wind*. The

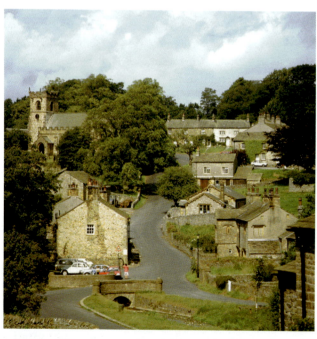

Downham Village

village also provides location scenes for BBC-TV's period drama series *Born & Bred*. Thanks for Downham's unspoilt appearance must go to the Clitheroe family which has owned the whole village since 1558 – the same year in which they acquired Whalley Abbey.. It was the present Lord Clitheroe's grandfather who paid for the electricity supply cables to be laid underground back in the 1930s and the present squire, Lord Clitheroe of Downham, still refuses to permit the skyline to be spoilt by television aerials, satellite dishes, and even dormer windows. The village phone box has also come under the influence of the family and is not painted a distinctive pillar box red but grey, to tone in with the surroundings.

Sawley
4 miles N of Clitheroe off the A59

At the centre of this historic village, easily missed as the main road by-passes it, are the slight remains of **Sawley Abbey,** founded in the 13th century by the Cistercian monks of Fountains Abbey. As well as building their religious house, the monks had great influence over the whole of the surrounding area. Clearing their immediate surroundings, the monks cultivated the land and their ridge and furrow patterns can still be made out in the fields.

Although during the reigns Edward I and II the abbots of Sawley were called to the House of Lords, none of the abbots were men of note except, perhaps, William Trafford, the last head of the community. With his colleague and neighbour, the last Abbot of Whalley, Trafford took part in the Pilgrimage of Grace in 1536 and, for his part in the failed uprising, was taken prisoner. Tried for treason at Lancaster in 1537, Trafford, with others like him, was found guilty and executed.

Although little of the abbey remains – much of the stone was cannibalised for village buildings – the site is wonderfully quiet and peaceful.

Rimington
5 miles NE of Clitheroe off the A59

This small hillside village has twice won Lancashire's Best Kept Village competition. Its name means "farmstead

RAIKES BARN
Beck Side Farm, Rimington, Clitheroe, Lancashire BB7 4EE
Tel: 01200 445287
e-mail: beckside@talk21.com
website: www.raikesbarn.co.uk

with lots of character. Double-glazed throughout, the cottage has a lounge with open fire, colour television and

Standing in the middle of a green field, **Raikes Barn** enjoys wonderful views of the surrounding countryside. Tastefully converted from an 18th century barn, Raikes Barn provides quality self-catering accommodation video; three bedrooms, bathroom, separate w.c.; a well equipped kitchen and a utility room. Outside, there's a paved area with garden chairs and ample parking for two cars.

on the boundary" and as the Lancashire/ Yorkshire boundary has changed over the years the village has been transferred from one county to the other. The most recent transfer was made in 1974 when people who had been Yorkshire born and bred suddenly found themselves Lancastrians.

This pleasant rural village was the home of Francis Duckworth, the famous composer of hymn tunes including one he named *Rimington*. His parents ran the village post office and shop next door to the Methodist chapel and a plaque on the chapel, now a private house, commemorates him.

Gisburn

7 miles NE of Clitheroe on the A59

Like Rimington, this village was also once in Yorkshire and, as many locals would like to believe, still is! One of the Ribble Valley's most pleasant and picturesque villages, Gisburn's history is dominated by the Lister family who, from humble beginnings rose to become the Lords of Ribblesdale. Their house, built in the early 17th century in

Gisburne Park, is still standing though it is now a private hospital. Over the years, many people were given shelter by the family and, in 1648, Cromwell is said to have rested at the house whilst on his way to fight at Preston.

During the late 1700s when the current lord of the manor raised an army against Napoleon he was rewarded for his loyalty to king and country by being raised to the peerage with the title Lord of Ribblesdale. Coincidentally, the 4th and last Lord of Ribblesdale, who died in 1925 after having lost both his sons in World War I, shared the same name, Thomas, as the 1st Lord.

Paythorne

10 miles NE of Clitheroe off the A682

Although the source of the River Ribble lies to the north in Yorkshire, near the famous Three Peaks of Whernside, Ingleborough, and Pen-y-ghent, this village is the first on its banks on this side of the county boundary. It also marks the end of the river's journey through the rugged limestone scenery of

moorlands and the start of its picturesque course through a lush green valley.

Barnoldswick
10 miles NE of Clitheroe on the B6251

If you approach this former cotton town from the south, off the A56, you may wonder why the road is so straight. The answer is that it was specially constructed in the 1930s to service the new Rolls Royce factory in the town. The B in the names of jet engines such as the RB211 stands for Barnoldswick.

At the western end of the town is **Bancroft Mill Engine Museum**. The mill was the last weaving shed to be built in Lancashire, in 1922. The mill closed in 1978 but the grand 600hp cross-compound steam engine was preserved and there are regular demonstrations of it in action. The museum also displays tools and documents connected with the weaving industry.

West of Clitheroe

Waddington
2 miles NW of Clitheroe on the B6478

This is one of the area's best known villages – its attractive Coronation Gardens have appeared on many postcards and even on biscuit tin lids. King Henry VI spent a whole year here in 1464/5, not because he particularly

appreciated its charms but because he was hiding at Waddington Hall from the Yorkists who had defeated him at the Battle of Hexham. When his hiding place was discovered he escaped by a secret tunnel that led from the Hall's dining room but he was quickly captured at Brungerley Bridge, down river near Clitheroe, then imprisoned in the Tower of London where he died in 1471.

Waddington has several times won first prize in Lancashire's Best Kept Village competition and it's easy to see why. Waddington Brook splashes the length of the village and 18th century almshouses cluster around the green.

About ten years ago Waddington's villagers enjoyed a certain amount of fame when, for the sake of a television series, they agreed to renounce their TVs for a whole month. This cold turkey treatment proved too much for some and they had to be resuscitated by having their sets returned.

Great Mitton
3 miles SW of Clitheroe on the B6246

Standing opposite the Three Fishes Hotel, which takes its name from the three fishes on the Whalley Abbey coat of arms, is the attractive **All Hallows' Church.** Housing some of the finest relics to be seen in any British church, this is most certainly worth a visit. Built in around 1270, though undoubtedly there was a wooden Saxon structure hereabouts, little has been done to the building since, although a tower was added in 1438 and the pews are Jacobean. However, it is the Shireburn Chapel that draws most visitors to the church. It was added in 1440 by the Shireburn family of Stonyhurst who claimed to be the direct descendants of the first rector, Ralph the Red of Mytton. The family tombs here are regarded as the best in the county. One of the earliest is the fine alabaster tomb of Sir Richard Shireburn (who died in 1594) and his wife Maude who is dressed in capacious petticoats. The latest is of another Richard who died in 1702 at the age of 9 after eating poisonous berries. Following the fashion of the time the monument displays copious macabre items – a skull, hour glass, sickle, more bones than seem necessary and, emerging from the ground, two skeletal hands.

Confirmation that a settlement existed here before the days of the land ownership by the abbey comes with the name of the village itself. Mitton is derived from the Saxon word 'mythe' which means a farm at the junction of

two rivers – perfectly describing the location as, close by, the River Hodder feeds into the River Ribble.

Hurst Green

5 miles SW of Clitheroe on the B6243

This pretty village of stone-built cottages nestling in the Ribble Valley is best known for its nearby public school. **Stonyhurst College**, the world famous Roman Catholic school, began life as the residence of the local lords of the manor. The present building, begun in around 1523, was the work of Hugh Shireburn although additions were made in 1592 by Sir Richard Shireburn. The core of this imposing building set beside a lake is late-Elizabethan but there have been major additions almost every century, all of them blending remarkably well with their predecessors.

Sir Richard Shireburn was an ambitious man who served the Tudor monarchy well. As well as being the Chief Forester of Bowland he was also one of Henry VIII's commissioners studying the state of the monasteries. He

Stonyhurst College, Hurst Green

was an eager participant in the suppression of Whalley Abbey. Though the family publicly adopted the new Protestant religion under Elizabeth I, it was with little enthusiasm and in a short time the Shireburn family, like many other Lancashire families, returned to their Catholic faith. It seems strange then that Cromwell, on his way to and from the Battle of Preston, should take shelter at Stonyhurst although rumour has it that the ardent Puritan slept with a pistol at his side and his guards around him.

In 1794, after the house had been left for some considerable time and had fallen into a state of disrepair, the owner, Thomas Weld, offered the property to the Jesuits who had set up an English Catholic School in Flanders.

Unwelcome in France following the revolution, the Jesuits gladly accepted and after restoring the original building they extended it during the 19th century. Their finest addition must be the replica of King's College in Cambridge: **St Peter's Church** was built in 1835 and contains many treasures including a 7th century copy of St John's Gospel and a cope of Henry II that was used by Henry VIII at the battle of the Field of the Cloth of Gold. One of the college's most famous sons was Sir Arthur Conan Doyle, the creator of Sherlock Holmes.

Stonyhurst College is occasionally open to the public during the summer holidays. The exterior of the College can always be seen from the minor road that runs through its grounds.

Stydd

7 miles SW of Clitheroe off the B6245

Just to the north of Ribchester lies the small hamlet of Stydd. All that remains of the monastery founded here by the Knights Hospitallers of St John of Jerusalem is the Norman **Chapel**, standing alone surrounded by meadows. It contains effigies of some of the knights. A crusading and military order established in 1113, the Knights Hospitallers provided help and assistance to pilgrims travelling to the Holy Land. Their commandery, as their religious houses were called, at Stydd was dissolved by the mid 14th century and, although at one time there were over 50 of their small monasteries in the country, only 15 survived to the 1530s.

Longridge

10 miles SW of Clitheroe on the B6243

After Clitheroe, bustling Longridge is the only other town of any size in the area. Like Clitheroe it offers a good selection of independently owned shops along with a range of antique galleries, and is widely known for its Lancashire Cheese Dairies.

The village lies at the foot of **Longridge Fell** from whose 1150ft elevation, especially at Jeffrey Hill or Kemple End, there are superb views northwards over the Loud Valley to Chipping: to the south the land drops away towards the River Ribble. For many years this area was an important source of building stone and several of Preston's civic buildings, including the Harris Library and Museum, and the docks at Liverpool were constructed with Longridge stone.

In the 1790s the stone was also used to build a row of 20 terraced cottages in Longridge – numbers 4 to 44 Higher Road, which now have listed building status. They were erected by a group of quarrymen who formed a club into which each member paid a fixed weekly sum. The money was used to pay the cost of materials, £138.3s.6d (£138.17p), for building each cottage. When a cottage was completed, the members drew lots as to who should occupy it. Known as **Club Row**, these mutually funded cottages are the earliest known example of properties built on the principles of a Building Society and have earned themselves an entry in the *Guinness Book of Records*.

Goosnargh

12 miles SW of Clitheroe on the B5269

Just to the west of the village lies **Chingle Hall**, a small moated manor house that was built in 1260 by Adam de Singleton. A Catholic family, the Singletons are said to have a chapel with three priest hides and, so the story goes, Cromwell once climbed down one of the hall's chimneys to spy on the Royalists below. As well as being the birthplace of St John Wall, one of the last priests to die for his faith, in 1620, it enjoys the reputation of being one of the most haunted houses in Britain and, as such, the hall has featured on countless television and radio programmes.

Grimsargh
11 miles W of Clitheroe on the B6243

As well as having one of the largest village greens in Lancashire, covering some 12 acres, Grimsargh is also home to **Tun Brook Wood**. Following the line of the brook until it meets the River Ribble, this is one of the largest areas of deciduous woodland in the country.

PLACES TO STAY, EAT AND DRINK

⬤ Denotes entries in other chapters

3 The Fylde

The Fylde derives its name from the Anglo-Saxon word *gefilde* meaning level, green fields, an apt description of this low-lying area that extends from Fleetwood in the north to Lytham St Anne's in the south. It was once known as "Windmill Land" but nowadays windmills are few and far between. A notable exception is the striking example on the waterfront at Lytham. It was built in 1805, worked until 1929, and now houses a small museum.

This historic area of coastal Lancashire is known to many as the home of Blackpool: the brash, seaside resort that has been entertaining holidaymakers for generations. To the south lies another resort, Lytham St Anne's, which is not only somewhat more genteel but also the home of one of the country's most well known golf courses and host to the British Open Championships. Both places grew up as a result of the expansion of the railway system in the Victorian age, when they were popular destinations for the mill workers of Lancashire and Yorkshire.

However, the Fylde is also an ancient region that was known to both the Saxons and the Romans. To the north of this region, around the Wyre estuary, the salt marshes have been exploited for over 2,000 years and the process continues at the large ICI plant. Fishing and shipping too have been important sources of revenue here. Fleetwood is still a port though smaller than it was whilst, surprisingly though it might seem today, Lytham was also an important port along the Ribble Estuary.

Sunset at Fleetwood

Inland, the fertile, flat plain has been farmed for many centuries and, with few major roads, the quiet rural communities lie undisturbed and little changed by the 21st century. A haven for wildlife, and particularly birds and plants, the two estuaries, of the Ribble and the Wyre, provide habitats that abound with rare and endangered species of plants and birds. A relatively undiscovered region, the Fylde has much more to offer than a white knuckle ride and candy floss and is well worth taking the time to explore.

Blackpool

Blackpool is as unique to England as Las Vegas is to the United States. Everyone is familiar with Blackpool's brash, warm-hearted attractions but did you know that this single town has more beds available for the 16 million people who visit each year than the whole of Portugal has for its visitors?

Today, Blackpool is the largest town in the present county of Lancashire. Little more than a fishing village among the sand dunes of the Fylde coast 150 years ago, Blackpool's huge expansion followed the arrival of the railway. Up until then, travel to and from the village involved considerable discomfort, taking a day from Manchester and two days from York. The great Victorian railway companies put Blackpool well and truly on the map by laying the railway lines right to the coast and building the grand stations – the town had three. The quiet fishing village was quickly transformed

Blackpool Tower

into a vibrant resort as day-trippers from the mill towns of Lancashire and Yorkshire took advantage of the cheap excursion rail fares. Local developers enthusiastically began creating new attractions for their visitors. The first pier was constructed in 1863, followed by two more over the next twenty years. A glass-domed Winter Gardens opened in 1875, and ten years later the town's electric tram system began operating, the first in Britain and today the only one. The Pleasure Beach with its permanent fairground rides and amusements arrived in 1890 with the aim of providing "an American-style amusement park where adults could feel like children again".

But the developers' real master-stroke was the construction of the world-famous **Blackpool Tower**. Modelled on the Eiffel Tower and completed in 1894, the Tower stands some 518 feet high, incorporates a Ballroom and Grand Theatre, both of which are decorated in a wonderfully over-the-top rococo style. The **Tower Ballroom** is a much loved institution where tea dances are still a regular feature. It was, for many years from the 1960s to the 1980s, the venue for BBC-TV's enormously popular *Come Dancing* competition. The Tower's centenary celebrations in 1994 were numerous and extravagant and included painting the tower gold.

The introduction of the Blackpool Illuminations helped extend the summer season into autumn, and the late 20th century saw yet more visitor attractions added to the mix. **The Pleasure Beach** is an attraction that continues to be extended and improved. However some of its delights are certainly not for the fainthearted. It not only boasts its own railway station, but also the tallest, fastest and, it is claimed, the most thrilling roller-coaster ride in the world. In the summer of 2002 yet another seafront attraction was installed - the world's largest mirror ball. Weighing four and a half tons and 18 feet across, it is made up of 47,000 different pieces.

The Sandcastle is an all-weather indoor complex where visitors can enjoy waterslides, wave pools and water flumes in sub-tropical temperatures; and **The Sea Life Centre** provides close-up views of a wide range of marine creatures.

The **North Pier,** designed by Eugenius Birch, was opened at the beginning of the 1863 season. It soon became the place to promenade and is now a listed building.

Blackpool Pier

Despite its reputation as a brash and lively resort, Blackpool also has its quiet, secluded corners where visitors can escape the hustle of the crowds. There are seven miles of sea front, from the North Shore down as far as Squire's Gate and Lytham, where the pace of life is gentler and the beaches are quieter. **Blackpool Tramways** have provided a most enjoyable way of exploring these less busy sides of the town and its environs for many years. And it should also be remembered that the world's first electric street tram system opened here in 1885. The route was extended along the Lytham road in 1895 and later connecting with other routes in nearby Lytham and St Anne's. However bus services, which put paid to many town's tram routes, left by the 1960s Blackpool's tram system as the only commercial route in the country.

Still a popular means of transport here today, many of the tramcars date from the 1930s or 1950s and the managing company has a special selection of vintage cars which they run on special occasions. One of these occasions is the now annual **Illuminations** which, following a ceremonial lighting much like that of the Christmas lights in London, is a splendid end to the season. An eagerly awaited free show, running the full length of the promenade, the lights have, over the years, provided many spectacular shows and incorporated many themes.

A couple of miles inland from The

THE SHOVELS

260 Common Edge Road, Marton,
Blackpool, Lancashire FY4 5DH
Tel: 01253 762702
Fax: 01253 699635

The local CAMRA branch voted **The Shovels** "Pub of the Season" in 2000 and "Branch Pub of the Year" in 2001 so, as you might expect, it's a popular place with devotees of real ale. There are always 6 real ales on tap – Theakston's permanently, the others regularly rotating.

During their six years as landlords here, Stephen and Helen Norris calculate that they've offered their customers nearly 3000 different real ales to sample. They also host an annual Beer Festival each year at the end of October, a celebration that lasts a whole week.

The Shovels is also highly regarded for the quality of its food which is served everyday from noon until 9.30pm. Mark the Chef is Australian which explains some of the more adventurous dishes on the menu, but you'll also find a wide choice of more traditional meals with steaks served in a wide variety of ways as the speciality of the house. Meals are served in the charming conservatory but can also be enjoyed anywhere in the rest of this comfortable inn.

On weekdays, there's a substantial discount of one third off the price of meals served between 2.30pm and 6pm, except on Bank Holidays. And if you are visiting on a Thursday evening, feel free to take part in the regular weekly quiz.

Thornton Windmill

high and was constructed in 1794. The grinding of corn ceased here soon after World War I but the building has been restored and it is now a tourist attraction.

At this point the Wyre estuary is wide and provides shelter for shipping, an advantage that was utilised by both the Romans and the Scandinavians. They both took advantage of the salt deposits here and, today, the large ICI plant is still extracting salt. The **Wyre Estuary Country Park**, taking the whole estuary from Fleetwood up river as far as Shard Bridge, is an excellent place from which to discover the area. An initial stop at the **Wyreside Ecology Centre,** which provides all manner of information about the estuary, is a sensible starting point. From here a number of footpaths take in many of the places along the river as well as leading visitors through important areas of salt marsh which contain a wide range of plants, insects, and birds.

Pleasure Beach, **Marton Mere** bird sanctuary is a 10 acre lake, which is the year round home for many geese, swans and ducks, and a temporary resting place for many more. Nearby, Stanley Park is spacious, well-maintained and peaceful.

North of Blackpool

Thornton

5 miles N of Blackpool on the B5268

Situated in the west bank of the Wyre estuary, this small town is dominated by **Marsh Mill**, which stands over 100 feet

Cleveleys

5 miles N of Blackpool on the A584

This popular seaside resort is less boisterous than its neighbour, Blackpool, to the south and it is altogether more attractive – architecturally. This is hardly surprising as the town began to grow after an architectural competition, organised in 1906, in which Sir Edwin Lutyens, the designer of modern Whitehall, London, was involved.

Fleetwood

8 miles N of Blackpool on the A587

Cleveleys in turn links up with Fleetwood which until 1836 was just a small fishing village. Local landowner Sir Peter Hesketh-Fleetwood decided to develop the area as a seaside resort and employed the leading architect, Decimus Burton, who had designed London's Regent Street as well as large parts of St Leonards on Sea and Hove.

Prior to the commencement of the building work in 1836, Fleetwood was a small settlement of a few fishermen's cottages. The opening of the railway

extension from Preston to Fleetwood was a key player in the town's development and the impressive North Euston Hotel, which opened in 1842, reflects those railway links. Queen Victoria used Fleetwood as she travelled to Scotland for her annual holiday. However, this was all before the railway companies managed to lay a railway over Shap fell in Cumbria in 1847 and thus provide a direct rail link to Scotland. Sir Peter was bankrupted but the town itself continued to flourish as a port and seaside resort.

The town's **Museum**, overlooking the River Wyre, illustrates the town's links with the fishing industry which suffered greatly from the Icelandic cod wars of the 1970s.

The town's most famous product is known around the world. In 1865, a

Fleetwood Harbour

local chemist named James Lofthouse created a compound of liquorice, capsicum, eucalyptus and methanol designed to relieve the sore throats and bronchial troubles endured by fishermen at sea. He called the

Waverley Paddle Steamer, Fleetwood

mixture **Fisherman's Friend** and it was remarkably successful. The only problem was that the bottles in which it was sold frequently shattered in the rough Atlantic seas. So Lofthouse transformed the liquid into a lozenge which is still produced by his descendants and has enormous sales world-wide.

Upstream from Fleetwood, ICI continues an industry that was well-established in Roman times – extracting salt from the extensive salt marshes lining the river Wyre.

Rossall Point

7 miles N of Blackpool off the A587

Situated at the northern tip of the Fylde coast, this was where the Hesketh-Fleetwood family, the force behind the creation of Fleetwood, had their home. Their impressive mansion is still standing and is now part of Rossall School.

Preesall

8 miles N of Blackpool on the B5270

The village's original name, Pressoude, as it was mentioned in the *Domesday Book*, is thought to mean a salt farm near the sea and certainly in 1872 rock salt deposits were discovered beneath the village. From then on, for around 30 years, Preesall became a centre for salt mining and in 1883 the Fleetwood Salt Company was established to develop the field. The bulk of the salt was extracted in the form of brine and by the end of 1891 there was a reliable pipeline pumping the salt under the River Wyre to Fleetwood. However, as much of the salt was extracted from underneath the expanding village, subsidence soon became a problem. In 1923 this led to the opening up of a huge pit, known locally as "Bottomless" to the west of the village.

Knott End-on-Sea

8 miles N of Blackpool on the B5270

This small coastal resort on the River Wyre estuary grew into a substantial fishing settlement in the 17th and 18th centuries. It was also a pilot base for the upstream ports of Wardleys and Skippool and later developed into a ferry port. Today its broad flat sands and bracing sea air, along with the decline in the fishing industry, have turned the town into a small, quiet holiday resort that is also favoured by those who have retired.

Looking out to sea, at low tide, a rocky outcrop can be seen which, some historians have suggested, is the remains of the masonry of a Roman harbour. Whether this is the port that in the 2nd century Ptolemy marked on a map as Portus Setantiorum is certainly in doubt but it is undeniable that such a building existed as the Romans were planning an invasion of Ireland from this stretch of coast.

Pilling

10 miles N of Blackpool off the A588

This quiet scattered village, on the edge of rich, fertile marshland, was for many years linked to the market town of Garstang by a little, winding, single-track railway known affectionately as the "Pilling Pig" because the train's whistle sounded like a pig having its throat cut. The last passengers were

carried in 1930; the last goods train ran in 1950.

Said to be the second largest village in Britain, Pilling boasts no fewer than 5 churches. One of them, **Old St John's** is notable as a "time-warp" church, virtually unchanged since its completion in 1717. Flagged floors, pews and box-pews of unvarnished oak, and a three-decker pulpit have all survived unscathed thanks to the building of a new church in the village in 1887.

There has been a watermill at Pilling since 1242. The present windmill dates back to 1808 and was built on a raft of brushwood. It is now a private residence.

Another building of interest is The Olde Ship Inn, built in 1782 by George Dickson, a slave trader. Now a listed building, the inn is reputed to be haunted by a lady dressed in Georgian attire wandering around with a pale and worried look on her face.

Garstang

12 miles N of Blackpool on the A6

This is an ancient, picturesque town whose market dates back to the time of Edward II and is still held every Thursday in the central square with its handsome former Town Hall of 1755. A bell is rung at 10am to signify the opening of trading. Another long-standing institution is the Garstang Agricultural Show which was founded in 1809 and is held on the first Saturday in August.

The town is also home to an excellent **Discovery Centre** which deals with a variety of aspects of the region, including the history of the nearby Forest of Bowland and the natural history of the surrounding countryside.

Just to the east of the town, on the top of a grassy knoll, are the remains of **Greenhalgh Castle**, built in 1490 by Thomas Stanley, the first Earl of Derby. Severely damaged during a siege by Cromwell's troops in 1645-46, the castle was one of the last strongholds in Lancashire to have held out and only surrendered when its Governor died.

Nearby Gubberford Bridge is reputedly haunted. It was during the Civil War siege that a Roundhead soldier named Peter Broughton was standing on the bridge one winter evening when he was approached by a beautiful woman dressed all in white. To his amazement, he recognised the wife who had left him for another man some five years earlier.

She was advancing towards him, smiling and with her arms outstretched, when a Royalist captain, Robert Rowton, burst onto the bridge. In the altercation that followed it emerged that she had bigamously married the captain. Enraged, Rowton stabbed her in the breast and she died within minutes. The two soldiers from opposing sides then joined forces to bury beside the bridge the body of the woman they had both known as wife. It was only a death-bed confession by Peter Broughton many years later that brought the deed to light. By then Rowton was dead but the unquiet soul of the White Lady has

THE KENLIS ARMS

Kenlis Road, Barnacre, Garstang,
Lancashire PR3 1GD
Tel/Fax: 01995 603307

Built in 1856 as a hunting lodge on the Barnacre Estate, **The Kenlis Arms** occupies a scenic location just 50 yards from the Lancaster Canal.

Mine hosts are Andrea and Terry, with Andrea – an excellent cook – in charge of the kitchen. Freshly prepared food is available Friday to Sunday and Bank Holiday Mondays, every lunchtime and evening, with wholesome traditional fare as the speciality of the house. The choices on the regular menu are supplemented by daily specials. Andrea is also happy to cook for private parties. The inn hosts food themed evenings with music and there's also country music twice a month on Saturdays.

Beverages served include a rotating guest ale along with a wide selection of draught keg beers, lagers and stouts. Outside, there's a delightful country garden with a children's play area. The inn also has 3 excellent en suite guest rooms available all year. All are doubles with one room large enough to be called a family room. The tariff, which remains the same throughout the year, includes a hearty full English breakfast and there are discounts for stays of more than one night.

The Kenlis Arms is closed at lunchtime, Monday to Thursday, except on Bank Holiday Mondays. All major credit cards apart from American Express and Diners are welcome.

found no rest and on misty winter evenings she paces silently up and down the bridge.

A little to the north of Garstang, on the B6430, are the remains of a stone-built **Toll House** which probably dates from the 1820s when parts of the turnpike from Garstang to Lancaster were realigned. Although a ruin, the toll house is more than usually interesting as the posts for the toll gates can still be seen on either side of the road. This stretch of road also features some of the finest **Turnpike Milestones** in the county. To the south of Garstang they are round-faced stones with cursive lettering dating from the 1750s but to the north the stones are triangular, with Roman lettering, and date from the time of the turnpike's realignment in the early 19th century.

Hambleton

6 miles NE of Blackpool on the A588

A centre for ship building in medieval times, Hambleton is now a quiet village set around a bend of the River Wyre. A network of narrow lanes radiate from the village and wind through the charming north Fylde countryside.

The village stands on one of the narrowest parts of the river and there was certainly a ford in Roman times, as relics have been found here. However, it is probable that the ford goes back even further, to the Iron Age around 500 BC. On the site of the ford now stands the 325-yard **Shard Bridge**, built in 1864 and still operating as a toll bridge.

East of Blackpool

Poulton-le-Fylde

4 miles E of Blackpool on the A586

This is one of the oldest towns in the ancient area known as Amounderness. The Romans were known to have been in the area and it was probably their handiwork that constructed the **Danes Pad**, an ancient trackway. The town developed as a commercial centre for the surrounding agricultural communities and its Market Place remains its focal point. In 1732, a great

---

THE SHARD RIVERSIDE INN

Old Bridge Lane, Hambleton,
Poulton-le-Fylde, Lancashire FY6 9BT
Tel/Fax: 01253 700208
e-mail: info@shardriversideinn.co.uk
website: www.shardriversideinn.co.uk

Occupying a delightful position overlooking the River Wyre, **The Shard Riverside Inn** was originally ferrymen's cottages and parts of the premises date back to the 1600s. Family owned and run by a father and son team both

named Paul Hurst, this welcoming old inn is noted for its outstanding food, freshly prepared using only the finest ingredients.

Beverages on offer include two real ales and a good selection of wines. The Hurst family are currently planning to provide 10 superior guest rooms, all en suite, and these may well be available by the time you read this.

fire, started by sparks from the torches of a funeral procession, destroyed most of the thatched cottages that surrounded the market square in those days and a nationwide appeal was launched to help meet the rebuilding costs. Consequently, little of old Poulton can be seen in the centre of the town.

The present **Church of St Chad** dates from the early 17th century, though the majority of the building is Georgian, and it stands on the site of the original Norman church. Inside there's a splendid Georgian nave from which a magnificent staircase leads to typically Georgian galleries running around three sides. As Poulton was a key town in the area for centuries, it is not surprising that there are several magnificent memorials to the local Fleetwood-Hesketh family also to be found here.

Fire seems to have played an important role in the life of the town and one ancient custom still kept is **Teanlay Night**, which involves the lighting of bonfires on Hallowe'en. Each bonfire is encircled with white-coloured stones which are then thrown into the flames by the onlookers and left until the next day. The successful retrieval of one's own stone is considered a good omen for future prosperity.

Strolling around Poulton-le-Fylde now, it is hard to imagine that the town was once a seaport. But, until relatively recently ships sailed up the River Wyre to **Skippool Creek**. Today, the creek is home to the Blackpool and Fleetwood Yacht Club and from here the ocean-going yachts compete in major races around Britain.

The town had a rail link long before Blackpool and it was here that the early holidaymakers alighted from their trains to take a horse and trap the remaining few miles. Fortunately for Poulton, in 1846, the railway reached Blackpool and the town could, once again, return to a more peaceful existence. It is this quiet and charm, as well as sensitive approaches to planning, that have led it to become, in recent years, a much sought after residential area for businessmen now able to travel the M55 to Manchester and Liverpool.

Incidentally, Poulton's "le-Fylde" tag was added to distinguish the town from Poulton-le-Sands – nowadays better known as Morecambe.

Singleton

5 miles E of Blackpool on the B5260

Singleton's most famous son is Robert Gillow who lived here in the first half of the 18th century. He left to become an apprentice joiner at Lancaster and later founded the cabinet making business that became Waring & Gillow of Lancaster.

The village Gillow knew was completely demolished in 1853 after it was bought for £70,000 by Alderman Thomas Miller, a cotton manufacturer from Preston. He then rebuilt it as a model village complete with a church, school, public house – *The Millers Arms*, naturally, and an ornate black-and-white shed for the village fire engine which still stands although it is now an electricity sub-station.

The parish church of this quiet little Fylde village, **St Anne's Church**, was built as part of Miller's model village in 1860. In the sanctuary is a black oak chair which bears the inscription "John Milton, author of Paradise Lost and Paradise Regained 1671" but no-one seems to know where the chair came from and whether the great author did indeed use it. The Miller family home, Singleton Hall, lies tucked away out of sight behind a pair of impressive gates. The house is not open to the public.

Great Eccleston
8 miles NE of Blackpool off the A586

This quiet traditional agricultural community on the banks of the River Wyre was, during the 17th and 18th centuries known locally as Little London because it was the social centre for the surrounding area. This was probably directly linked to the generous number of public houses and inns in the village at that time.

Every Wednesday, a bustling open air market is held in the charming village square. However, unlike most markets Great Eccleston's first took place in 1974 following a campaign started by the parish council a few years previously. The wide variety of stalls attract visitors from not only the immediate surroundings but also coaches from outside the rural area.

St Michael's on Wyre
10 miles NE of Blackpool on the A586

The River Wyre at this point is still tidal and for centuries the inhabitants of St Michael's and other villages in the area have suffered the threat of flooding. An old flood bank has been constructed from the village bridge and below, beyond the overgrown banks, are the fertile fields of the flood plain.

Mentioned in the *Domesday Book* as Michelscherche, is it likely that the first church in the village was founded in the 7th century. As well as many memorials to the Butler family the church also contains a splendid 14th century mural that was only discovered in 1956 when repair work was being undertaken in the sanctuary.

The Butler family, whose home – Rawcliffe Hall – lies a few miles down river, are known to have been in this area for 800 years and their house is built on the site of a Saxon dwelling. Another of the staunchly Catholic Lancashire families, the Butlers finally lost their house and the influence that they had in the area. The house is now part of a private country club.

Churchtown
12 miles NE of Blackpool on the A586

This delightful village has many buildings of both architectural and historic interest and none more so than the **Church of St Helen** which dates back to the days of the Norman Conquest. Featuring architectural styles from almost every period since the 11th century, this church is well worth exploring. The oldest parts of the building are the circular pillars near the nave which date from around 1200. The roof is the original Tudor structure. Built on the site of a Saxon church, St Helen's is dedicated to the mother of Emperor Constantine and the circular churchyard is typical of the Saxon period.

Known as the "Cathedral of the Fylde", the church has been subjected to flooding by the River Wyre and in 1746 such was the damage caused by the rising waters that the rebuilding of the church looked necessary. However, the builder brought in to survey the scene, suggested that moving the river would be a cheaper option and this method of preserving the church was undertaken. The original course of the river can be seen by taking the footpath from the churchyard in the direction of the new river course.

Woodplumpton

12 miles E of Blackpool off the B5269

This charming little village, centred around its church still has its well preserved village stocks behind which is a mounting block that is now designated as a historic monument. **St Anne's Church** is also a building of historic note and the keen-eyed will be quick to spot the octagonal cupola shape of tower

that is reminiscent of the architecture of Christopher Wren. Completed in 1748, the tower was built to house a new timepiece, a clock, which replaced the sundial that for many years adorned the old tower. Bearing the date 1637, this can now be found in the churchyard.

Many small towns and villages in Lancashire have their own tale of witches to tell and Woodplumpton is no exception. In St Anne's churchyard a huge boulder marks the grave of Margaret Hilton, better known in her day as "Meg the Witch". It's said that one day the local squire made a wager with her that she could not turn herself into a hare and outrun their pack of dogs. (This transformation into a hare was apparently a standard feature of any self-respecting witch's repertoire). Meg accepted the bet, stipulating only that one particular black dog should be excluded.

The race duly took place but the squire cheated, letting slip the black dog which managed to nip the hare's back legs just before it vanished into thin air. From that day, Meg suffered from a severe limp – and a nasty temper. Every kind of rural mishap was attributed to her black arts. She was eventually found dead in her cottage, crushed between a water barrel and a well, and her body was buried in the churchyard by torchlight on May 2nd, 1705. But her body kept rising to the surface so a massive boulder was rolled over her grave. (Similar measures were taken at Samlesbury, to the east of Preston. In

HAND AND DAGGER

Treales Road, Salwick, Preston,
Lancashire PR4 0SA
Tel/Fax: 01772 690306

The Hand and Dagger, in addition to its loyal regulars, is also popular with travellers cruising along the Lancaster Canal who can stop off at the moorings here. Others walk to it along the towpath. This charming old country inn dates back to the late 1600s and

its interior is full of character with lots of exposed beams and plenty of interesting memorabilia displayed around the walls. Mine hosts, Jennifer Rayton and Gary Campsty, took over here in December 2000, just in time for the first Christmas of the new millennium. Jennifer has extensive experience in the hospitality business and is also an excellent cook who offers a menu that many top restaurants would be proud of. It offers a wide choice of appetising dishes based on locally produced seasonal meats and vegetables and cooked to perfection. To accompany this enticing fare the inn stocks an extensive selection of wines, spirits and beers, including several hand-pulled ales and a number of guest beers which alter every two weeks or so. Customers can enjoy their refreshments beside one of the open log fires or, in summer, sit outside in the patio-style beer garden. Good food, fine ales – and plans are under way for the Hand and Dagger to also offer quality accommodation which may well be already available by the time you read this.

the churchyard there's a witch's grave through which iron spikes have been driven to prevent her from returning to plague her neighbours).

Clifton and Salwick
11 miles SE of Blackpool off the A583

Both Salwick and its neighbour, Clifton, were formed from part of the old Clifton estate. As well as the pleasant walks along the banks of the canal, visitors can also enjoy the delights of The Windmill pub which is, unlike most pubs of that name, housed in a converted windmill.

Treales
9 miles SE of Blackpool off the A583

Although the M55 runs close by the village lies in an area of quiet country lanes, small woods, and farms. As well as the tastefully restored cottages, some of which have managed to retain their thatched roofs, this rural village's old windmill also has been converted into a beautiful home.

Kirkham
8 miles SE of Blackpool off the A583

Mentioned in the *Domesday Book*, there was a settlement here in Saxon times, known as Ciric-ham, and before that the Romans had a fort though it is now lost under a modern housing estate. Kirkham was first granted a charter to hold a

weekly market in 1287 and since then it has been serving the needs of the surrounding farming communities. Some fine Georgian inns and houses reflect the town's importance in stagecoach days and steep main street contains a number of old-fashioned family-run shops. In the cobbled market square, used for markets and fairs since 1296, The Fishstones are still to be seen – flat stone slabs set on stone uprights to form a broken circle and were the counters from which fish was sold.

Freckleton
9 miles SE of Blackpool on the A584

This is the largest village in the Fylde with a population of more than 7000. The name is derived from the Anglo-Saxon *Frecheltun* meaning 'an enclosed area' and this is how it featured in the *Domesday Book*. Situated on the northern banks of the River Ribble, the long straggling village was, until the river was canalised, surrounded by marshland.

During World War II the village suffered an appalling tragedy. On a sweltering, thundery day in August 1944 an American Liberator plane took off from nearby Warton aerodrome but because of the adverse weather, the pilot decided to turn back. As it descended over Freckleton it clipped some trees and crashed into the village school. Thirty-six children and 36 adults perished. A disaster fund was set up but villagers bitterly disagreed about how it should be spent. It wasn't until 33 years later that the money was used to build the village's Memorial Hall.

Lytham St Anne's

4 miles E of Blackpool on the A584

Located on the northern bank of the Ribble Estuary, Lytham St Anne's is based on a much older community, already well established by the time of the Norman Conquest. It has a short pier, a gracious Victorian Promenade, and an attractive grassy expanse called the Beach. Here stands a handsome white-washed windmill, one of very few to have survived from the days when the flat plain of the Fylde was dotted with hundreds of them.

There are actually two towns here: Lytham, which is mentioned in the *Domesday Book*, and St Anne's, which was largely developed in the 1870s as a rather upmarket resort. Before the development of the resort, in the Victorian age, Lytham was an important port on the Ribble estuary and was home

to the first fishing company on this stretch of the northwest coast. Shipbuilding also continued here until the 1950s when the last vessel constructed in the shipyards was the Windermere Car Ferry. During the 1940s, parts of the famous Mulberry harbour were constructed in secret here in preparation for the invasion of Normandy in 1944.

The arrival of the railway linking Lytham with Preston prompted a group of Lancashire businessmen to plan the construction of a health resort between the old established port and the rapidly expanding town of Blackpool to the north. There was scarcely a cottage on their chosen site when the work began in 1875 but the growth of the carefully planned town was spectacular. In just 30 years the population increased from 1,000 to 17,000 inhabitants.

The **Promenade**, running the full length of the seafront from St Anne's to Lytham was constructed in 1875 and on the landward side there are several fine examples of Victorian and Edwardian

seaside villas. Beyond the attractive Promenade Gardens, laid out by a local character, Henry Gregson, is **St Anne's Pier**. Opened in 1885, the elegant pier was built in a mock Tudor style and up until 1897

Lytham at Sunset

fishing smacks and pleasure boats were able to tie up at the end of the jetty. Lytham also had a pier, built in 1865, but during a gale in 1903 two sand barges dragged their anchors and sliced the structure in two. Undeterred, and with the Pavilion still standing at the far end, the pier was rebuilt only to be almost entirely destroyed by fire in 1928.

In fact, the town has had its fair share of disasters associated with the sea. By far the worst of these occurred in 1886 and it is still Britain's greatest lifeboat disaster. The crew of the St Anne's lifeboat, with the help of the Southport lifeboat, set out to answer a distress signal put up by a German ship, the *Mexico*. The sea was so rough that 15 members of the lifeboat crew were lost. The tragedy led to the improvement of lifeboat design. In the **Alpine Garden** on the Promenade is a monument which pays tribute to the men who lost their lives. The statue features the stone figure of a coxswain looking out to sea

with a rope in one hand and a lifebelt in the other.

As well as being an elegant place full of fine Victorian and Edwardian architecture, Lytham St Anne's also contains some reminders to the more distant past. **Lytham Hall**, now privately owned by a large insurance company, started life as a farming cell of the Durham cathedral in 1190. After the Reformation, the estate changed hands several times, until in 1606 it became the property of Sir Cuthbert Clifton, the first squire of Lytham. The fine Georgian hall standing today was the building that John Carr of York built for Thomas Clifton between 1757 and 1764. The extensive grounds, once part of the estate, are now **Lytham Hall Country Park**, where visitors can follow several nature trails to discover the birds and wildlife living here which includes three species of woodpecker, the lesser whitethroat, and the hawfinch.

There has been a **Windmill** at Lytham

Lytham Hall, Lytham

House is home to the **Lifeboat Museum**. Both buildings have limited opening times. Two other museums worthy of a visit are the **Lytham Motive Power Museum**, with its large model railway layout and an outdoor display of rolling stock, and the **Toy and Teddy Museum**, housed in the Porrit Victorian building with a varied collection of childhood memorabilia.

for more than 800 years though the present structure dates from 1805. A well known landmark along the coast, the building has a solid white tower with a cap that looks rather like an upturned boat. In 1929 the wind set the four sails turning the wrong way, ruining the machinery and firing the mill, which has never worked since. Now renovated, the windmill is home to a permanent exhibition on the building's history and on the process of breadmaking. Adjacent to the windmill, and the original home of the Lytham lifeboat, Old Lifeboat

For those interested in discovering more about the abundant wildlife of the dune system here, a visit to **Lytham St Anne's Nature Reserve** is a must. Established in 1968, the reserve is an important scientific site as well as being just a small part of what was once a very extensive sand dune system. As well as the rich plant life, the dunes are home to several rare species of migrating birds

THE LAURELS

346, Clifton Drive North, St Annes,
Lancashire FY8 2PB
Tel: 01253 782934
e-mail: thelaurels@bigfoot.com
website: www.laurels.ic24.net

Quality self-catering accommodation in a prime location is on offer at The Laurels, a spacious Victorian house which has recently been refurbished. It's almost opposite the attractive Ashton Gardens while St Anne's Square with its excellent shops and

restaurants is just a 3 minute walk away. The local beach, indoor swimming pool, cinema and casino are also within walking distance. The Laurels has 8 apartments on three floors and 2 Mews cottages. They accommodate from 1 to 5 persons and all are furnished and decorated to a very high standard and comprehensively equipped.

including osprey, black redstart, and Lapland buntings.

No description of Lytham St Anne's is complete without a mention of the **Royal Lytham and St Anne's Golf Course**. The club originated after a meeting held in 1886 when a group

Lytham Windmill at Sunset

of 19 keen golfers sought to furnish themselves with suitable facilities. The course opened in 1898 and it is still considered by many to be one of the finest golf links in the country and is a regular host of the British Open.

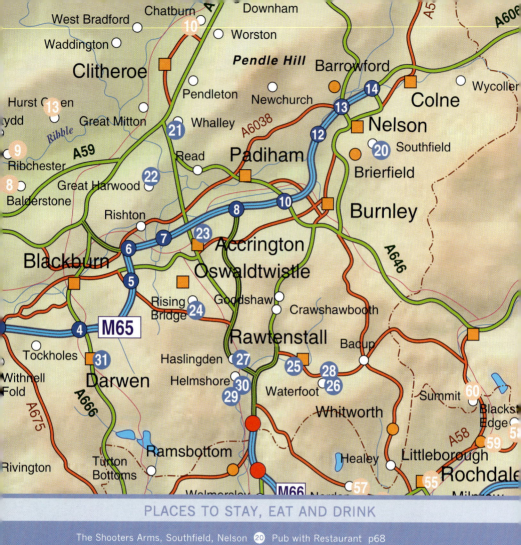

PLACES TO STAY, EAT AND DRINK

● Denotes entries in other chapters

4 The Forests of Pendle & Rossendale

The Pennine Hills, the *backbone of England*, are such a well-known geographical feature that it comes as something of a surprise to find that the name was created as recently as 1750 by a fraudulent professor. Charles Bertram claimed to have discovered a medieval chronicle describing Britain as it was in Roman times. In this non-existent tome, he said, the Romans had named this range of hills 'Alps Penina' because they resembled the Apennine Hills of central Italy. The professor's fake chronicle was soon discredited but his spurious name, the 'Pennines', has been universally adopted.

In the 1720s, Daniel Defoe jogged on horseback through the area and wrote it off as 'a howling wilderness....the English Andes'. A century later the wild, poverty stricken area Defoe had travelled through was throbbing with the sound of churning mill wheels, its sky murky with the smoke of thousands of coal fuelled factories. That sooty, industrial image lingers on despite the fact that this area of Lancashire has re-invented itself in the past few decades. The waste from coalpits has been transformed into smoothly landscaped country parks and energetic local councils are also striving to make the most of the region's natural attractions: swooping hills, stark moorlands and contrasting wooded valleys.

But the area still takes pride in its industrial past, now recognised by its designation as an official Heritage Area. Bacup, for example, as well as being the highest town in Lancashire at 827ft above sea level, is also acknowledged by English Heritage as the best preserved cotton town in Britain. And the Queen Street Mill at Haile Syke near Burnley is the only surviving steam-powered cotton mill in the country. Here, more than 300 deafening Lancashire looms clatter away in the imposing weaving shed where hundreds of metres of cotton cloth are produced weekly. In Burnley itself, the Weavers Triangle is one of the finest examples of a Victorian industrial townscape still in existence.

Southeast Lancashire also possesses some grand buildings from an earlier era. Gawthorpe Hall at Padiham is a Jacobean gem; Towneley Hall, dating back to the 1400s, houses Burnley's excellent Museum & Art Gallery, and Turton Tower, north of Bolton, is a lovely old building which began as a medieval pele.

Despite its industrial history, the southern border of Lancashire boasts some attractive villages. Withnell Fold, 5 miles southwest of Blackburn, is an idyllic model village entirely built by the Parke family in the mid 1800s to house the workforce employed at their paper mill. Rivington, near Chorley, is a captivating small village set around a village green and alongside a huge reservoir beneath whose waters half of the old village lies submerged.

Burnley

This cotton town is rich in history as well as being the largest town in this area of East Lancashire. Incorporating some 50 square miles, the town offers visitors a wealth of contrasts, from some of the best preserved industrial landscapes in Britain to the magnificent, untouched moorlands just to the east. First established at the beginning of the 9th century, the town nestles in a basin between the River Calder and the River Brun, from which it takes its name.

With the Industrial Revolution and the building of the Leeds and Liverpool Canal, Burnley not only expanded but grew in stature until, by the end of the 19th century, it was the world's leading producer of cotton cloth. Burnley's fine Victorian **Town Hall** of 1888, is one of many monumental public buildings in the area erected during that period of unparalleled English prosperity.

A walk along the towpath of the canal, through an area known as the **Weavers' Triangle** is like taking a step back in time. This is an area of spinning mills and weaving sheds; foundries where steam engines and looms were made; canal-side warehouses; domestic buildings, including a unique row of workers' cottages; and a Victorian school house. The Weavers' Triangle Visitors Centre is housed in the former wharfmaster's house and canal toll office. The centre is open to the public on several afternoons a week during the summer months and on most bank holidays. A short walk from the Visitors' Centre is **Oak Mount Mill** engine house. The splendid old steam, originally installed in 1887, has recently been restored and is now operated by electric motor. Opening times are variable.

Even more impressive is the **Queen Street Mill** which is the only surviving steam-powered cotton mill in Britain. A visit here provides a unique insight into Victorian factory life as the 300 deafening looms are powered by the magnificent steam engine, Peace. The mill was recently designated by the government as a museum with an outstanding collection – one of only 53 in the country to receive the award.

The history of Burnley can also be explored by boat along the Leeds and Liverpool Canal. This famous waterway leaves the Weavers' Triangle via a huge embankment which carries the canal across the town. Known as the 'straight mile', it is in fact less than that but no less exciting and, at 60 feet above the

Gawthorpe Hall, Burnley

around. Subjects include a giant magpie, a crocodile emerging from the water, and a huge cricket. The grounds also include a natural history centre, a **Museum of Local Crafts and Industries** and facilities for golf, tennis, bowls, and other outdoor pursuits.

Two other interesting places to visit whilst in Burnley are the **Burnley Heritage Centre**, where memorabilia on display from the town's past includes old photographs, a Lancashire loom, and a replica 1930s kitchen and living room. **The Stables Museum**, open at the weekends, is one of the town's more recent attractions and can be found at the wharf. Run by the Horses and Ponies Protection Association, the museum is a must for horse lovers and the exhibitions include information of the rescue and care of neglected horses, ponies, and donkeys as well as a display of the life of the canal horse.

Lovers of ghost stories will want to visit the **Rosehill Hotel** which has a resident ghost. She's called Rose and she was an employee at the hotel. In 1860, Rose had an affair with a relative of the hotel proprietor and became pregnant. This was an era when Victorian sexual

ground, it is one of the most impressive features of the canal's length.

Situated on the Todmorden Road on the outskirts of Burnley is the **Towneley Hall Art Gallery and Museum**. The home of the Towneley family since the 14th century, right up until 1902, parts of the present building date from the 15th century. Visitors can not only view the art collections, the Whalley Abbey Vestments, and the museum of local crafts and industries, but also take in a tour of the house. The kitchens, with their open fires, the servants' hall, a priest's hole and the fascinating family rooms are all on display. The grounds too are open to visitors and contain a traditional Victorian flower garden, woodland nature trails, and a fascinating series of sculptures hewn from the trees

The Shooters Arms

Southfield Lane, Southfield, Nelson,
Lancashire, BB10 3RJ
Tel: 01282 614153

The Shooters Arms occupies a superb position high on a hillside overlooking the town of Nelson and enjoying a grand view across to famous Pendle Hill. This welcoming old hostelry stands on a former drovers road and was originally a farmhouse. The farmer began selling ale and in due course the premises was licensed as a public house.

Today the inn is run by landlord David Coffey who has been in the hospitality business nearly all his working life.

Continuous credit for the Poacher's Kitchen Restaurant must go to the chef. Here you'll find an outstanding choice of beautifully prepared and presented food, all home cooked and based on fresh local produce. Amongst the starters for example are a farmhouse pâté, an Indian snack selection, a soup of the day and Chicken Satay served with a side salad and raita dip. Main meals include traditional pub favourites such as Liver & Onions, Fish & Chips and Steak & Kidney Pie along with homemade lasagne verdi, chilli con carne, a Poacher's Big Breakfast and wholetail Whitby scampi. Alternatives include heartily filled hot sandwiches, jacket potatoes, salads, burgers, and cold sandwiches. For vegetarians there's a wholesome Mediterranean Wellington, a Porcini Ravioli in a

Mushroom Sauce and a meat free breakfast. Kids have their own menu which offers popular children's choices such as chicken nuggets or fish fingers. Senior Citizens are well served by a very modestly priced 2-course meal with a choice of main dishes. Steak lovers should try to arrive on a Wednesday. This is Steak Night and offers a 2-course steak meal, again at a remarkable value-for-money price. The Poacher's Kitchen is open from noon until 3pm (Monday to Thursday), and on Wednesday evening from 5.30pm to 9pm. On Friday and Saturday the restaurant is open from noon until 9pm; on Sunday from noon until 7pm. The restaurant seats 26 diners and bookings are strongly advised for Wednesday evening and Sunday lunch.

For ale, the inn is open all day, every day, and offers a full range of Thwaite's beers along with 3 quality draught lagers, Kingston Press cider and Guinness, as well as traditional hand pulled beer. Each Saturday there's a DJ leading the entertainment from around 8.15pm, and the pub arranges occasional live entertainment.

Please note that the Shooters Arms accepts cash or cheques only.

morality was at its most rigid (and hypocritical). If Rose's illicit pregnancy became known, the hotel's reputation would suffer disastrously. Rose disappeared, completely. The hotel owner said she had been dismissed and left the town but those who knew of her condition suspected murder. Beneath the hotel there were cellars which were later filled with tons of rubble and it's believed that poor Rose was buried there, emerging from time to time when her successors as chambermaids were cleaning the rooms. She has been heard talking to herself about the daily chores to be done but otherwise has never troubled either the maids or the guests.

North of Burnley

Brierfield
2 miles N of Burnley on the A682

This industrial town has magnificent views of Pendle Hill as it lies on a steep slope at the bottom of which is an attractive **Quaker Bridge** over Pendle Water. At the beginning of the 19th century, coal was discovered in the area. Within a few years three pits had opened, thus sealing Brierfield's fate as a place of industry. The laying of turnpike roads, followed by the opening of the Leeds and Liverpool Canal, gave the growing village a further boost and by 1833 a handloom weaving business was also flourishing here. The humid climate and expanding transport system made Brierfield an ideal place for the burgeoning cotton industry, which had become the main source of employment here by the end of the 19th century.

Nelson
3 miles N of Burnley on the A56

This town, along with its neighbours Colne and Burnley are now inseparable as they share the same valley running along the length of Colne Water. Nelson is a modern textile town which takes its name from the hotel, The Lord Nelson, which stands by the railway line running along the valley bottom. Although the town itself might have been the product of the Industrial Age, two of its suburbs, Little and Great Marsden, have been here for centuries. Here, above Nelson, lies **Marsden Park**, and once Marsden Hall, the home of the de Walton family until their line died out in 1912. Acquired by the local authority, much of the hall was demolished whilst the parkland was developed.

Colne
5 miles N of Burnley on the A56

Before the Industrial Revolution turned this area into a valley devoted to the production of cotton cloth, Colne was a small market town that specialised in wool. Unfortunately, there are few reminders of the days before industrialisation but **St Batholomew's Church**, founded in 1122, is still here and contains some interesting interior decorations and furnishings. In the centre of the town, next to the War

Memorial is another memorial. The statue is of Lawrence Hartley, the bandmaster on the ill-fated *Titanic* who, heroically, stayed at his post with his musicians and played *Nearer my God to Thee* as the liner sank beneath the waves of the icy Atlantic in 1912.

Colne is also the unlikely home of the **British in India Museum**, where exhibits covering many aspects of the British rule over the subcontinent, from the 17th century until 1947 can be seen. The collection includes coins, medals, uniforms, model soldiers and a working model of the railway from Kalka to Simla.

Collectors of curiosities will enjoy the unique form of punishment devised for minor malefactors in Colne and preserved in the **Town Museum.** Stocks and pillories enjoyed a long history as a way of humiliating offenders and providing innocent amusement for bystanders. But many of Colne's busy citizens could not spare the time to leave their work and make their way to wherever the stocks were fixed. So a movable cart was constructed, capable of seating three offenders side by side, and the Town Beadle would wheel it around the town so that everyone could join in the fun.

Wycoller
6 miles NE of Burnley off the B6250

This hamlet lies amidst the moorlands that rise to the east of the textile towns of the Colne valley and up to the bleak summits of the Pennines. Now almost deserted, this was once a thriving place as an important centre for the wool trade and as a handloom weavers' settlement but it lost most of its inhabitants to the new factories in the west.

Fortunately, the place has been saved by the creation of a **Wycoller Country Park,** surrounding the village, and many of the buildings have been restored. There is also a delightful old hump-backed packhorse bridge crossing a stream and, above the village, a single slab gritstone bridge, **Clam Bridge**, that is thought to date from the Iron Age. Now a ruin, **Wycoller Hall** was the inspiration for Ferndean Manor in

Wycoller Hall

Charlotte Brontë's *Jane Eyre*: Wycoller was one of the villages to which the sisters walked from their house at Haworth.

Earby

10 miles NE of Burnley on the A56

The town lies almost on the county border with Yorkshire and here can be found the **Earby Mines Museum** housed in the old Grammar School building. With the largest collection of lead mining tools and equipment used in the Yorkshire Dales on display, there is much to see, including examples of the minerals extracted, a lead crushing mill, and other working models.

Pendle Hill

5 miles N of Burnley off the A6068

Dominating the landscape here is the great whale-backed mass of Pendle Hill, rising to 1920 feet above sea-level. The hill became notorious in the early 1600s as the location where the **Pendle Witches** supposedly practised their black arts. It has a more uplifting association, though, since it was from the summit of Pendle Hill in 1625 that George Fox saw a vision which inspired him to found the Society of Friends, or Quakers.

Pendle Hill lies at the heart of Lancashire's 'Witch Country', so called because of the events of 1612. On the 18th March of that year, a Halifax pedlar named John Law refused to give some pins to a beggar, Alison Device.

She spat out the usual beggar's curse on him. He died almost immediately of a heart attack. The effect of a curse or just a co-incidence? The early 1600s were the years of the great witch-hunts so the authorities had little difficulty in attributing John Law's sudden death to Alison Device's supernatural powers.

Alison was arrested. Under torture, she incriminated eight other 'witches'. All of them were then charged with communing with the Devil and committing a total of sixteen murders. They were tried, found guilty and hanged at Lancaster Castle on August 20th, 1612. All except one: Old Mother Demdike, eighty years old and half-blind, escaped the gallows by dying in gaol. During their trial, the 'Pendle Witches' seem to have taken pride in implicating each other. In effect, they hanged themselves by their fanciful tales of spells, potions, and the coven's naked caperings, fuelling the popular imagination that there really were witches who could affect the lives of other people. The infamous witches were, in the main, old women who dabbled with plants and herbs, knowing which could heal and which, when ingested, would spell certain death.

The Victorian novelist W.H. Ainsworth was inspired to write a colourful melodrama based on the trial, *The Lancashire Witches – A Romance of Pendle Forest*, and although it's doubtful that 'witchcraft' was any more prevalent around Pendle Hill than anywhere else in the country at that time, the legend has proved very durable. Every year now, on the evening of October 31st, Halloween, Pendle Hill is flecked with the dark figures of masked, black-cloaked figures making their way to its summit.

The story of the Pendle Witches is known to everyone with an interest in the occult, but there has always been something of a mystery about why one of them, Alice Nutter, was involved. Unlike the others who were either very poor or even beggars, Alice was a lady of substance. She lived at Roughlee Old Hall, a captivating Elizabethan manor house of 1576 which still stands (but is not open to the public). A recent theory is that she was a Roman Catholic and on her way to a clandestine service when she was caught up with the witches. To avoid betraying her co-religionists she kept silent about her real motives for being on Pendle Hill on the crucial night.

Something of this old, dark tragedy still broods over Pendle and many memories and places which hark back to those grim days remain. Those interested in finding out more about the trials should visit the **Pendle Heritage Centre** at **Barrowford**, to the southeast of the hill. The Centre is housed in a sturdy 17th century farmhouse built by the Bannister family, one of whose descendants was Roger Bannister, the first man to run a mile in less than four minutes. Historically, witches aside, the hill was one of the many beacon hills throughout the country that, forming a

chain, were lit in times of national crisis, such as the sighting of the Spanish Armada.

To the west of the hill's summit lies **Apronfull Hill**, a Bronze Age burial site, that is said to be the place from which the Devil threw stones at Clitheroe Castle, creating what is known as the Devil's Window.

Newchurch

4 miles N of Burnley off the A6068

This charming Pendle village was named following the consecration of a new church in 1544 by John Bird, Bishop of Chester. Earlier, during the Middle Ages, Newchurch was a cow and deer rearing centre, as well as part of the old hunting forest of Pendle but by the reign of Elizabeth I the area was becoming de-forested and farming was beginning to take over as the primary source of income.

Newchurch did not escape from stories of witchcraft that surrounded the notorious Pendle witches trial in the 17th century, and many ghostly tales and shadowy traditions are said to be associated with the village. Though those times were a frightening experience for anyone living in the area, by the 18th century, the witch hunts were over and the village grew rapidly as part of the expanding textile industry, first with handloom weavers and then with the construction of a factory for washing and dyeing wool.

An old tradition continues here – the **Annual Rushbearing** when dry rushes are scattered on the church floor and in the pews. Originally this was to keep parishioners warm and although the advent of central heating makes it no longer necessary the villagers still process through the village carrying rushes and singing hymns accompanied by a brass band. A Rushbearing Queen is crowned and after a short service in the church everyone repairs to the school for a grand tea.

Padiham
2 miles W of Burnley on the A646

This charming small town of narrow winding lanes and cobbled alleyways still retains characteristics typical of the early days of the Industrial Revolution. However, there was a settlement here long before the Norman Conquest and Padiham was also the market town for the western slopes of Pendle. A market is still held here every Wednesday and Friday.

One of Lancashire's most impressive stately homes is **Gawthorpe Hall** (National Trust) which stands on the bank of the River Calder, surrounded by gardens and woodland. The Shuttleworth family have lived at Gawthorpe since the early 1400s but the present house is a gracious 17th century mansion, restored and extended in the 1850s by Sir Charles Barry. This was the era of High Victorian extravagance and no expense was spared on the opulent decorations and furnishings. The Hall has many pictures on loan from the National Portrait Gallery which add

extra lustre to the already notable collection. Open to the public between Easter and October, the house has beautiful period furnishings, ornately decorated ceilings and the original wood panelled walls and is also home to the nationally important Kay-Shuttleworth collection of fine needlework and lace.

Read
5 miles W of Burnley on the A671

Situated on the banks of the River Calder it was during a skirmish near **Read Old Bridge** in April 1643 that the Royalist cause in Lancashire was lost.

Read Hall, privately owned and no longer in the hands of the original family, was the home of one of Lancashire's most famous families, the Nowells. It was Roger Nowell, in 1612, who committed the Pendle witches to trial. The Nowells left the hall in 1772 and in 1799 the house was completely rebuilt in the Georgian style seen today.

Whalley
7 miles W of Burnley on the B6246

One of Lancashire's most attractive villages, Whalley grew up around a crossing of the River Calder, between Pendle Hill and the Nab. There are old cottages and Tudor houses, Georgian houses in the main street and three out of the four inns at the crossroads date from the 1700s. Soaring above the village is the **Whalley Viaduct,** an impressive 48-arched structure built in 1850 to carry the Blackburn to Clitheroe

TOBY JUG TEA SHOP

20 King Street, Whalley, Clitheroe,
Lancashire BB7 9SL
Tel/Fax: 01254 823298

The delightful **Toby Jug Tea Shop,** a Grade II listed building, stands in the heart of Whalley's Conservation Area and is one of the oldest buildings in the village. It's not known exactly when the house was built but it has stood on the main road to the Fylde coast for some 300 years. A mill race excavated in 1300 for the Cistercian monks of Whalley Abbey borders the tea room and, inside the house, the oak beams and upstairs panelling

is believed to have come from the Abbey. Old stone fireplaces testify to the antiquity of the building which for many years was a farmhouse. In 1810, farmer Thurston Tomlinson won an award at Whalley's first Agricultural Show. He also traded as a miller, grocer and butcher. In recent years the house has served as a sweet shop, a café and an ice cream parlour but now seems to have found its real purpose as a top quality tea shop.

The menu offers some delicious teatime treats such as home-made scones with butter, jam and cream, and a selection of gateaux and cakes that varies both on a daily basis and with the changing seasons. The cakes and scones are all baked in Marie Ireland's family kitchen, using only the finest ingredients including free range eggs. Between 11.30am and 2.30pm,

the Toby Jug also offers an appetising choice of lunchtime savouries – home-made soup served with a freshly baked granary roll, open or closed sandwiches (large succulent Greenland prawns with celery and a special dressing, for example), warm ciabatta rolls and baked jacket potatoes. Other choices include a Miller's Lunch (tasty Lancashire cheese with apple, home-made chutney, granary roll and salad), and an Angler's Lunch of melt-in-the-mouth smoked trout fillet accompanied by a bowl of mayonnaise, granary roll and salad. Everything is freshly prepared for the day, attractively presented and served with courtesy and efficiency.

Given the quality of the food served here, it comes as no surprise to learn that the Toby Jug recently received the accolade of a prestigious Award of Excellence from the Tea Council – one of only 12 tea rooms in the country to be so honoured. The Tea Shop is open all year round, Tuesday to Saturday, from 10.30am to 4.30pm (4pm in the winter months).

railway line across the broad valley of the Calder. Rather touchingly, where the viaduct crosses the lane leading to **Whalley Abbey** the arches have added Gothic details that harmonise with the nearby 14th century gatehouse to the abbey.

The abbey was the last to be built in Lancashire, started in the early 1300s, but for the Cistercian monks whose work it was, Whalley was not their first choice. They had already established a religious house at Stanlow, on the banks of the River Mersey and now under a huge oil refinery, in 1172.

Seeking somewhere less harsh and more fertile land, the monks moved to Whalley in 1296 but their attempts to build were hampered as Sawley Abbey felt threatened by the competition for the donations of land and goods expected from the local population. Building finally began in 1310 and by 1400 the imposing and impressive abbey had taken shape. The demise of the abbey came, as it did to all religious houses, under Henry VIII but Whalley's abbot, joining forces with the abbot of Sawley, took part in the Pilgrimage of Grace in an attempt to save their houses. This failed and the abbots were both executed.

Now owned and cared for by the Diocese of Blackburn, Whalley Abbey is one of the best preserved such places in the country and its future secure as it also acts as a conference centre.

Whalley's **Parish Church** is almost a century older than the abbey, its oldest parts dating back to 1206. Built on the site of an even older place of worship, the churchyard is home to three ancient crosses and the church itself contains a set of some of the finest choir stalls anywhere. They were brought here from the abbey after the Dissolution and though they are not elaborate there are some intriguing carvings on the lower portions. Even more intriguing though are the puzzling tombstones in the churchyard, each one inscribed with impossible dates such as April 31st 1752 and February 30th 1839.

Pendleton
6 miles NW of Burnley off the A59

Recorded in the *Domesday Book* when the village was part of the vast parish of Whalley, this small settlement of cottages and working farms has retained much of its traditional air – only seven new houses have been built here in the last 100 years. A beck runs through the middle of the village which was designated a Conservation Area in 1968. The discovery of a Bronze Age burial urn in the village in 1969 would indicate that there were settlers here as long ago as 1600BC.

From the village there is a steep road, to the southeast, that climbs up to the **Nick of Pendle** from where there are magnificent views.

Rishton
7 miles W of Burnley on the A678

Originally a Saxon settlement, the name means the fortified village or dwelling place amid the rushes, and, during the

Middle Ages, the village grew in importance as an early textile centre with the operation of its fulling mill. By the 17th century, Rishton had gained a name for the manufacture of linen cloth and, in 1766, it became the first village to weave calico. As the Industrial Revolution advanced, the industry moved from the weavers' homes into newly built mills.

The manor of Rishton, once owned by the Petre family, was part of the larger estate of Clayton-le-Moors and the manor house, **Dunkenhalgh Hall**, is said to have been named after a Scottish raider called Duncan who made his home here. Elizabethan in origin, the hall is now a private hotel.

Oswaldtwistle

7 miles W of Burnley on the A679

This typical Lancashire textile town has produced many miles of cotton cloth over the years. You can still hear the deafening clatter of looms at Oswaldtwistle Mills in Collier Street, one of the last working cotton mills in the country. Cotton has been woven here for more than 200 years under the watchful eyes of just two owners – the Walmsleys and the Tattersall/Hargreaves family. The town can justifiably be considered the heart of the industry since it was whilst staying here, at what is now Stanhill Post Office, that James Hargreaves invented his famous 'Spinning Jenny' in 1764. Although he was forced to leave the area after sometimes violent opposition to his

machine from local hand spinners, the town's prosperity is largely due to textiles and, in particular, calico printing. However, Oswaldtwistle is a much older settlement than its rows of Victorian terraced houses would suggest as the name means the boundary of the kingdom of Oswald, who was a 7th century Northumbrian king.

Great Harwood

6 miles W of Burnley on the B6535

Before the Industrial Revolution, this was a quiet village of farms and cottages nestling between two streams. Famous for its fine woollen cloth, at the beginning of the 19th century cotton handloom weaving and then, by the 1850s, the introduction of the factory system and the cotton mills took over. Today only one mill remains but at the industry's height the town supported 22 mills. Not surprisingly, Great Harwood's most famous son was very much linked with cotton. In 1850, John Mercer, an industrial chemist, developed the technique of processing cotton to give it a sheen and the technique, mercerisation, is still used today. The free-standing clock tower in the Town Square was erected in 1903 to commemorate Mercer's contribution to the life of his home town.

Accrington

5 miles SW of Burnley on the A680

This attractive Victorian market town, as is typical in this area, expanded as a

DOG & OTTER

Cliffe Lane, Great Harwood,
Lancashire BB6 7PG
Tel: 01254 885760 Fax: 01254 882600

Close to the parish church, the **Dog & Otter** has an inviting black and cream exterior with colourful hanging baskets. Simon Price, who runs the inn with his business partner Catherine Fielding-Darnley, is an interior designer and has completely redesigned and refurbished the inn with very pleasing results. A major attraction here is the excellent food, served every lunchtime and evening, from noon until 9pm on Friday, Saturday and Sunday, with fish dishes and the Sunday roast as the specialities. To complement your meal, a wide range of beverages are available including 3 real ales.Monday is quiz night with gallons of ale to be won.

result of the boom in the textile industry of the 18th and 19th centuries. Of all Lancashire's indoor markets, Accrington enjoys the grandest surroundings, housed in a magnificent **Market Hall** built in 1868. Accrington is also the place to visit for a real flavour of the old Lancashire: in April it hosts the Lancashire Food Festival, followed in May by the annual Clog Dancing Festival. The town is the home of the **Haworth Art Gallery**, one of the most appealing galleries in the country – a charming Jacobean-style house built in 1909 and set in beautiful parkland. The gallery owns the largest collection of Tiffany glass – there are 130 pieces – in Europe. The collection was presented to the town by Joseph Briggs, an Accrington man, who emigrated to New York and worked with Louis Tiffany for nearly 40 years. Briggs joined the studio in 1890 and rose through the company ranks to become the manager of the Mosaic department before finally becoming Tiffany's personal assistant.

After the First World War, the fashion for Tiffany glassware waned and during the economic depression of the 1920s Briggs was given the sad job of selling off the remainder of the Tiffany stock. Returning to his native Accrington in 1933 with his collection of glass, Briggs gave half to the town and distributed the remainder amongst his family.

To the west of the town centre, the

THE WHITAKERS

322 Burnley Road, Accrington,
Lancashire BB5 6HG
Tel: 01254 392999

The Whitakers "for food with attitude" says the menu and indeed you will find a wide choice ranging from Cumberland Sausage Ring, Indian, Chinese and Thai dishes to filled baguettes, sandwiches, jacket potatoes and toasties. Mine hosts, Louise McVety and Danny Haskey, also make sure their customers have an extensive choice of beverages that includes 3 real ales. When they took over here in July 2001 the pub was in a sad way but they very quickly made The Whitakers a lively social centre. Especially popular are their themed parties – "Wacky Whitakers Fun Themes" – which include Medieval Madness, School Dinners for which guests arrive in their old school uniforms, a Shipwrecked evening as well as special Christmas themed parties.

RISING BRIDGE INN

600 Blackburn Road, Rising Bridge,
Accrington, Lancashire BB5 2SB
Tel: 01706 215891

A good place to stop off for a well-pulled pint and some wholesome home-cooked food is the **Rising Bridge Inn** at the village of Rising Bridge near Haslingden. Brett Powell and his sister Pamela Eden took over here in 2000 with Brett, an experienced chef, in charge of the kitchen and Pamela presiding over the bar. The inn has been totally refurbished recently and offers a full range of wines, beers, spirits and cask ales. Brett's menu offers a varied choice with Roast Beef, Lamb and Chicken as specialities but also including vegetarian options. Senior Citizens enjoy permanent discounts on all the meals.

Accrington Railway Viaduct is another magnificent monument to Victorian builders. Erected for the former East Lancashire Railway it sweeps across the River Hyndburn in a graceful curve of 19 arches sixty feet high. Also worth a visit are the imposing **Town Hall** with its Corinthian portico and the elegant glass-roofed Arcade of 1880.

South of Burnley

Bacup

7 miles S of Burnley on the A671

At 827ft the highest town in Lancashire, Bacup was built in the 19th century for the sole purpose of cotton manufacture. It remains one of the best examples of a textile town in England even though the town suffered more than most when the mills began to close. A stroll through the town centre will reveal carefully restored shops and houses, with the grander homes of the mill owners and the elegant civic buildings acting as a reminder of the town's more prosperous times. Also, look out for what is claimed to be the shortest street in the world –

Elgin Street off the Market Place which is just 17ft long.

An excellent time to visit the town is during the Easter weekend when the town's famous troop of Morris dancers take to the streets. Known as the **Coconut Dancers**, their costume is unique and involves wearing halved coconut husks strapped to their knees and blackening their faces. Maintaining that the correct name is Moorish not Morris Dancers, the tradition is thought to go back to the times of the Crusades.

Rawtenstall

7 miles S of Burnley on the A682

The town first developed as a centre of the woollen cloth trade with the work being undertaken by hand workers in their own homes before steam-powered mills were introduced in the early 19th century. The introduction of the cotton industry to the town happened at around the same time. Lower Mill, now a ruin, was opened in 1840 by the Whitehead brothers who were some of the area's first manufacturing pioneers. The **Weaver's Cottage**, purpose-built for a

ROSSENDALE MUSEUM

Whitaker Park, Haslingden Road,
Rawtenstall, Rossendale,
Lancashire. BB4 6RE
Tel: 01706 217777/244682
Fax: 01706 250037

Rossendale Museum is a former 19th century mill owner's house set in Whitaker Park. Displays include a Victorian drawing room, fine and decorative art, local and natural history, and costume. Temporary exhibitions held throughout the year. Disabled access to ground floor. Audio and large print guides available. Admission is free.

home weaver, is one of the last buildings remaining of its kind and is open to visitors at weekends during the summer.

Also in the town, and housed in a former Victorian mill owner's house called Oakhill, is the **Rossendale Museum** (see above). Naturally, the area's industrial heritage is given a prominent position but collections of the region's natural history, fine art and furniture, and ceramics are on display too.

At one end of the town stands a new railway station which marks the end of a very old railway line – the **East Lancashire Railway**. Opened in 1846 and run commercially until 1980, when the last coal train drew into Rawtenstall, the line is now in the hands of the East Lancashire Railway Preservation Society. Running a passenger service (at weekends with additional summer services), the steam trains offer an enthralling 17 mile round trip along the River Irwell between Rawtenstall and Bury, via Ramsbottom. The railway also operates regular Red Rose Diner trains with Pullman style dining cars offering travellers a gourmet meal and an evening of pure nostalgia.

Rawtenstall itself is noted for having the only remaining temperance bar in Britain – Herbal Health on Bank Street which serves traditional drinks such as

THE OLD STABLES

Tippett Farm, Cowpe Road, Waterfoot,
Rossendale, Lancashire BB4 7AE
Tel/Fax: 01706 224741
e-mail: wdcowpe@aol.com

With lovely views from every room, **The Old Stables** is a handsome Grade II listed building which its owners, Wendy Davison and John Earnshaw, have beautifully restored and renovated providing top quality self-catering accommodation. There are 4 double bedrooms, a fully equipped kitchen with wood burning stove and a charming living room. Outside, there's a pleasant sitting area with a barbecue. Guests can

book the whole house, half of it or even a single room. Wendy and John are happy to supply free range eggs and goat's milk from their own smallholding and if you just want to stay one night they will provide breakfast ingredients for you to cook yourself.

SYKESIDE COUNTRY HOUSE HOTEL

Rawtenstall Road End, Haslingden,
Rossendale, Lancashire BB4 6QE
Tel: 01706 831163 Fax: 01706 830090

Easily accessible from either the M66 or
M62, **Sykeside Country House Hotel** is an
impressive 19th century mansion surrounded
by 3 acres of idyllic gardens. Now enjoying
Grade II listed building status, the house has
seen some interesting visitors. A blue plaque
on an outside wall records that the influential
Lancashire composer Alan Rawsthorne lived
here as a boy between 1908 and 1913. More
recently, the house was owned by William
Roache, better known to millions as Ken

Barlow in TV's *Coronation Street*.

The house became a hotel in 1989 and
after being run by the Turner family for some
years is now owned and run by sisters Muriel
McEvoy and Bernadette Gisbourne. Their
parents were also in the hospitality business
and at Sykeside they continue the family
tradition of providing personal service,
excellent food and quality
accommodation.

Guests arriving at Sykeside pass
through a magnificent entrance porch
with leaded stained glass windows
and after checking in mount a huge
sweeping staircase with a polished
mahogany handrail, then walk along
chandeliered landings and passages
to their room. The luxurious
accommodation with its period
atmosphere comprises 10 guest
bedrooms, all en suite (some with
Jacuzzi or sauna baths), and all with

direct dial telephone, TV, trouser press and
hospitality tray. One of the rooms has been
specially designed and equipped with
facilities for the disabled.

Back again downstairs, guests can enjoy a
pre-dinner drink in the lounge, originally the
dining room of the house. It enjoys views of
the beautifully maintained gardens and if
the evening is a little chilly the open fire will
be blazing away. A perfect place to relax
before progressing to the elegant, high-
ceilinged dining room where the tables are
laid with crisp linen tablecloths and napkins
and only the finest English fare is served.

In the morning, there's a choice of a full
traditional English or a Continental
breakfast, and guests can later enjoy
morning coffee in the Victorian style
conservatory. With its lovely grounds and
extensive facilities, it's not surprising that
Sykeside has become a popular venue for
weddings, conferences and other events.

It's always enlightening to browse through
a hotel's Visitors' Book and there's one
comment in Sykeside's book that sums it all
up. A clearly satisfied customer has written
simply: "Perfection has been achieved".

THE ROYAL HOTEL & THE CELLAR BAR

729 Bacup Road, Waterfoot,
Rossendale BB4 7EU
Tel: 01706 214493 Fax: 01706 215371
e-mail: info@theroyal-hotel.co.uk
website: www.theroyal-hotel.co.uk

The Royal Hotel is in the centre of Waterfoot in the picturesque valley of Rossendale. Built in 1841 to accommodate workers building a nearby railway, this fine old hotel has been run for the past 30 years by the Stannard family. The 14 en suite bedrooms, three with 4-poster beds, all have colour tv, phone and hospitality tray. A popular attraction is The Cellar Bar with its snooker table, pool table, table football and large screen television. There is also a restaurant serving light snacks to full meals, a well-stocked bar and a function room for up to 150 guests.

sarsaparilla or dandelion & burdock.

At Rawtenstall, you can also join the **Irwell Sculpture Trail**, the largest public art trail in the United Kingdom. New sculptures are appearing all the time and more than 50 regional, national and international artists are being commissioned to produce sculptures with an environmental theme. The Trail follows a well-established 30 mile footpath stretching from Salford Quays through Bury into Rossendale and on up to the Pennine Moors.

Haslingden
7 miles S of Burnley on the A56

The market in this town, which serves much of the Rossendale Valley, dates back to 1676, when the charter was granted by Charles II. Tuesdays and Fridays, market days, still bring the town alive as people flock to the numerous stalls. In Victorian times a familiar figure at the market was Miles Lonsdale, better known as the Haslingden Miser. To avoid spending money on food he would gather up discarded fish heads from the fishmonger's and fry them up for an unpalatable, if inexpensive, meal.

After his death in 1889 it was discovered that Miles owned stocks and shares worth more than £16,000 - about £1.2m in today's money.

Goodshaw
5 miles S of Burnley on the A682

Just to the north of Crawshawbooth in the small village of Goodshaw and set high above the main road lies **Goodshaw Chapel**, a recently restored Baptist house of worship that dates from 1760.

Helmshore
8 miles S of Burnley on the B6214

This small town still retains much evidence of the early Lancashire cotton industry and, housed in an old cotton mill, is the Museum of the Lancashire Textile Industry, **Helmshore Textile Museum** (see panel above). The building dates from 1789 and was one of the first fulling mills to be built in the Rossendale area.

Crawshawbooth
5 miles SW of Burnley on the A682

Once an important settlement in the old

HELMSHORE TEXTILE MUSEUM

Holcombe Road, Rossendale,
Lancashire BB4 4NP

Tel: 01706 226459

An 18th Century water powered fulling mill and a Victorian cotton spinning mill, both in working order on one site. Newly designated as a museum with a collection of outstanding national importance, this museum has recently developed an interactive gallery for families on the history of the Lancashire cotton industry. Spinning mules, water wheel, an original Arkwright's Water Frame and other machinery dating from the Industrial Revolution can also be seen. Easily reached from Junction 5 of M65 (Haslingden) or from end of M66. Open from Easter to October every afternoon, closed Saturdays.

THE HOLDEN ARMS TAPAS BAR

Crane Road, Helmshore, Rossendale BB4 4PB
Tel: 01706 228997 Fax: 01706 218380

Located about a mile from the centre of Haslingden, **The Holden Arms Tapas Bar** is housed in a fine old coaching inn. Nick and Denise Hogan only took over here in May 2002 but 50 years earlier Nick's grandmother was the licensee. A major attraction here is the excellent food served every lunchtime and evening except on Mondays. The menu offers a wide choice of tasty tapas dishes and, in the evenings, paellas for a minimum of two diners. Amenities include a recently erected non-smoking Conservatory, an attractive beer garden and off road parking. Entertainment is generous – either live music or a disco every evening from Thursday to Sunday, starting around 9pm.

hunting forest of Rossendale, the village's oldest house, Swinshaw Hall (now privately owned), is said to have played a part in the destruction of the last wild boar in England. The influence of non-conformists can also still be seen in the village, where a number made their home, in the old **Quaker Meeting House** dating from 1716.

Blackburn

The largest town in East Lancashire, Blackburn is notable for its modern shopping malls, its celebrated three day market, its modern cathedral, and Thwaites Brewery, one of the biggest independent brewers of real ale in the north of England. Hard though it may be to imagine today, at the height of the textile industry, Blackburn was the biggest weaving town in the world. At that time there were one hundred and twenty mills in operation, their multiple chimneys belching out soot and smoke.

In 1931, the town received arguably its most influential visitor when Mahatma Gandhi toured the area on a study trip of Lancashire's textile manufacture. Examples of the early machines, including James Hargreaves' Spinning Jenny and his carding machine, invented in 1760, can be seen at the **Lewis Textile Museum**, which is dedicated to the industry. The town's **Museum and Art Gallery** has, amongst its treasures, several paintings by Turner, the Hart collection of medieval manuscripts, and the finest collection of Eastern European icons in Britain.

Mentioned in the *Domesday Book*, the town was originally an agricultural community before the production of first woollen and then cotton cloth took over. Much of the town seen today was built on the prosperity brought by the cotton trade, a fact symbolized on the dome of **St John's Church** (1789) where there's a weathervane in the shape of a weaving shuttle.

The town's old manor house, Witton House, has long since been demolished but the grounds have been turned into an excellent local amenity. The 480 acres of **Witton Country Park** contain nature trails through woodlands up on to heather covered hill tops. Closer to the town centre, the 60-acre **Corporation** Park is one of the county's most attractive urban parks.

South and West of Blackburn

Hoghton
4 miles W of Blackburn on the A675

Originally a collection of hamlets with handloom weavers' cottages, the village was, during the 17th century, a place where Roman Catholics still practiced their faith in defiance of the law. It was at **Arrowsmith House** that Edmund Arrowsmith said his last mass before being captured and sentenced to death for being a Catholic priest and a Jesuit.

It is however, today, best known as the home of Lancashire's only true baronial residence **Hoghton Tower** which dates from 1565. The de Hoghton family have owned the land in this area since the time of the Norman Conquest and the house was built in a style in keeping with their social position and importance. The famous banqueting hall, on the ground floor, is where James I is said to have knighted the Sir Loin of Beef in 1617. The name of the house is today rather misleading since the tower was blown up by

Hoghton Tower, Hoghton

Cromwell's troops in 1643 when they overran the Royalist garrison stationed here. Another famous visitor, who caused less disruption, was William Shakespeare who came to perform with William Hoghton's troupe of players. The grounds, too, are well worth a visit and are as perfectly preserved as the house.

Brindle

5 miles SW of Blackburn on the B6256

An ancient village itself, Brindle's **St James' Church** celebrated its 800 year anniversary in 1990. The church was originally dedicated to St Helen, the patron saint of wells. 'Bryn' is the Old English word for a spring and there are still numerous springs in the village.

Withnell Fold

5 miles SW of Blackburn off the A674

A short walk from Brindle, crossing the Leeds and Liverpool Canal is the village of Withnell Fold whose name comes from 'withy knool' – a wooded hill. It was developed as a model village in the 1840s with 35 terraced cottages each with its own garden. The whole village was owned by the Parke family who also owned the cotton mills and paper mill for whose workers the houses were provided. The mills have long since closed but the old mill chimney still towers above the village. Withnell Fold does have a small claim to fame. The paper mill, built in 1844 overlooking the canal, was once the world's biggest exporter of high-quality bank note paper.

Tockholes

3 miles SW of Blackburn off the A666

This interesting, textile village was once an isolated centre of nonconformism. Standing next to a row of cottages is the **United Reformed Chapel**, founded in 1662, though it has been rebuilt twice, in 1710 and in 1880. The **Parish Church** also has some unusual features. As well as the unique lance-shaped windows, there is an outdoor pulpit dating from the days when the whole congregation could not fit inside the building. Close to the pulpit is the grave of John Osbaldeston, the inventor of the weft fork, a gadget that allowed power looms to weave intricate patterns.

Just to the south of the village lies **Roddlesworth Nature Trail**, a path that follows the line of an old coach drive. Along the trail, for which details can be obtained at the information centre, can be found the ruins of **Hollinshead Hall**. Built in the 18th century and once very grand, the ruins were tidied up in the early 1990s but, fortunately, the wishing well has withstood the ravages of time and neglect. Reminiscent of a small Georgian chapel, the well inside dates back to medieval times when its waters were thought to cure eye complaints.

Darwen

3 miles S of Blackburn on the A666

Visitors to the town may be forgiven for thinking they have been here before as Darwen will be familiar to all viewers of the BBC series *Hetty Wainthropp Investigates*, which stars Patricia Routledge. Dominating the town from the west and situated high on Darwen Moor, is **Darwen Tower**, built to commemorate the Diamond Jubilee of Queen Victoria in 1897. The view from the top of the tower, which is always open, is enhanced by the height of the hill on which it stands (1,225 feet) and with the help of the plaques at the top much of the Lancashire landscape, and beyond, can be identified.

A striking landmark, very visible from the tower, and standing in the heart of Darwen is the chimney of the **India Mill**. Constructed out of hand-made bricks, it was built to resemble the campanile in St Mark's Square, Venice.

To the west of Darwen lies **Sunnyhurst Wood** and visitor centre in the valley of a gentle brook that originates on Darwen Moor to the south. Acquired by public subscription in 1902 to commemorate the coronation of Edward VII this area of woodland, covering some 85 acres, is rich in both bird and plant life. The visitor centre, housed in an old keeper's cottage, has an ever changing exhibition and there is also the Olde England Kiosk, built in 1912, which serves all manner of refreshments.

ASTLEY BANK HOTEL

Bolton Road, Darwen, Lancashire BB3 2QB
Tel: 01254 777700 Fax: 01254 777707
e-mail: sales@astleybank.co.uk
website: www.astleybank.co.uk

Built in the early 1800s as a splendid private residence, **Astley Bank Hotel** enjoys a reputation as one of the premier hotels in the North West, providing outstanding service within the beautiful surroundings of a superbly maintained mansion house. During its long history, Astley Bank has been home to three Members of Parliament and three Mayors of Darwen while its visitors have included many government figures such as Herbert Morrison, Selwyn Lloyd, Lady Violet Bonham Carter, Hartley Shawcross and many others. Standing in 7 acres of its own grounds and easily accessible from both the M6 and M65, the hotel is the perfect venue for either business or a vacation.

It has its own restaurant, Othello's, which offers excellent cuisine rivalling that of 4 or even 5 star hotels. It seats up to 80 diners

and there are also smaller private dining rooms for special occasions. Astley Bank boasts 37 newly refurbished rooms, some with interconnecting doors to serve as family suites. Guests can stay on either a bed & breakfast or dinner, bed & breakfast basis. It can also claim to have the best equipped conference rooms in the North West, all designed to cater for the most demanding of conferences. The friendly atmosphere of the house, the immaculately maintained gardens and first class service make Astley Bank an experience not to be missed.

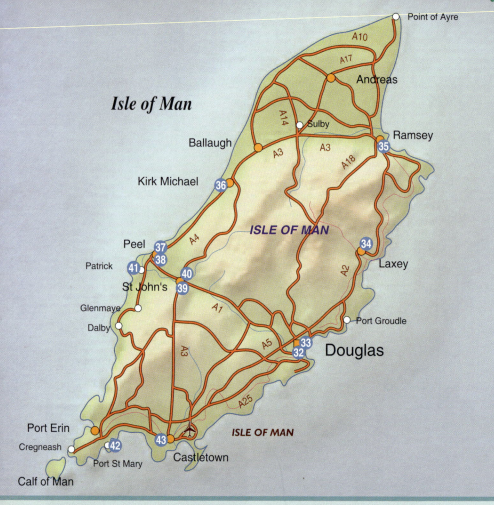

PLACES TO STAY, EAT AND DRINK

● Denotes entries in other chapters

5 The Isle of Man

lthough only 33 miles long and 13 miles wide, the Isle of Man contains a rich diversity of scenery and heritage and, perhaps best of all, exudes a sense of peacefulness epitomised by the Manx Gaelic saying: *traa-dy-liooar* – "Time enough".

Most British mainlanders are surprised to discover that the island is not part of the United Kingdom but a Crown Protectorate with the Queen as Lord of Mann represented in the island by the Lieutenant Governor. Its Parliament, the Tynwald, dates back more than a thousand years – the oldest continuous parliament in the world. The island issues its own coins and notes with the currency having an equivalent value to that of the UK. Recently issued coins include Harry Potter crowns (2001) and another crown marking the Chinese Year of the Horse, 2002.

This island is perhaps best known for its annual TT motorcycle races, its tailless cat, Manx kippers,

and as a tax haven for the wealthy. However, there is much more to this beautiful island which, set in the heart of the Irish Sea, is truly a world apart. With around 100 miles of coastline and several resorts, each with its own individual style and character, although the Isle of Man is by no means large, there is plenty to interest the visitor.

This magical place became an island around 10,000 years ago when the melt water of the Ice Age raised the sea level. Soon afterwards, the first settlers

Spooyt Vane Waterfall, Isle of Man

arrived, working and developing the island into the landscape seen today. The distinctive influences of the various cultures who have lived here still remain, leaving a land with a unique and colourful heritage.

Among the first arrivals were the Vikings and evidence of their era, from the early chieftains to the last Norse King, abounds throughout the Isle of Man. Against the skyline on the seaward side of road between Ballaugh and Bride are some ancient hilltop Viking burial mounds and, at the ancient castle in Peel, an archaeological dig revealed many hidden Viking treasures which are now on display at the Manx Museum in Douglas.

Despite their reputation for plunder, rape, and pillage, the Vikings also made some positive contributions to life on the island, not least of which was the establishment of the Manx governmental system, known as Tynwald. The Manx name for Tynwald Hill is 'Cronk Keeill Eoin', the hill of St John's Church. Although there is no evidence to confirm the story that it contains earth from all of the 17 parish churches here, it is not unlikely that token portions of soil were added to the mound in accordance with Norse tradition.

The Tynwald ceremony continues today with an annual meeting of the island's governors on Midsummer's Day at the ancient parliament field at St John's, where Manx citizens can also petition parliament.

The island's famous three-legged symbol seems to have been adopted in the 13th century as the armorial bearings of the native Kings of the Isle of Man, whose dominion also included the Hebrides. After 1266, when the native dynasty ended and control of the island passed briefly to the Crown of Scotland and then permanently to the Crown of England, the emblem was retained, and among the earliest surviving representations are those on the Manx Sword of State, thought to have been made in 1300. The Three Legs also appeared on Manx coinage from the 17th to the 19th century, and are still seen in everyday use in the form of the official Manx flag.

Why the Three Legs were adopted as the Royal Arms of the Manx Kingdom is unknown. Many heraldic emblems have no meaning and are simply chosen because they are distinctive. This may be the case with the Three Legs, though the emblem as such - something between a cross and a swastika - has a long history reaching far back into pagan times and was originally a symbol of the sun, the seat of power and light.

Douglas

The island's capital, Douglas is also a lively resort with a sweeping sandy beach and a two-mile long promenade, the focus of the island's nightlife. There's excellent shopping around Strand Street, a fine park, Noble's Park, on the edge of town with facilities for

Douglas Harbour

the Douglas Tramway has survived into the 21st century is remarkable especially since, in the early 1900s, attempts were made to electrify the line and extend the Manx electric railway along the promenade.

There is a story often told about the horses that pull the trams, which concerns a parrot that lived in a cage at a hotel close to one of the tram's stops. The bird learnt to mimic the sound of the tram's starting bell and used to practise this skill constantly. The tram horses would stop when they heard the bell and start off again immediately before the passengers could alight as the bird joined in the fun.

The Manx Electric Railway, completed in 1899, is the longest narrow-gauge vintage line in the British

tennis, bowls, putting, crazy golf and a children's play area. Other attractions include the magnificently restored Victorian Gaiety Theatre, the Manx Superbowl, a casino, the Summerland sport and leisure centre which hosts live entertainment during the summer, a cinema complex and an Aquadrome.

From dawn to dusk, visitors can take a leisurely ride along the wonderful promenade aboard the **Douglas Bay Horse Tramway**, a remarkable and beautiful reminder of a bygone era. It was the brainchild of a civil engineer, Thomas Lightfoot, who retired to the island and, seeing the need for a public transport system along this elegant promenade, designed in 1876 the system still in use today. That

The Manx Electric Railway

Isles and operates the oldest working tramcars in the world. The 18 mile journey departs from the northern end of Douglas promenade, stops at Laxey, terminus of the Snaefell Mountain Railway, and then continues to Ramsey.

Another delightful means of travel is the narrow-gauge Victorian **Steam Railway** that runs between Douglas and Port Erin. Following the line of the cliff tops, the memorable journey also travels through bluebell woods and through steep-sided rocky cuttings. This section of line is all that remains of a railway that once served the whole of the island. Many miles of the old railway network have been developed as footpaths. From Quarterbridge in Douglas **The Heritage Trail** is a 10.5 mile former railway route that cuts across the island to Peel on the west coast. It's a scenic but undemanding trail that passes close to historic Tynwald Hill. Picnic sites and useful information boards are situated along the way.

The Isle of Man's most famous export is probably the Manx cat, notable for having no tail. There are several stories of how the cat lost its tail but one, in particular, is delightful. At the time that Noah was building the Ark there were two Manx cats, complete with tails. Noah sent for all the animals to come to the Ark, two by two, but the Manx cats replied that there was plenty of time and continued to play outside. Finally, when the cats did decide to board the Ark, Noah was just slamming the door and the cats lost their tails. A variation on this tale is that one of the cats reached the Ark safely, the other had its tail chopped off by the closing doors. The tailless cat went on to become the Manx cat and the one who managed to keep its tail became the ever grinning Cheshire cat.

No trip to the island is complete without a visit to the **Manx Museum** where the award-winning *Story of Mann* audio-visual presentation uncovers 10,000 years of the island's history. The Manx Museum complex also contains the superb National Art Gallery, the National Library & Archives, as well as exhibits portraying many other aspects of life on the island, including the

JAK'S

43 Loch Promenade, Douglas,
Isle of Man IMI 2LZ
Tel: 01624 663786 Fax: 01624 677859
e-mail: jakspub@aol.com
website: www.jakspub.com

Occupying a superb position overlooking the bay, **Jak's** is a stylish bar/restaurant created by Andrew Gibbs and now established as one of the town's most popular venues. Food is served every lunchtime and evening and customers can eat in the bar or in the restaurant downstairs. The menu offers a mix of traditional favourites such as Steak & Stout Pie or Golden Scampi, along with appetising vegetarian dishes and a kiddie's menu. An extensive choice of lighter meals – filled baguettes, jacket potatoes, burgers, salads and sandwiches – is also available.

Horsedrawn Tram, Douglas

Miraculously, all the crew of the *St George* were saved without the loss of one lifeboat man despite the extremely treacherous conditions. It was following this incident that Hilary decided that a form of refuge should be built for shipwrecked mariners to shelter in and so, with Hilary laying the foundation stone in 1832, the Tower of Refuge was built on Conister Rock out in the bay.

Perched on a headland overlooking Douglas Bay is a camera obscura known as the **Great Union Camera**. The camera was originally situated on the old iron pier, but when this was demolished in the 1870s the camera was re-sited on Douglas Head. In the camera, the natural daylight is focused on to a white panel through a simple system of lenses and angled mirrors and so provides a living image of the scene outside. At first apparently still, as with a

famous TT races.

One of the Isle of Man's most famous landmarks, the **Tower of Refuge**, looks out over Douglas Bay. Sir William Hilary, founder of the Royal National Lifeboat Institution, lived in a mansion overlooking the bay and, following a near disaster in 1830 when the Royal Mail Steam Packet *St George* was driven on to rocks in high seas, Hilary launched the Douglas lifeboat.

THE SEFTON HOTEL

Harris Promenade, Douglas,
Isle of Man IM1 2RW
Tel: 01624 645500 Fax: 01624 676004
e-mail: info@seftonhotel.co.im
website: www.seftonhotel.co.im

With its eye-catching creamy white façade, **The Sefton Hotel** is immediately impressive but this outstanding hotel offers much more than good looks. It occupies a superb position overlooking Douglas Bay, a spectacular view that is enjoyed by many of the luxuriously appointed rooms. An attractive ground floor feature of the hotel is the Atrium Water

Garden where Indoor Gardening Weekends are held throughout the year. Amenities include a private car park for hotel residents only, a library with free internet, swimming pool, steam rooms, saunas, gym, conference room, lecture theatre, a breakfast room with fine views over the bay and an award winning restaurant. Booking on the hotel's own website is recommended where you will find the best rates available and links to ferry and airline reservation sites.

photograph, viewers soon become fascinated as the 'picture' begins to move.

North of Douglas

Port Groudle

3 miles N of Douglas on the A11

Close to Port Groudle lies **Groundle Glen**, a deep and in places rocky valley with a bubbling stream running through its length. Excellent specimens of beech grow in the upper sections of the glen whilst, lower down, pines and larches are abundant. There is also a small waterwheel in the lower half of the glen. Railway enthusiasts will be delighted to learn that on certain days in the summer the **Groudle Glen Railway** operates. Running on a track just 2ft wide for three-quarters of a mile along the cliffs, the railways lovingly restored carriages are pulled by Sea Lion, the original 1896 steam engine.

Laxey

5 miles N of Douglas on the A2

Set in a deep, wooded valley, this village is one of interesting contrasts. Tracing the river up from its mouth at the small tidal harbour leads the walker into **Laxey Glen**, one of the island's 17 National Glens that are preserved and maintained by the Forestry Department of the government

Further up the glen is one of the island's most famous sights, the **Great Laxey Wheel** that marks the site of a once thriving mining community. Known as the Lady Isabella Wheel, with a circumference of 228 feet, a diameter of 72 feet, and a top platform some 72 feet off the ground, it is the largest working waterwheel in the world.

It was Robert Casement, an engineer at the mines, who constructed this mechanical wonder and designed it to pump 250 gallons of water a minute from a depth of 200 fathoms. Officially opened in 1854, it was named the Lady Isabella after the wife of the then Lieutenant Governor of the Isle of Man. After considerable repair and reconstruction work, the wheel now operates just as it did when it first opened and it stands as a monument to Victorian engineering as well as the island's industrial heritage.

The Great Laxey Wheel

THE BRIDGE INN

6 New Road, Laxey, Isle of Man
Tel: 01624 862414
Fax: 01624 862779

An excellent place to stay in Laxey is **The Bridge Inn** which has 8 first class en suite rooms, all very comfortable and equipped with all modern facilities. The bar offers 3 real ales and is open from 4pm, Monday to Friday; from noon on Saturday and Sunday. An 80-seat function room is also available. Nearby is the Snaefell Mountain Railway and adjacent to

the station, the Mines Tavern entices customers with the slogan "Rude Landlord. Grotty Food. Lousy Beer". None of which, thankfully, is true. It is owned and run by Derek and Sandra Black-Kay who also own The Bridge Inn. Derek is the chef and his menu offers a good choice of wholesome and appetizing food, available every lunchtime and evening.

Situated above Laxey, in a beautiful natural glen, are the magnificent **Ballalheanagh Gardens**. The valley, of steep sides with winding paths and a crystal clear stream running through the bottom, is packed with rhododendrons, shrubs, bulbs, and ferns and is certainly a gardeners' paradise well worth seeking out.

From Laxey station, the **Snaefell Mountain Railway** carries visitors to the top of the island's only mountain. Built in 1895, the six original tram cars still climb the steep gradients to Snaefell's 2,036 foot summit and this is certainly the way to travel for those unwilling to walk. Those reaching the top are rewarded with outstanding views of the whole island and out over the sea to Ireland, Scotland, and England. There is also a café at the summit offering welcome refreshments.

Ramsey

12 miles N of Douglas on the A18

The second largest town in the island, Ramsey occupies a scenic location at the foot of North Barrule. This northernmost resort on the island has a busy working harbour, a long stretch of beach and a wide promenade. A popular amenity is **Mooragh Park,** a 40 acre expanse of gardens and recreational facilities with a 12 acre boating lake and lakeside café. During the summer months there's live musical entertainment in the park and around the 3rd week of July each year the park is one of several venues hosting events during Yn Chruinnaght, an inter-Celtic festival of music, dance and literature.

Other major crowd-pullers are the Round the Island Yacht Race, held each summer and starting and finishing in Ramsey, and the Ramsey Motorcycle Sprint, part of the T.T. festival, when bikers show off their skills along Mooragh Promenade.

In the mid 1800s the town assumed the title of "Royal Ramsey" following an unscheduled visit by Queen Victoria and Prince Albert in 1847. The royal yacht anchored in Ramsey Bay following a stormy crossing from Scotland so that the seasick Queen could recover. While Her Majesty recuperated on board,

Prince Albert walked to the top of Lhergy Frissel and was much impressed by the view. A few years later the Albert Tower was erected to commemorate the Prince Consort's visit.

Just to the north of the town, lies the **Grove Rural Life Museum**, housed in a pleasantly proportioned Victorian house. Built as the summer retreat of Duncan Gibb, a wealthy Victorian shipping merchant from Liverpool, and his family, the rooms within the house have all been restored to their Victorian splendour and stepping into the museum is just like taking a step back in time. The outbuildings have not been neglected and they contain an interesting collection of vehicles and agricultural instruments that were seen on Manx farms in the late 19th century.

Ramsey is the northern terminus of the Manx Electric Railway, built in 1899. The **Manx Electric Railway Museum** tells the fascinating story of this world-famous Victorian transport system. From Ramsey the railway follows a scenic route southwards to Douglas, accompanied most of the way by the equally delightful coastal road, the A15/A2.

For serious walkers, there's the **Millennium Way** which starts about a mile from Parliament Square in Ramsey. Established in 1979 to mark the millennium year of the Tynwald parliament, the 28 mile long path passes through some magnificent countryside, picturesque towns and villages, before ending at the island's former capital, Castletown.

Point of Ayre
18 miles N of Douglas on the A16

This is the northernmost tip of the island and, not surprisingly, there is a lighthouse situated here. The area around the point is known as **The Ayres** and, at the Ayres Visitor Centre, a whole wealth of information can be found about this fascinating part of the island. Amongst the inland heath moorland, a variety of species of birds can be found nesting whilst, on the pebbled beaches, can be seen terns. The offshore sandbanks provide a plentiful supply of food for both the diving gannets and the basking grey seals.

THE SWAN

Parliament Square, Ramsey,
Isle of Man IM8 2LN
Tel: 01624 814236

In the heart of the town, **The Swan** is a stylish modern pub built in 1993 by Isobel and Alan Christian who have made it a popular venue for those who appreciate good food and well-maintained ales. Isobel is the chef and her home-cooked delicious food is served every lunchtime, Monday to Saturday. Fresh fish and local gammon dishes are the specialities but there's a wide choice from the regular menu or the specials board. The Swan is a free house with an extensive selection of beverages including 2 real ales – Okell's Bitter and Mild – along with Carling and Cooil lagers (the latter is an Isle of Man brew). Children are welcome in the lounge until 6pm; cash and cheques only.

Andreas

5 miles N of Ramsey on the A17

Andreas was originally a Viking
settlement and the village church
contains intricately carved crosses dating
back to the days of these early
occupants. The church tower's mutilated
spire goes back to the 1940s when part
of it was removed in case it proved to be
dangerous to aircraft from the nearby
wartime airfields.

Sulby

11 miles N of Douglas on the A3

Situated in the heart of the island, the
village lies on the famous TT course, a
circular route on the island's roads that
takes in Douglas, Ramsey, Kirk Michael,
and St John's. There are several scenic
and picturesque walks from the village
which take in **Sulby Glen** and **Tholt-y-
Will Glen**, both of which are renowned
beauty spots, and to the south, over
moorland, to Sulby reservoir. Bird
watchers particularly will enjoy the walks
over the higher ground as it provides the
opportunity to see hen harriers, kestrels,
peregrines, and curlews.

Ballaugh

7 miles W of Ramsey on the A3

The village, which lies on the TT race
course, is close to the island's most
extensive area of marshland, the perfect
habitat for a range of birds, including
woodcock and grasshopper warbler, as
well as being the largest roost for hen
harriers in Western Europe.

Situated on the edge of the Ballaugh
Curraghs, **Curraghs Wildlife Park** is
home to a wide variety of wetland
wildlife that come from all over the
world. Curraghs is the Manx word for
the wet, boggy, willow woodland that is
typical of this part of the island and the
site, which was opened in 1965, gives
visitors the opportunity to see the
animals in their natural environments.
This world-renowned wildlife park has
been divided into several different
habitats, including The Pampas, The
Swamp, The Marsh, and the Flooded
Forest, and here endangered animals
from around the world, such as
Canadian otters, Spider monkeys, Rhea,
and Muntjac deer, live as they would in
the wild.

The Curraghs Wildlife Park also has
an enviable breeding record and, as
many of the species are becoming rare in
the wild, this is a very important aspect
of the park's work. Not only have they
successfully bred bald ibis, one of the
most endangered birds in the world, but
tapirs, lechwe antelope and many others
also flourish in this environment. Not
all the animals and birds are exotic –
there are a great number of native
species to be seen here too.

Visitors to the park are able to wander
around the various habitats, following a
well laid out path, and, aided by the
illustrated brochure the whole family
will find this an interesting and
informative trail. There is also an
adventure play area for young children
and, during the summer, a miniature

THE OLD STABLE

Berk, Peel Road, Kirk Michael,
Isle of Man IM8 1AP
Tel/Fax: 01624 878039
e-mail: theoldstable@manx.net
website: http://homepages.manx.net/
theoldstable

The self-catering property, known as **The Old Stable**, is located on the west coast at Berk, a smallholding of 100 acres of pastureland and grazing which enjoys glorious scenic views in every direction. It stands about half a mile from Kirk Michael, set back from the A4. (To find it, from the junction of the A4 and A3 at Kirk Michael take the A4 road towards Peel for half a mile and The Old Stable is on your left). Parts of the building date back more than 200 years. It was originally a farm worker's house, later a byre and now, after recent conversion, a superb 2-bedroom cottage. It sleeps up to 4 guests in 2 en suite rooms, 1 double and 1 twin. No expense has been spared on the décor and furnishings and the tourist board classification is in the highest grade. Everything you could possibly need for your stay has been provided. The Old Stable is available all year round; children are welcome but pets are not, and the house is non-smoking. The price is fully inclusive.

railway runs around the park. The lakeside café is open during the day for refreshments and, during the main summer season when the park is open until 9pm, barbecues are held here. *Tel: 01624 897323*

Kirk Michael
10 miles N of Douglas on the A3

Close to the village lies **Glen Wyllin**, another of the island's 17 National Glens, and one that certainly deserves exploration. The varied woodland contains elm, ash, sycamore, alder, beech, lime, holm oak and chestnut and in spring the woodland floor is carpeted with bluebell, primrose, wood anemone and wild garlic. Kirk Michael also lies on a 16 mile footpath that follows the route of an old railway line from Peel to Ramsey. After following the coast, and part of the Raad ny Foillan, the footpath branches off through pastoral countryside before reaching the port of Ramsey on the other side of the island.

West of Douglas

Peel
12 miles W of Douglas on the A1

Located on the western side of the island, Peel is renowned for its stunning sunsets and the town is generally regarded as best typifying the unique character and atmosphere of the Isle of Man. Traditionally the centre of the Manx fishing industry, including delicious oak smoked kippers and fresh shellfish, Peel has managed to avoid any large scale developments. Its narrow winding streets exude history and draw the visitor unfailingly down to the busy harbour, sweeping sandy beach, and magnificent castle of local red sandstone.

THE CENTRAL HOTEL

14 Castle Street, Peel,
Isle of Man IM5 1AL
Tel: 01624 844143

The Central Hotel stands on a meandering road that leads down to the picturesque harbour, sandy beach and mighty castle. Parts of the hotel date back to the 1600s and the interior has a real old world charm. The owners, Linda and Barry Gelling, are both local islanders and their son Mark is the chef, serving up appetizing home cooked food with Queenies and steaks as the specialities of the house. Food is served every lunchtime and evening, Monday to Friday; from noon until 8pm on Saturday and Sunday. There's always a minimum of 2 real ales on tap along with many other brews. The hotel is particularly busy on Thursday evenings when musicians are invited to bring along their instruments for a jam session.

Peel Castle, one of Isle of Man's principal historic monuments, occupies the important site of St Patrick's Isle. The imposing curtain wall encircles many ruined buildings, including St Patrick's Church, the 11th century Round Tower and the 13th century Cathedral of St Germans – the cathedral of Sodor and Mann and the very first diocese established in the British Isles, pre-dating even Canterbury. The great curtain wall also encloses the later apartments of the Lords of Mann. In the 11th century the castle became the ruling seat of the Norse Kingdom of Man and the Isles, first united by Godred Crovan – the King Orry of Manx folklore. Today, the castle provides a dramatic backdrop for a variety of plays and musical events during the summer.

Recent archaeological excavations have discovered exciting new evidence relating to the long history of the site. One of the most dramatic finds was the Norse grave of a lady of high social status buried in pagan splendour. The jewellery and effects buried with her can be seen on display, with other excavation finds, at the Manx Museum. The castle is also said to be haunted by the Black Dog, or Mauthe Dhoo. On dark windy nights, it can be heard howling in the castle's dungeons.

The Isle of Man

QUAYSIDE RESTAURANT

East Quay, Peel, Isle of Man IM5 1AR
Tel: 01624 844144

The Quayside Restaurant offers both a stunning location on Peel's east quay and outstanding cuisine. Seafood is the speciality here with delicious dishes based on locally caught fish and shellfish – roast sea bass fillets, for example, served on a vegetable tagliatelle with a roast garlic and pepper dressing, or crab filo parcels served on a lemon saffron and ginger cream sauce. Owners Paul Galloway and Penny Hardman also offer meat dishes –fillet steak, roast lamb or pan seared duck amongst them. During the season the restaurant is open every lunchtime (11.30am to 2.30pm) and evening (6.30pm until 10pm); out of season it is closed on Sunday and Monday. Children are welcome and all major credit cards are accepted.

SANDHOUSE & SANDHOUSE LODGE

Peel Road, St John's, nr Peel,
Isle of Man IM4 3NE
Tel/Fax: 01624 878528

The area around St John's is reckoned by many to be the most typically Manx in character which makes it an ideal place to stay for those who want to enjoy the full "Manx experience". Within a short distance of the town are two excellent self-catering properties, both of them available all year

round. **Sandhouse** and **Sandhouse Lodge** stand on opposite sides of the A1 about a mile to the west of St John's. These are top of the range properties, beautifully furnished and decorated, and comprehensively equipped. Sandhouse sleeps up to 8 guests in 2 double rooms, 2 singles and 1 twin. Children are welcome and cots and high chairs are available if required. Sandhouse Lodge can accommodate up to 7 people in 3 bedrooms – 1 large room with a double and 2 single beds, 1 twin and 1 single. Both properties are oil centrally heated which is included in the price. Electricity is paid for by a £1 slot meter.

THE FARMERS ARMS

Station Road, St John's, nr Peel,
Isle of Man IM4 3AN
Tel: 01624 801372
website: www.ruraltrader.com

The Farmers Arms is a handsome black and white, two storey building dating back some 200 years, with picnic tables outside and an inviting traditional atmosphere within. A free house, the inn is situated on the original TT race course and is a very popular spot with motorcyclists and visitors to the races. Pictures of local interest adorn the walls of the bar where owners Kevin and Jane Rogers, ably assisted by their nephew Darren, offer a menu of satisfying home-cooked fare – soup of the day or garlic mushrooms could precede cod cooked in beer batter, lasagne (meat or vegetarian), chicken Kiev or a mixed grill. Sandwiches provide lighter bites and there is a special menu for children.

Food is served every lunchtime

(noon until 2pm) and evening (6pm to 8pm), and to accompany your meal a wide range of beverages is on offer including 3 real ales – Cairns, plus real ales from local micro brewers. On Friday and Saturday evenings the inn hosts either a live music session or a karaoke evening. And if you are planning to stay in this scenic corner of the island, the Farmers Arms has 4 guest bedrooms, 2 of which have en suite facilities. Only opened in April 2002, the rooms are attractively furnished and decorated, and very comfortable.

Peel Harbour

Connoisseurs of kippers speak highly of the tasty Manx kipper. At **Moore's Traditional Museum** you can watch a kipper curing process that remains unchanged since the late 1700s. Another major museum is **The House of Manannan**, a state of the art heritage attraction which was voted British Isles Museum of the Year in 1998. And for those researching their family history, **The Leece Museum** has an archive of documents and photographs of the town along with a varied display of artifacts connected with the life of a busy fishing port.

St John's
3 miles E of Peel on the A1

Roads from all over the island converge at the village of St John's because this is the site of the ancient **Tynwald Day Ceremony**, held on July 5th which is a public holiday throughout the island. This grand open-air event takes place on Tynwald Hill just north of the village. Here the Tynwald Court – a parliament that can trace its origins to the 9th century – assembles and the new laws of the land are proclaimed in both Manx and English. The serious business over, the rest of the day is devoted to various celebrations and activities culminating in a firework display.

Adjoining Tynwald Hill, the 25 acre **Tynwald Arboretum** was established in 1979 to mark the millennium of the island's parliament.

Glenmaye
3 miles S of Peel on the A27

A spectacular bridged gorge and waterfall dominate this glen which is one of the most picturesque on the island. Comprising over 11 acres, its beautiful sheltered woodland includes some relics of the ancient forests that once covered much of the Isle of Man. Another feature of this glen is the Mona Erin, one of the many waterwheels which once produced power for the Manx lead mines.

Dalby
4 miles S of Peel on the A27

Just southwest of Dalby village, **Niarbyl Bay** takes its name from the Manx Gaelic, Yn Arbyl, meaning "the tail", so named because of the long reef that curves out from the shoreline. There are stunning views to the north and south, and the grandeur of the southwestern coast is seen at its best from this typically Manx setting. The beach here is an ideal place for picnics, relaxing and enjoying the tranquillity of the setting.

Port Erin
16 miles S of Peel on the A5

Port Erin Harbour

Situated between magnificent headlands, Port Erin's beach is certainly a safe haven. It is also a place of soft sands cleaned daily by the tide with rock pools to one side and a quay to the other. A long promenade above the sheltered sandy beach has a number of cafés and other amenities include bowls, tennis, putting, nearby Rowany golf course and some superb walks along coastal paths out to Bradda Head. Port Erin is also the terminus for the Steam Railway which runs from here to Douglas.

The town has its own Erin Arts Centre which since 1975 has hosted the annual **Mananan International Festival of Music and the Arts**, now recognized as one the island's most prestigious cultural events. The two week long festival takes place from mid to late June and the eclectic programme ranges

The Calf of Man

those days it was called The Mansion. Known as the Calf Crucifixion Cross, the stone is believed to date from the 8th century and it is one of the earliest Christian finds in Europe. The cross can be seen in the Manx Museum in Douglas.

In 2002, a new **Visitor Centre** was opened at the southernmost top of the island. The scenic 4 acre site also has a shop, café and car park and provides grand views of Spanish Head, the Calf of Man and the Irish Mountains of Mourne.

Calf Sound, the stretch of water between the island and the Isle of Man has seen many ships pass through and it was here that the largest armada of Viking longships ever assembled in the British Isles congregated before setting off to invade Ireland. Centuries later, men from nearby Port St Mary were granted a gallantry medal by Napoleon, thought to be the only such medal he presented to British subjects, when they

through classical music, opera and ballet, jazz and theatre, to films, Indian music and art exhibitions as well as special events for children.

Calf of Man
18 miles S of Peel

This small island, situated just off the southwestern tip of the island, is now a bird sanctuary owned by the National Trust. The puffins should be grateful – one of the previous owners, the Dukes of Athol, requested that his tenants living on the Calf pickled the nesting puffins! In 1777, a stone was found on the isle in the garden of Jane's Cottage, though in came to the rescue of the crew of the *St Charles* schooner from France which foundered in the sound.

Cregneash
19 miles S of Peel off the A31

Perched close to the southwestern tip of the island this village is now a living museum, **Cregneash Village Folk Museum**, which offers a unique experience of Manx traditional life within a 19th century crofting community. Its isolated position led the village to become one of the last strongholds of the island's ancient skills and customs and all this is beautifully preserved today.

By combining small scale farming with other occupations, a small settlement of Manx men and women have successfully prospered here since the mid 1600s. In the carefully restored buildings, visitors can see the conditions in which they lived and managed to sustain life in this rugged landscape. The centrepiece of Cregneash is without doubt **Harry Kelly's Cottage**. Kelly, who died in 1934, was a renowned Cregneash crofter and a fluent speaker of the Manx language. Opened to the public in 1938, his cottage, still filled with his furniture, is an excellent starting point to any tour of the village. There are various other buildings of interest, including Turner's Shed, a smithy, and the Karran Farm.

The village is also one of the few remaining places where visitors get a chance to view the unusual Manx Loaghtan four-horned sheep, a breed which, thanks to Manx National Heritage and other interest groups, now has a secure future.

Port St Mary
13 miles SW of Douglas off the A31

This delightful little working port has both an inner and outer harbour, two piers, and excellent anchorage for visiting yachts. The beach, along a scenic walkway from the harbour, is no more than two miles from the beach at Port Erin but it faces in almost the opposite direction and lies in the most sheltered part

Cregneash Village

THE ALBERT HOTEL

Athol Street, Port St Mary,
Isle of Man IM9 5DS
Tel: 01624 832118
Fax: 01624 834263
e-mail: albert.hotel@manx.net

Overlooking the quayside of this small working port, **The Albert Hotel** was originally built in the mid-1800s as a Temperance Hotel. The interior is very olde worlde with lots of charm and character – and a minimum of 3 real ales always on tap. Owner Peter Holt has been the landlord here for 10 years and in 2001 he opened the restaurant which has a reputation for excellent food. Two chefs are employed and specialities of the house are fresh fish dishes, notably the delicious crab claws. The hotel hosts occasional live entertainment sessions on Saturday evenings and has 4 guest bedrooms which, because of their popularity, should be booked well ahead.

of the island.

One of the finest walks on the Isle of Man is the cliff-top route from Port St Mary to Port Erin along the **Raad ny Foillan** - the road of the gull - a long distance footpath that follows the coastline right around the island. From Port St Mary, the first part of the walk takes in **The Chasms**, gigantic vertical rifts that, in some places, descend the full 400 feet of the cliffs.

Castletown
9 miles SW of Douglas on the A7

The original capital of the island, Castletown is full of character and charm, especially around the harbour area. Here, in August, is held the **World Tin Bath Championship,** one of the sporting world's more unusual contests, as well as snake racing and many other aquatic events.

The harbour lies beneath the imposing battlements of the finely preserved **Castle Rushen,** once home to the Kings and Lords of Mann. The present building was mostly constructed between 1340 and 1350 and has recently been restored to provide today's visitors with a vivid impression of what life was like in the fortress many years ago by presenting in authentic detail the sights, sounds, and smells of its heyday. Among the various points of interest is a unique one-fingered clock that was presented to

FRANCORCHAMPS GUEST HOUSE

Fishers Hill, Castletown, Isle of Man IM9 4PN
Tel: 01624 823635
e-mail: dot&stuart@francorchamps.co.uk
website: www.francorchamps.co.uk

Named after the Belgian motor racing circuit, **Francorchamps Guest House** stands on the main A5, a mile or so west of Castletown. It enjoys a picturesque setting with Carrick Bay to the south and attractive countryside all around. Francorchamps is the home of Dot and Stuart Butler who began welcoming bed & breakfast guests in May 2002 and have already established a reputation for warm hospitality.

They have a 4-diamond rating from the English Tourist Board and the 3 guest bedrooms comprise 1 ground floor double en suite; and upstairs a double and a twin, both with private facilities. A splendid breakfast is included in the tariff; children are welcome.

the castle by Elizabeth I in 1597 and which still keeps perfect time.

The castle is also still used as a courthouse, for the swearing-on of new governors, and for registry office weddings. During the summer months there are regular spectacular displays re-enacting scenes from the castle's history, especially the events of 1651 when Royalists were forced to surrender Castle Rushen to Cromwell's parliamentary troops.

Like Peel Castle, Rushen too is said to be haunted, by a ghost known as the White Lady. Believed to be the ghost of Lady Jane Gray who travelled to the island from Scotland with her family, the spectre has been seen walking the battlements at night and occasionally passing straight through the castle's closed main gate during the day.

Also recently restored to its 19th century state of grace is the **Old House of the Keys**, the seat of the Manx parliament until it removed to Douglas in 1874. In the rather cosy former debating chamber visitors can vote on various issues which the parliament faced in the past, and some they may face in the future.

Castletown is also home to the island's **Nautical Museum**, where the displays centre around the 1791 armed yacht *Peggy* which sits in her contemporary boathouse. Part of the original building is constructed as a cabin room from the time of the Battle of Trafalgar and there are many other artifacts on display, all with a maritime theme.

A mile or so northeast of Castletown

Castle Rushden

is Ronaldsay, the island's principal airport and nearby, in the village of **Ballasulla**, is **Rushen Abbey** – the most substantial medieval religious site in the Isle of Man. This ancient Cistercian monastery now has an interpretive centre that explains the abbey's past importance and illustrates the daily life of the monks.

A couple of miles further along the A5 road towards Douglas, visitors should look out for the **Fairy Bridge**. For centuries, Manx people have taken no chances when it comes to the little people and it is still customary to wish the fairies who live under the bridge a "Good Morning" when crossing.

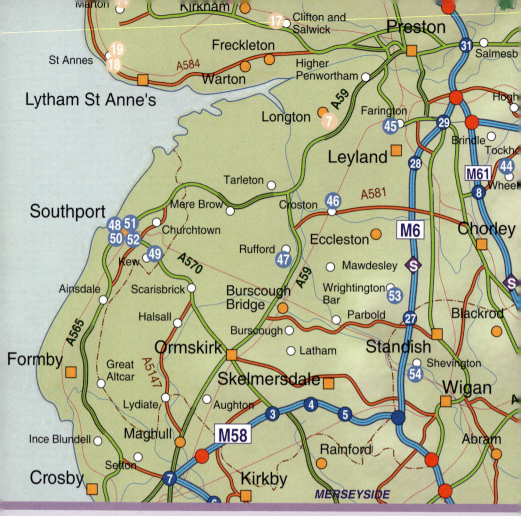

PLACES TO STAY, EAT AND DRINK

● Denotes entries in other chapters

6 West Lancashire

This area of Lancashire, with its sandy coastline and flat fertile farmland, is home to the elegant Victorian seaside resort of Southport, the ancient market towns of Chorley and Ormskirk, and Wigan, another ancient place with a rich industrial past. Following the reorganisation of the county boundaries in the 1970s and the creation of Merseyside, much of the coast and the southwestern area of Lancashire became part of the new county but the individual character and charm of this area has certainly not been lost.

As well as offering a step back in time, the broad promenades of Southport, its elegant tree-lined streets, and its superb shopping still makes this one of the most visited towns in this region. Though the silting up of the Ribble estuary, to the north, has caused the sea at this resort to recede, further south, at Ainsdale and Formby, not only is there paddling but also a vast expanse of sand dune and pine forest that is now an important nature reserve.

Behind the coast, the flat lands of the West Lancashire plain were once under water. Now with an extensive network of ditches, drainage has provided the old towns and quaint villages with rich fertile land that now produces a wealth of produce all year round and roadside farm shops are very much a feature of the area.

Although there are several rivers flowing across the land, the chief waterway, which is hard to miss, is the Leeds to Liverpool Canal. Linking the port of Liverpool with industrial Leeds and the many textile villages and towns in between, this major navigation changed

Rivington Reservoirs

the lives of many of the people living along its length. The section through West Lancashire, passing rural villages, is perhaps one of the more pleasant stretches. There are plenty of charming canal side pubs in the area and walks along the towpath,

Astley Hall, Chorley

through the unspoilt countryside, have been popular for many years. There is also, in this section, the wharf at Wigan Pier, now a fascinating living museum that brings the canal to life.

Chorley

A bustling and friendly place, Chorley is a charming town that is locally famous for its market that dates back to 1498. Today, there are two markets – the covered market and the open, 'flat iron' market. This peculiar and intriguing name stems from the ancient practice of trading by displaying goods on the grounds without the use of stalls.

Dating back to 1360 and standing on the site of a Saxon chapel, the **Church of St Lawrence** is the town's oldest building. The church is said to contain the remains of St Lawrence, brought back from Normandy by Sir Richard Standish, and whether they are his relics or not, during the Middle Ages the

saint's shrine certainly brought pilgrims to the parish.

The Civil War also brought visitors to the town, albeit less welcome ones. Following defeat at the nearby Battle of Preston, Royalist troops were twice engaged in battle here by Cromwell's victorious forces. Though not a happy time for both the Royalists and the town, the skirmishes did place Chorley on the historical map of England.

Chorley was the birthplace, in 1819, of Henry Tate. The son of a Unitarian minister, Henry was apprenticed in 1832 to the grocery trade in Liverpool and by 1855 he had not only set up his own business but also opened a chain of six shops. Selling the shops, Henry entered into the world of the competitive sugar trade and founded the world famous business of **Tate and Lyle**. Opening a new sugar refinery equipped with the latest machinery from France, Henry cornered the refining business in Britain and amassed a huge fortune. A great benefactor, Henry not only gave away vast sums of money to worthy causes but also to the London art gallery which now bears his name.

The jewel in Chorley's crown is undoubtedly **Astley Hall**. Built in the late 16th century and set within some beautiful parkland, the hall is a fine example of an Elizabethan mansion. A notable feature is its south wing – "more glass than wall". Inside, the moulded ceilings of the main hall and the drawing room are quite remarkable, as are the painted panels dating from the 1620s and representing a range of heroes that includes Elizabeth I, Philip II of Spain and the Islamic warrior Tamerlane.

Extended in 1666, and again in 1825, this is truly a house of history and the rooms, which reflect the passing of the centuries, contain superb items of furniture from 1600 to the Edwardian period. Whether or not Cromwell stayed at the hall following the Battle of Preston is open to debate but his boots are here on display.

The hall was given to the borough in 1922 by Reginald Tatton and it was he who insisted that the building should incorporate a memorial to those who had died in World War I. As a result, a small room has been devoted to the local men who fought and died for their country. Along with the display of photographs, there is a Book of Remembrance.

Golden Lion Hotel

369 Blackburn Road, Higher Wheelton, Chorley, Lancashire PR6 8HP
Tel: 01254 830855
website: chorleyonline.co.uk

With the Liverpool and Leeds Canal passing close by, the Golden Lion Hotel in the village of Higher Wheelton is a popular watering-hole for canal and towpath users along with fishermen, golfers and hillwalkers.

In the summer of 2002 the hotel was taken over by Sandra and Martyn White who have been busy refurbishing the bar and guest bedrooms as well as converting the stables at the rear into self-catering accommodation. All of these amenities should be available by the time you read this.

A charming and friendly couple, Sandra and Martyn have made this traditional old hostelry a welcoming social venue for locals and a treat for visitors. Sandra looks after the catering with snacks designed to suit local tastes – such as hot beef butties and home-made chips – served in the bar, and full meals based on top quality local produce available in the restaurant every lunchtime and evening. There's a wide choice of local and international beers, including cask beers and a guest brew. For those who prefer wine, the hand-picked wine list offers a good selection at very affordable prices.

With their detailed local knowledge, Sandra and Martyn are happy to give advice on the best walks and fishing nearby and information on other amenities such as the local golf course.

FARINGTON LODGE

Stanifield Lane, Farington, Leyland,
Lancashire PR5 2QR
Tel: 01772 421321 Fax: 01772 455388
e-mail: enquiries@farington.co.uk
website: www.faringtonlodge.co.uk

Farington Lodge is a stately Grade II listed building dating back to early Georgian times and now swathed in colourful creeper. It was originally built for a wealthy mill owner and later became the private residence of James Todd, the chairman of the Sunbeam Motor Company. Following his death in the early 1930s, the house was purchased by another motoring magnate, Sir Henry Spooner of Leyland Motors, and was used to entertain visiting dignitaries, amongst them members

of the Royal Family. It was converted into a hotel in 1989 and acquired by its present owners in 1994. During 2001/2002 a complete refurbishment was carried out and the Lodge is now one of the premier hotels in Lancashire, offering luxurious accommodation, an excellent restaurant and superb service.

The Lodge stands in three acres of mature trees and lawns, close to Leyland and some delightful Lancashire countryside. Despite the peaceful setting, the hotel is only a 2-minute drive away from the intersection of the M6, M65 and M61. Open all year round, the Lodge has eleven beautiful bedrooms, all exquisitely furnished and decorated, and equipped with all modern amenities. For that romantic occasion, some have elegant 4-poster beds.

Good food is taken very seriously at Farington Lodge. The superb Garden Restaurant is a chandeliered room with tall windows overlooking the beautifully maintained gardens. Various menus are available, including à la carte, and although the restaurant seats 40, booking is advisable at all times. Children are welcome and all major credit cards apart from Diners are accepted. The restuarant is open every day from noon until 2pm, and from 7pm to 9.30pm.

In addition to the Garden Restaurant, there are two private dining rooms available for smaller parties. One seats 24, the other 16. For larger parties, there's a Function Room that can accommodate up to 250 people for any occasion.

Farington Lodge's excellent facilities and its attractive location have made the hotel a popular venue for weddings. It is licensed for civil ceremonies and its lovely grounds provide the perfect setting for those wedding photographs.

North of Chorley

Leyland

4 miles NW of Chorley on the B5253

The town is probably best known for its associations with the manufacture of cars and lorries and the **British Commercial Vehicle Museum**, the largest such museum in Europe, is well worth a visit. It stands on the site of the former Leyland South Works, where commercial vehicles were produced for many years. On display are many restored vans, fire engines and lorries along with exhibits ranging from the horsedrawn era, through steam-powered wagons right up to present day vans and lorries. Perhaps the most famous vehicle here is the one used by the Pope and irreverently known as the Popemobile.

Leyland is, however, an ancient settlement and documentary evidence has been found which suggests that the town was a Crown possession in Saxon times, owned by Edward the Confessor. The village cross marks the centre of the old settlement around which the town expanded and it is in this area of Leyland that the older buildings can be seen. Founded in the 11th century, much of the present **St Andrew's Church** dates from 1220 although there was some restoration work undertaken in the 1400s. The Eagle and Child Inn is almost as old, said to date from around 1230, and it served the needs of travellers journeying along the ancient

highway which passed through the town.

Whilst not one of the town's oldest buildings, the old Grammar School, parts of which dates from the late 16th century, is hardly modern. Today it is home to the town's **Heritage Museum**, a fascinating place that describes, through interesting displays and exhibits, the history of this ancient market town.

Tarleton

8 miles W of Chorley off the A59

This pleasant rural village, now by-passed by the main road to Preston, is home to **St Mary's Church**, one of the finest buildings in Lancashire. Built in 1719, it is constructed from brick except for the cut-stone belfry. No longer the village church, it was replaced in the late 19th century by a larger building, it is still maintained and its churchyard has remained in use.

Croston

6 miles W of Chorley on the A581

This historic village in the heart of rural West Lancashire has been a centre for local farmers since it was granted a weekly market charter in 1283. Set beside the banks of the River Yarrow, a tributary of the River Douglas, much of the village, including the 17th century almshouses and the lovely 15th century church, are part of a conservation area. Church Street is a fine example of an 18th century Lancashire street, some of the houses bearing the date 1704; even older is the charming packhorse bridge

MEMORY LANE

24 Town Road, Croston, Leyland,
Lancashire PR26 9RB
Tel: 01772 601927

Memory Lane is a tea room with a difference – and a character all its own. Owner Carol Parkinson has always had a strong interest in antiques and collectable so when she bought this well-established business she decided to furnish it with items from her collection. So you'll find two splendid old rocking horses set between the tables with their lace tablecloths, while mounted on one wall is a vintage grocer's delivery bicycle complete with basket, and on another a magnificent penny-farthing. Carol has a range of collectables and small antiques for sale at very affordable prices, along with greetings cards and other gifts.

The décor is one good reason for visiting; Carol's excellent cooking is another. Self-taught, Carol considers herself a "good, wholesome cook" and after several years cooking in other establishments she decided to open her own. In addition to the extensive choice of delicious home-made cakes and other traditional teatime treats, the menu also offers a varied range of appetising meals such as a tasty Smoked Mackerel Salad with Apple Sauce.

To complete your meal, there's a choice of scrumptious desserts, accompanied perhaps by some of the locally produced speciality ice cream. Both for its distinctive décor and delicious food, Memory Lane is indeed a place that will stay in the memory.

dated 1682. The strong links with agriculture are still apparent in this area and the open farmland actually extends right into the village centre.

On **Coffee Day** the village turns out with decorated farm horses and carts to take part in a procession led by a band and morris dancers. The name is derived from the former "Feoffing Day" when tenants paid their fees, or rents, to the squire.

Ormskirk

In the days when Liverpool was just a small fishing village, the main town in this area was Ormskirk, founded around 840 AD by a Viking leader called Orme. Surrounded by rich agricultural land, the town has always been an important market centre with the locally-grown potatoes, 'Ormskirks', a firm favourite right across the north-west. The market is still flourishing, held every day except Wednesday and Sunday. In late Victorian times one of the traders in Ormskirk market was a certain Joseph Beecham who did a roaring trade selling his medicinal 'Little Liver Pills'. Joseph became a millionaire through the sales of his little pills; his son, the conductor Sir Thomas, went on to become the most popular and flamboyant figure of English musical life during the first half of the 20th century.

The town received its first market charter from Edward I in 1286 and today the market is still a key event in the region. The partial drainage of Martin

Mere in the late 18th century, to provide more rich, fertile agricultural land, as well as the growth of nearby Liverpool, increased the prosperity of the town. Ormskirk was also touched by the Industrial Revolution and, whilst the traditional farming activities continued, cotton spinning and silk weaving also became important sources of local income. Today, the town has reverted to its traditional past.

The **Church of St Peter and St Paul**, in the centre of the town, unusually has both a steeple and a tower. The tower, added in the 16th century, was constructed to take the bells of Burscough Priory after the religious community had been disbanded by Henry VIII. However, the oldest feature found in the church is a stone carving on the outer face of the chancel's east wall that was probably the work of Saxon craftsmen.

Ormskirk too has a famous son: a market trader called Beecham who sold his own brand of liver pills that customers' described as 'worth a guinea a box'. His pills and powders made Beecham's fortune although his son, Thomas, a musical genius, brought world-wide fame to the family.

North of Ormskirk

Burscough
2 miles NE of Ormskirk on the A59

Situated on the banks of the Leeds and Liverpool Canal, the village's Parish Church was one of the Million, or Waterloo, Churches built as a thanks to God after the final defeat of Napoleon in 1815. A later addition to the church is the Memorial Window to those of the parish who died for their country during the First World War.

Little remains of **Burscough Priory**, founded in the early 1100s by the Black Canons. Receiving lavish endowments from the local inhabitants, the priory was at one time one of the most influential religious houses in Lancashire.

Rufford
5 miles NE of Ormskirk on the B5246

This attractive village of pretty houses is notable for its church and its beautiful old hall. Built in 1869, the church is a splendid example of the Gothic revival period and its tall spire dominates the skyline.

Rufford Old Hall (National Trust) is an enchanting building. Its medieval part is constructed of richly decorated black-and-white timbering enclosing a glorious Great Hall where angels bearing colourful heraldic shields float from massive hammer-beam trusses. The Hall's 17th century additions are less spectacular but still very attractive and contain displays of historic costumes as well as an interesting local folk museum.

Generally regarded as one of the finest timber-framed halls in the country, the hall was the ancestral home of the Hesketh family who lived at this site from the 1200s until Baron Hesketh gave the hall to the National Trust in 1936. From the superb, intricately carved movable wooden screen to the solid oak chests and long refectory table, the atmosphere here is definitely one of wealth and position.

Later additions to the house were made in the 1660s and again in 1821. Parts of these are now devoted to the **Philip Ashcroft Museum of Rural Life** with its unique collection of items illustrating village life in pre-industrial Lancashire. Another attraction here is the spacious garden alongside the canal.

Mere Brow
7 miles N of Ormskirk on the B5246

Just to the south of the village lies the Wildfowl and Wetlands Trust at **Martin Mere** (see below), over 350 acres of reclaimed marshland which was established in 1976 as a refuge for thousands of wintering wildfowl. Until Martin Mere was drained in the 1600s to

WWT MARTIN MERE

Nr Rufford, Lancashire

WWT Martin Mere is one of nine Wildfowl & Wetlands Centres run by the Wildfowl & Wetlands Trust (WWT), a UK registered charity. Visit WWT Martin Mere and come in close contact with wetlands and their wildlife. You can feed some of the birds straight from your hand. Special events and exhibitions help to give an insight into the wonder of wetlands and the vital need for their conservation.

People of all ages and abilities will enjoy exploring the carefully planned pathways. You can go on a journey around the world, from the Australian Riverway, through the South American Lake, to the Oriental Pen with its Japanese gateway, observing a multitude of exotic ducks, geese, swans and flamingos along the way. In winter, WWT Martin Mere plays host to thousands of Pink-footed Geese, Whooper and Bewick's Swans and much more. Visitors can see swans under floodlight most winter evenings.

Covering 150 hectares, the reserve (one of Britain's most important wetland sites) is designated a Ramsar Site and SSSI for its wealth of rare wetland plants.

The Wildfowl & Wetlands Trust is the largest international wetland conservation charity in the UK. WWT's mission is to conserve wetlands and their biodiversity. These are vitally important for the quality and maintenance of all life. WWT operates nine visitor centres in the UK, bringing people closer to wildlife and providing a fun day out for all the family.

provide rich, fertile farmland, the lake was one of the largest in England. Many devotees of the Arthurian legends believe that the pool into which the dying king's sword Excalibur was thrown, (to be received by a woman's arm *clothed in white samite, mystic, wonderful'*), was actually Martin Mere.

Today, the stretches of water, mudbanks, and grassland provide homes for many species of birds and, with a network of hides, visitors can observe the birds in their natural habitats. There are also a series of pens, near to the visitors centre, where many other birds can be seen all year round at closer quarters. The mere is particularly famous for the vast numbers of pink-footed geese that winter here, their number often approaching 20,000. Although winter is a busy time at Martin Mere, a visit in any season is sure to be rewarded. The visitor centre caters for everyone and, as well as the shop and café, there is a theatre and a wealth of information regarding the birds found here and the work of the Trust.

Churchtown
7 miles NW of Ormskirk on the A5267

This charming village, now a small part of Southport, has retained much of its village feel and is certainly worthy of exploration in its own right. Considerably predating the seaside resort, Churchtown is, as its name suggests, centred around its church. Since it is dedicated to St Cuthbert, it's

possible that whilst fleeing from the Danes, the monks of Lindisfarne rested here with the remains of their famous saint.

However, it is likely that the village was, for many years, known by the name of North Meols and a chapel of Mele is mentioned in the *Domesday Book*. Derived from the Norse word 'melr' meaning sand dune, there was certainly a thriving fishing village here in the early 1100s. In 1224, Robert de Coudrey granted the village the right to hold a market, the likely place for which is the cross standing opposite the church in the heart of the village.

As the settlement lay on a crossroads and at the start of a route over the sands of the Ribble estuary, it was a place of considerable importance. It was also here that the tradition of sea bathing in this area began, when, in 1219 St Cuthbert's Eve was declared a fair day, which later became known as Bathing Sunday.

There is still plenty to see in this small village. The present **Meols Hall** dates from the 17th century but its appearance today is largely thanks to the work carried out by the late Colonel Roger Fleetwood Hesketh in the 1960s. When the colonel took over the house in the late 1930s, the older and larger part of the hall had been demolished in 1733 and the remaining building was rather nondescript. Taking the gabled bay of the late 17th century, extensions were added to give the house a varied roofline and a three dimensional frontage.

Meols Hall

little has changed here since the day the gardens were first opened by the Rev Charles Hesketh. Built in 1938, following the gardens' restoration, the **Botanic Bowling Pavilion** mimics the style of the late Regency architect Decimus Burton. Here too is the Botanic Gardens Museum, with its fine exhibition on local history and its gallery of Victoriana.

The hall is the last home of the Hesketh family who at one time had owned most of the coastal area between Southport and Heysham. Originally, the manor had been granted to Robert de Coudrey, coming into the Hesketh family by marriage in the late 16th century. There has been a house on this site since the 13th century. Occasionally open to visitors, the hall has a fine art collection and, in the entrance hall, are three carved chairs that were used in Westminster Abbey during the coronation of Charles II. During World War I, Moels Hall was used as a military hospital.

Planned on the site of the old Churchtown Strawberry Gardens in 1874, the **Botanic Gardens**, restored in 1937, are beautifully maintained and present a superb example of classic Victorian garden design. With magnificent floral displays, a boating lake, wide, twisting paths, and a fernery,

Southport

8 miles NW of Ormskirk on the A570

The fashion for sea-bathing is usually reckoned to have originated with George III's regular dips at Weymouth in the late 1700s, but at Southport they'd already been doing it for generations. Only once a year though, on St Cuthbert's Eve, the Sunday following August 20th. The holiday became known as 'Bathing Sunday, when folk travelled some distance to throw off their clothes and frolick naked in the sea'. The tradition was associated with the legend, or fact, that St Cuthbert had once been shipwrecked but had miraculously been able to swim to the shore and safety.

Southport's history as an all-year, rather than a one-day-a-year resort began in 1792 when its first hotel was built. A local man, 'Duke' Sutton, went to the beach, gathered all the driftwood he could find, nailed it together, put in the minimum of furniture, and opened for business.

Within a few years other houses and hotels had sprung up amongst the dunes and by 1802 'Duke' Sutton felt confident enough to rebuild his makeshift, if environmentally-friendly hotel, in stone. Over-confident as it turned out. The following year he was thrown into Lancaster gaol for debt and later died a pauper.

Southport though continued to thrive and by the 1860s was by far the most popular seaside resort in Lancashire. The town's only problem was that its main attraction, the sea, was getting further and further away as silt from the Ribble estuary clogged the beach. The town council's response was to build the second-longest pier in the country, complete with a miniature railway which is still operating, create numerous parks and gardens, and construct elegant boulevards such as Lord Street. All that activity in Victorian times imbued the town with an appealingly genteel atmosphere which, happily, it still retains.

The town's central, main boulevard, **Lord Street**, is a mile long wide road that was built along the boundary bordering the lands of the two neighbouring lords of the manor. A superb shopping street today, the

SQUIRES HOTEL & RESTAURANT

78/80 King Street, Southport PR8 1LG
Tel/Fax: 01704 544462
e-mail: enquiries@squireshotel.com
website: www.squireshotel.com

Only minutes from the famous Lord Street shopping area and well known for being the Golfing Capital of the UK with championship golf courses close by, **Squires Hotel & Restaurant** offers comfortable accommodation and intimate dining at reasonable rates combined with a friendly atmosphere.

There are 11 guest bedrooms, doubles, twins and family all with a 3-Diamond rating from the English Tourist Board. They are non-smoking and well-appointed with colour TV and en suite facilities. The hotel has its own licensed bar and an award-winning restaurant serving an extensive menu each evening from 6.30pm onwards, Tuesday to Saturday.

The non-smoking restaurant is famed for its steaks, lamb shanks and fish, plus an á la carte and vegetarian menu with a daily Specials Board. Children are welcome and all major credit cards are accepted. Guests at Squires Hotel, which is open throughout the year, can stay on either a bed & breakfast or bed, breakfast and evening meal basis.

THE PAGEANT

70 Folkstone Road, Kew,
Southport PR8 6JW
Tel/Fax: 01704 544629

The Pageant stands on the site of the old Southport Zoo and the boating lake and although it's only some 15 years old the atmosphere in this friendly hostelry is as traditional as you could hope to find. Phil Rayment and Mike Evans who run the pub with their partners Danielle and Jayne, are local people who took over here in early 2001. They have made The Pageant a genuine hub of the community with something going on, it seems. almost every evening. There's a Quiz on Tuesday from 9.15pm, a disco/karaoke on Friday starting about 9pm, and alternate Saturdays live tribute bands perform. In summer, there is a Fun Day once a month on a Saturday with a children's circus, clowns, Punch & Judy, a magician, bouncy castle and other attractions.

Mike who is bar manager is responsible for the keeping of the fine ales for which the pub is well-known. There are always two or three real ales available with Websters Green Label as the permanent brew, accompanied by one or two rotating guest ales. Also available are John Smith's Smooth, Fosters, Carling, Miller, Stella, Kronenberg plus a rotating guest lager, Strongbow, Guinness and Chestmnut Dark Mild. From 3pm to 5pm, Monday to Thursday, and from 7.30pm to

11pm on Monday and Wednesday, there's a Happy Hour for draught and bottled beers, while on Saturday evening customers get two bottled drinks for the price of one.

"We must eat to live, and live to eat" is the message inscribed above the food service counter. Phil, landlord and chef of 23 years experience is responsible for all the home-cooked delights. A good selection of wholesome food is available every lunchtime (noon to 2.30pm) and evening (5.30pm to 9pm), Monday to Friday. On Saturday food is served from noon through to 9pm; on Sunday from noon until 6pm. Choose from either the printed menu or the specials board - you'll find a very varied choice. Specialities of the house are Kleftico, a Greek style Lamb dish, Pageants Mixed Grill,fresh fish dishes and homemade desserts like Bread and Butter Pudding or Banoffee Pie. Children are welcome in the dining area and parts have been designated as non-smoking areas.

Open all day, everyday The Pageant accepts all major credit cards apart from American Express and Diners.

THE THATCH & THISTLE

147 Norwood Road, Southport,
Merseyside PR8 6EF
Tel: 01704 514513 Fax: 01704 531597

With its neat thatched roof and colourful hanging baskets **The Thatch & Thistle** looks really inviting and the interior is just as appealing with its beamed ceilings and open fire. Although built in 1998, the Thatch & Thistle has all the characteristics of a traditional inn, including friendly hosts, John and Diane Taylor, an excellent choice of ales with a minimum of 8 cask ales on tap, and outstanding food. The 4-page menu offers a huge choice, with Lamb Devonshire as a speciality of the house and the extensive wine list has sensibly priced choices. Entertainment includes a Quiz on Thursday and Sunday evenings, and live performances on the second Friday of each month.

exceptionally wide pavements, with gardens along one side and an elegant glass-topped canopy along most of the other side, make this one of the most pleasant places to shop in the country. Many of the town's classical style buildings are found along its length and it has been designated a conservation area. Off Lord Street, there is one of the town's several covered arcades – **Wayfarers Arcade**, built in 1898 and a fine example of these popular shopping malls. The modest entrance opens out into a beautiful cast iron and glass conservatory with a first floor gallery and splendid central dome. Originally named the Leyland Arcade after the town's Member of Parliament, it took its present name in 1976 after the arcade's most successful leaseholder.

In a central position along Lord Street stands Southport's rather modest Town Hall. Built in 1852 and of a classical design, its façade includes a beautiful carving in bold relief of the figures of Justice, Mercy, and Truth picked out in white against a Wedgwood blue background. Further along, the Atkinson Central Library was built in 1879 as the premises of the Southport and West Lancashire Bank. The original ceiling of the banking hall can still be seen as can its fireplace. On the first floor is the **Atkinson Art Gallery** which contains collections of British art and Chinese porcelain.

However, not all the buildings in Southport are Victorian and the Top Rank Bingo Club, originally called the Garrick Theatre, was held to be the finest theatre when it was opened in 1932. With much of its exterior as it would have appeared when it first opened, it is a wonderful example of the Art Deco style. Finally, Lord Street is also home to the town's war memorial, **The Monument**. Opened on Remembrance Day 1923 by the Earl of Derby, this is a large and grand memorial that remains the town's focal point. Its design was the subject of a competition and the winning entry was submitted by Garyson and Barnish, designers of the famous Royal Liver Building in Liverpool. The central obelisk is flanked by twin colonnades on

BRITISH LAWNMOWER MUSEUM

106-114 Shakespeare Street, Southport,
Lancashire
Tel: 01704 501336
Fax: 01704 500564

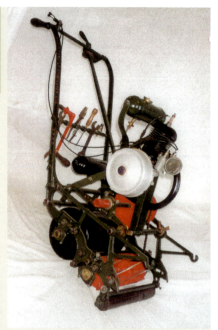

The **British Lawnmower Museum** located in
the picturesque Victorian seaside holiday
resort of Southport, Lancashire, houses a
private collection of over 200 pristine
exhibits of special interest (part of 400) built
up over a period of 50 years and is now a
tribute to the garden machinery industry
which has developed over the past 170 years
from the Industrial Revolution, when modern
technology was not available, to the present
day. Many of the machines have been
rescued from the scrap yard and restored to
their present very high standard. In addition
to early grass cutting and garden machines
dating from the 1830's, the exhibition houses
the largest collection of vintage toy
lawnmowers and games in the world.

The lawnmower was invented in 1830 by
Edwin Budding of Gloucester, thought of as a
madman testing the strange contraption at
night. Originally designed to trim the nap
from cloth, the cylinder machine he devised
has not changed in principle since that date
and has been the only traditional lawnmower
for formal lawns used throughout Great
Britain, although somewhat unique in so far
as every other country in the world use the
more recently introduced (circa 1930) rotary
grass cutter.

The museum has now become one of the
world's leading authorities on vintage
lawnmowers and is now the largest
specialists in antique garden machinery,
supplying parts, archive conservation of

manuscript materials including 500 original
patents from 1799, and valuing machines
from all over the world. The museum retains
a character not often seen in these modern
times.

Included in this unique national collection
are manufacturers not normally associated
with the garden industry, names such as
Rolls Royce, Royal Enfield, Daimler, Hawker
Sidley, Perkins Diesel, British Leyland and
many more. A lot of the exhibits memorabilia
and industrial artifacts are from the Victorian
and Edwardian era and have been restored
and keep a small part of British engineering
heritage alive.

which the names of the town's more
than 1,000 dead are inscribed.

As every Victorian resort had a
Promenade, so does Southport and this
is a typical example: flanked by grand
hotels on the land side and a series of
formal gardens on the other. As the
silting up of the Ribble estuary

progressed unchecked the **Marine Lake**
was constructed at the northern end of
the promenade. At over 86 acres, this
man-made lake is the largest in Britain
and as well as being an attractive site
and a place for the pursuit of all manner
of watersports it is also host to an annual
24-hour yacht race.

CONISTON HOTEL

41 Bath Street, Southport PR9 0DP
Tel: 01704 530441 Mobile: 07765 671890
website: coniston-hotel.com

Located just a short walk from both the town centre and the Promenade, the **Coniston Hotel,** which has parking spaces, is a friendly hotel where proprietor Jacquie Winfield makes guests feel immediately at home by providing welcoming trays, tea trays ,sandwiches and pre ordered breadfasts, described by one guest as "out of this world". There are 12 excellent guest bedrooms, a mix of double rooms with en suite facilities and others with private bathroom or shower. Smoking is permitted. It's a child friendly hotel with cots and high chairs available. Pets are also welcome. Open, except Christmas Day and Boxing Day, the hotel is licensed and will cater for any age or occasion. Currently only cash or cheques are accepted.

From the centre of the promenade extends Southport's **Pier** which, at 1,460 yards long was the longest pier in the country until 1897. Following a fire in 1933 it was shortened but it remains the second longest in the country. Looking at the pier today it is hard to imagine that at the end of the last century pleasure steamers were able to depart from here to Barrow in Cumbria, Bangor, Wales, and the Isle of Man. Along the shore line, and opened in the spring of 1998, the new sea wall and **Marine Drive** is a wonderful modern construction, the length of Southport's sea front, that blends well with the town's Victorian heritage.

The normal attractions of a seaside resort have not been forgotten and **Pleasureland** is the obvious choice for those seeking thrills and hair-raising rides. Keen gardeners will know Southport for its splendid annual Flower Show, second only to Chelsea, and golfers will be familiar with the name of Royal Birkdale Golf Course, just south of the town centre. Southport has one more sporting association of which it is justly proud. From behind a car show room in the 1970s, Ginger McCain trained Red Rum on the sands of Southport to a record breaking three magnificent wins in the Grand National run at Aintree. A statue of the great horse can be seen in Wayfarers Arcade.

Grand National, Aintree

West Lancashire

Scarisbrick Hall

which is screened from the road by thick woodland, was extensively remodelled by the Victorian architect Augustus Welby Pugin for Charles Scarisbrick. In 1945, the hall and surrounding extensive grounds were sold by the last member of the family to live here, Sir Everard Scarisbrick. Today it is an independent boarding school and occasionally open to the public in the summer months. Pugin's flamboyant decoration is well worth seeing if you have the chance.

South and West of Ormskirk

Halsall

4 miles W of Ormskirk on the A5147

Scarisbrick

3 miles N of Ormskirk on the A570

Scarisbrick, which is part of the largest parish in Lancashire, lies in the heart of rich agricultural land that is intensively cultivated for vegetables, including carrots, Brussels sprouts, cabbages, and early potatoes. A feature of this area is the large number of farm shops by the side of the road selling the produce fresh from the fields.

The first **Scarisbrick Hall** was built in the reign of King Stephen but in the middle of the 19th century the hall,

This is a charming unspoilt village lying in the heart of fertile West Lancashire and close to the Leeds and Liverpool Canal – the longest canal in Britain with a mainline of 127.25 miles and 92 locks. **St Cuthbert's Church**, which dates from the middle of the 13th century is one of the oldest churches in the diocese of Liverpool and it remains one of the prettiest in the county. The distinctive spire, which was added around 1400, rises from a tower that has octagonal upper stages.

Ainsdale

7 miles W of Ormskirk on the A565

Towards the sea, from the centre of the village, lies what was Ainsdale-on-Sea with its old Lido and the more modern Pontin's holiday village. Between here and Formby, further down the coast, the sand dunes form part of the **Ainsdale National Nature Reserve**, one of the most extensive dune systems in the country. It's also one of the few remaining habitats of the endangered natterjack toad which breeds in the shallow pools that form in the sand dunes. As well as supporting the toads, the salt pools are the natural habitat for a variety of dune plants, including dune helleborine, grass of Parnassus and round-leaved wintergreen.

Formby

8 miles W of Ormskirk off the A565

Like Ormskirk, Formby has a connection with potatoes. It's said that sailors who had travelled with Sir Walter Raleigh to Virginia brought back potatoes with them and grew them in the fields around what was then a small village. There are still many acres of potato fields being cultivated in the area. To the west of the town, **Formby Point** and **Ainsdale National Nature Reserve** form the most extensive dune system in Britain, 450 acres of wood and duneland, one of the last refuges in the country for the quirky

natterjack toad, the only species of toad which runs rather than hops.

The origins of this small coastal town lie in the time of the Vikings and the name Formby comes from the Norse Fornebei meaning Forni's town. Between the Norman Conquest and the time of the Dissolution in 1536, there were a succession of landowners but, by the mid-16th century, the Formby and Blundell families emerged as the chief owners. Formby Hall, built for William Formby in 1523, occupies a site that was first developed in the 1100s.

Today, Formby is perhaps better known as a quiet and desirable residential area and also the home of an important red squirrel sanctuary at the National Trust **Freshfield Nature Reserve** and pine forest. Linked with Ainsdale's nature reserve, the two form over 400 acres of dunes and woodland, as well as shoreline, from which there are magnificent views over the Mersey estuary and, on a clear day, the hills of Wales and of Lakeland are also visible.

Great Altcar

6 miles SW of Ormskirk on the B5195

Standing on the banks of the River Alt, this old farming village is famous as the venue for the Liverpool Cup, an annual hare coursing event. In the churchyard of the present church, erected by the Earl of Sefton in 1879, are a pedestal font and a stoup which came from the earlier churches that occupied this site.

Ince Blundell

8 miles SW of Ormskirk off the A565

The village takes part of its name from the Blundell family who have for centuries exerted much influence on the village and surrounding area. Ince comes from the Celtic word 'Ynes' which means an island within a watery meadow and it would have perfectly described the village's situation before the surrounding land was drained.

The annual candlelight service at the village **Church of the Holy Family** is an ancient custom that appears to be unique to this country. The people of the parish decorate the graves in the cemetery with flowers and candles before holding a service there. Common in Belgium, this custom was brought to the village at the beginning of the 20th century.

Sefton

8 miles SW of Ormskirk on the B5422

This quiet old village stands at the edge of a rich and fertile plain of farmland that lies just behind the West Lancashire coast. It formed part of the estate of the Earls of Sefton (descendents of the Molyneux family) right up until 1972. The village has a pub, a 16th century corn mill and a delightful church, **St Helen's**, with a 14th century spire. Inside, there's a beautifully restored ceiling with bosses and moulded beams, 16th century screens, well-preserved box pews, two medieval effigies of knights, and an elaborately carved pulpit of 1635. A

Ince Blundell Hall

series of brasses recounts the history of the Molyneux family from their arrival in Britain with William the Conqueror.

Though this is a small village, its name has also been given to the large metropolitan district of north Merseyside which stretches from Bootle to Southport.

Lydiate

4 miles SW of Ormskirk on the A5147

This is another pleasant old village bordering the flat open farmland created from the West Lancashire mosses. Lydiate itself means an enclosure with a gate to stop cattle roaming and, though the age of the settlement here is uncertain, the now ruined **St Katharine's Chapel** dates from the 15th century. However, the most frequented building in the village is **The Scotch Piper**, a lovely cruck-framed house with a thatched roof that has the reputation for being the oldest pub in Lancashire.

Aughton

3 miles SW of Ormskirk off the A59

This picturesque village, surrounded by agricultural land, is dominated by the spire of St Michael's Church. An ancient place, it was mentioned in the *Domesday Book*, the register of church rectors goes back to 1246 and much of the building's medieval framework remains though it was restored in 1914.

Close by is Aughton Old Hall (private) which stands on a site that has

been occupied since Saxon times. The ruins of a 15th century pele tower are visible in the garden and, as well as having a priest's hole, the house is reputed to have been Cromwell's base whilst he was active in the area.

Lathom

3 miles NE of Ormskirk off the A5209

The stretch of the famous Leeds and Liverpool Canal which passes through this village is well worth a visit and it includes the **Top Locks** area, a particularly interesting part of this major canal route.

To the south of the village, in Lathom Park, is Lathom House (private), formerly home of Lord Stanley, Earl of Derby, a Royalist who was executed during the Civil War. Only one wing of the original house remains but within the grounds are the ancient **Chapel of St John the Divine,** consecrated in 1509, and ten adjoining almshouses built for the chapel bedesmen. It's a charming cluster of buildings in an attractive setting and visitors are welcome at the services held in the chapel every Sunday.

Parbold

5 miles E of Ormskirk off the A5209

This is a charming village of pretty stone cottages as well as grand, late-Victorian houses built by wealthy Manchester cotton brokers. The village houses extend up the slopes of **Parbold**

Hill, one of the highest points for miles around and from which there are superb views of the West Lancashire plain. At the summit stands a rough hewn monument, erected to commemorate the Reform Act of 1832, that is locally known, due to its shape, as Parbold Bottle.

Ashurst Beacon, another local landmark, was re-erected on Ashurst Hill by Lord Skelmersdale in 1798 when the threat of a French invasion was thought to be imminent.

Mawdesley

6 miles NE of Ormskirk off the B5246

A past winner of the Best Kept Village of Lancashire award, Mawdesley lies in rich farming country and was once associated with a thriving basket making industry. The village has a surprising number of old buildings. Mawdesley Hall (private), originally built in the 1500s and altered in the late 18th century, was for many generations the home of the Mawdesley family. At the other end of the village is Lane Ends House, built in 1590, which was occupied by a Catholic family and has a chapel in one of its attics. Other venerable buildings include Ambrose House (1577), Barret House Farm (1695), Back House Farm (1690) and Jay Bank Cottage (1692). By contrast, the oldest of the village's three churches only dates back to 1840.

THE TUDOR INN

117 Mossy Lea Road, Wrightington, Lancashire WN6 9RE
Tel/Fax: 01257 425977

The Tudor Inn is a really charming hostelry standing at the heart of the quiet village of Wrightington, little more than a mile from Junction 27 of the M6. The premises were originally two cottages with a smithy at the back and the neat, compact brick and stone exterior hides a wealth of olde worlde character and atmosphere – small-paned windows, black-and-white Tudor features, open brickwork, old beams, well-chosen pictures on yellow-painted walls, burnished copper and brass ornaments, a snug corner with comfortable sofas to sink into, a dining area with neatly laid tables and an elaborate chandelier.

Mine hosts, Norman and Wanda Gildart, offer their customers a good choice of appetising home-cooked food with steak dishes and beef pie amongst the specialities of the house. Wanda is a professional chef who has been in catering for some 30 years and has brought to perfection dishes such as a whole poussin in a honey and Dijon mustard sauce. Highly recommended! Children are welcome in the non-smoking restaurant. Food is served every lunchtime and evening except for Mondays, unless it's a Bank Holiday. Beverages on offer include 3 real ales – Tetley, John Smith's and a rotating guest ale – along with a wide selection of other beers, spirits and wines.

The inn has an attractive beer garden, large car park, and a disabled entrance and toilets. Wednesday is Quiz Night, starting around 9.30pm.

Wrightington

8 miles NE of Ormskirk on the B5250

Bypassed by most people as they travel up and down the nearby M6 and overshadowed by the delights of the **Camelot Theme Park** at nearby Charnock Richard, this is another pleasant, rural Lancashire village.

Rivington

13 miles E of Ormskirk off the A673

One of the county's prettiest villages, Rivington is surrounded by moorland of outstanding natural beauty that forms the western border of the Forest of Rossendale. Overlooking the village and with splendid views over West Lancashire, **Rivington Pike**, at 1,191 feet, is one of the area's high spots. It

was once a site of one of the country's chain of signal beacons.

Just to the south of the village lies **Lever Park**, situated on the lower slopes of Rivington Moor, which was made over to the public in 1902 by William Hesketh Lever, who later became Lord Leverhulme. The park comprises an awe-inspiring pot pourri of ornamental, landscaped gardens, tree-lined avenues, ancient cruck-framed barns, a Georgian hall, and a treasure trove of natural history within its 400 acres. The park's moorland setting, elevated position, and adjoining reservoirs provide scenery on a grand scale which leaves a lasting impression.

Standish

9 miles E of Ormskirk on the A49

This historic old market town has several reminders of its past and not

Rivington Moor

THE NAVIGATION INN

162 Gathurst Lane, Shevington,
Wigan WN6 8HZ
Tel: 01257 252856 Tel: 01257 254969
e-mail: peers@thenavigationinn.com
website: www.thenavigationinn.com

The Navigation Inn occupies a picturesque setting with the Leeds to Liverpool canal passing on one side (moorings are available) and the River Douglas just yards away on the other. The two waterways meet about half a mile away at Dean Lock. The inn is part of the tiny hamlet of Gathurst, a rural retreat just over 3.5 miles from Wigan and a few minutes drive from Junction 27 of the M6. Despite its miniscule size Gathurst even has its own

railway station on the Southport to Manchester line.

Dating back to the early 1800s this spacious old hostelry has been superbly furnished and decorated and is now run by Peers and Wendy Cawley who took over here in 2000 after some 7 years experience in the hospitality business. They have made a real success of the enterprise and The Navigation is now regarded as one of the best public houses in Lancashire. One of the major attractions is the quality of the food which is available every lunchtime (noon to 2.30pm) and evening (5.30pm to 8.30pm) on weekdays; from noon until 8.30pm on Saturdays; noon until 7.30pm on Sundays. The regular menu offers a wide choice of starters, main courses, jacket potatoes, sandwiches, filled hot baguettes with

chips, salads and desserts. There's a separate selection for children or those with a lighter appetite and the blackboard lists further options with daily specials and vegetarian dishes. One of Peers' specialities is Spicy Chicken Breast marinated in Jamaican jerk spices and dark rum and served with grilled pineapple. There are non-smoking areas and customers can dine throughout the inn – or outside if the weather is favourable. On Sundays a value for money 3-course roast meal is available with vegetarian alternatives also served. Such is the popularity of the cuisine here, booking is recommended at all times and especially in the summer months. During the winter, the inn hosts special themed food nights on Fridays – just ring for details.

The Navigation is also very popular with lovers of real ale and will be included in the 2003 CAMRA guide. There are 5 of them on tap, including Tetley's, Timothy Taylor Landlord and 3 rotating guest ales. A good selection of draught lagers, cider, stouts and wines are also available.

All major cards apart from American Express and Diners are welcome.

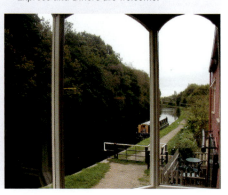

least of these is the splendid **St Wilfrid's Church.** Built in a size and style that befitted the importance of the town in the late 1500s, the building stands on the site of a church that was certainly here at the beginning of the 13th century. A look around the interior of the church will provide a potted history of the area: there are tombs and memorials to all the local families including the Wrightingtons, Shevingtons, and the Standish family themselves.

The Standish family came from Normandy and crossed the channel with William the Conqueror. One of the family members became the Warden of Scarborough Castle and another, Ralph de Standish, was knighted after his part in quelling the Peasants' Revolt. There was even a Standish at Agincourt. However, the most famous member of the family is Miles Standish who sailed to the New World on board the *Mayflower* with the Pilgrim Fathers in 1620. This may seem strange as the Standish family were staunch Catholics. Though there is little left in the way of monuments to the family in this country, their home (put up for sale in 1920 after the last family member died) was demolished and parts transported to America. Miles Standish is remembered in the town of Duxbury in America.

Wigan
10 miles E of Wigan on the A577

The American travel writer, Bill Bryson, visited Wigan in the mid 1990s and wrote "Such is Wigan's perennially poor reputation that I was truly astounded to find it has a handsome and well maintained town centre".

Although to many this town is a product of the industrial age, Wigan is one of the oldest places in Lancashire. As far back as the 1st century AD there was a Celtic Brigantes settlement here that was taken over by the Romans who built a small town called Coccium. Little remains of those far off days but during the construction of a gasworks in the mid 19th century various burial urns were unearthed during the excavation work. The town's name comes from Wic-Ham which is probably Anglo-Saxon or Breton in origin but, following the departure of the Romans, the settlement lay in that part of the country that was forever fluctuating between the kingdoms of Mercia and Northumbria so the derivation is uncertain.

The Middle Ages brought more settled times. By the end of the 13th century, the town had not only been granted a market charter but was also sending two members to Parliament. A staunchly Catholic town, Wigan fared badly during the Civil War. The Earl of Derby, whose home, Lathom House, lay on the outskirts of the town, was a favourite with the King and this was where Charles I made his base for his attacks on Roundhead Bolton. The bitter attacks on Wigan by the Cromwellian troops saw the fortifications destroyed and both the parish church and the moot hall were looted. The Battle of

Wigan Lane, the last encounter between the warring forces in Lancashire, is commemorated by a monument which stands on the place where a key member of the Earl of Derby's forces was killed.

Wigan's development as an industrial town

Winstanley Hall, Wigan

centred around coal mining, which began as early as 1450. By the 19th century, there were more than one thousand pit shafts in operation in the surrounding area, supplying the fuel for Lancashire's expanding textile industry. The Leeds and Liverpool Canal, which runs through the town, was a key means of transporting the coal to the cotton mills of Lancashire and **Wigan Pier**, the major loading bay, remains one of the most substantial and interesting features of the waterway. A well-known musical hall joke, first referred to by George Formby senior as he told of the virtues of his home town over Blackpool, it was the 1930s novel by George Orwell, *The Road to Wigan Pier*, that really put the old wharf on the map. Today, the pier has been beautifully restored and it is now a key attraction in the area. Visitors can see what locals did on holiday during the traditional Wakes Week break; witness a colliery disaster; sing along in the Palace of Varieties Music

Hall, or experience the rigours of a Victorian schoolroom. There's also a superb exhibition, The Way We Were, based on local social history and with costumed actors playing the part of the townsfolk of the 19th century. A short journey along the canal in a bateau mouche style Waterbus is **Trencherfield Mill** where not only is there the largest working mill steam engine in the world on display but also a collection of old textile machines and other engines. The Mill is also home to the award-winning **Opie's Museum of Memories**, a fascinating collection of actual products and brands, fashions, advertising and furniture from the last century. Incidentally, it was in Wigan that Michael Mark and Thomas Spencer first joined forces in 1894 and for three years the town was the headquarters of Mark's & Spencer.

As well as having a modern town centre with all the usual amenities, including a theatre and art gallery,

Wigan has some fine countryside on its doorstep, some of which can be explored by following the **Douglas Valley Trail** along the banks of the River Douglas. Even the town's coal mining past has interesting links with the natural world: **Pennington Flash** is a large lake formed by mining subsidence that is now a wildlife reserve and a country park. To the north of the town lies **Haigh Hall and Country Park**, one of the first to be designated in England and formed from the estate of the Earls of Crawford. With its 250 acres of lush and picturesque woodlands are a 15-inch gauge miniature railway; a very well-equipped children's playground; a crazy golf course; a model village and an art and craft centre in the original stables block. There are walks along the towpath of the Leeds to Liverpool canal which bisects the park or around the rose-filled Walled Gardens.

PLACES TO STAY, EAT AND DRINK

● Denotes entries in other chapters

7 East Lancashire

This area of the county, to the north of Manchester and west of the Pennines, is, perhaps, everyone's idea of Lancashire. A region dominated by cotton, East Lancashire has risen and fallen with the fluctuations in the trade over the years but, behind the dark, satanic mills is a population full of humour and wit as well as some splendid countryside.

Before the Industrial Revolution this was a sparsely populated region of remote hillside farms and cottages that relied, chiefly, on sheep farming and the wool trade. Many of the settlements date back to before the Norman Conquest and although little may have survived the rapid building of the 19th century

there are three surprisingly wonderful ancient houses to be seen here: Smithills Hall and Hall-i'-th'-Wood at Bolton and Turton Tower, just to the north.

However, there is no escaping the textile industry. Lancashire's ideal climate for cotton spinning and weaving – damp so that the yarn does not break – made it the obvious choice for the building of the mills. There are numerous valleys with fast flowing rivers and streams and then the development of the extensive coalfields around Wigan supplied the fuel to feed the power hungry machinery. Finally, there was a plentiful supply of labour as families moved from the hill top sheep farms into the expanding towns and villages to work the looms and turn the wheels of industry.

In a very short time, smoke and soot filled the air and the once clear streams and rivers became lifeless valleys of polluted squalor. There are many illustrations in the region of the harsh working conditions

Belmont Church, Bolton

the labourers had to endure and the dirt and filth that covered much of the area. Now that much of this has been cleaned up, the rivers running once again fast, clear, and supporting wildlife, the lasting legacy of those days is the splendid Victorian architecture of which every town has at least one example.

Bolton

Synonymous with the Lancashire textile industry, Bolton is also an ancient town that predates its expansion due to cotton by many centuries. First settled during the Bronze Age, by the time of the Civil War, this was a market town supporting the surrounding villages. The town saw one of the bloodiest episodes of the war when James Stanley, Earl of Derby, was brought back here by Cromwell's troops after the Royalists had been defeated. In a savage act of revenge for the massacre his army had brought on the town early in the troubles, Stanley was executed and his severed head and body, in separate caskets, were taken back to the family burial place at Ormskirk. Whilst in captivity in the town, Stanley was kept prisoner at Ye Olde Man and Scythe Inn which, dating from 1251, is still standing in Churchgate today and is the town's oldest building.

Bolton is fortunate in having two particularly fine old mansions, both on the northern edge of the town. **Hall-i'-th'-Wood**, is a delightful part-timbered medieval merchant's house dating from 1530 to 1648. A fine example of a wealthy merchant's house, Hall

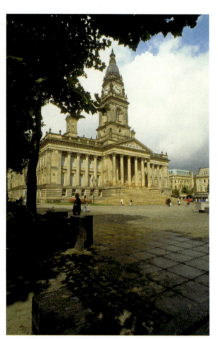

Albert Hall, Bolton

i'th'Wood was saved from dereliction by Lord Leverhulme in 1900 and has been restored and furnished with displays of fine 17th and 18th century furniture along with interesting items of local importance. The hall has a second claim to fame since, for a number of years one of several tenants here was Samuel Crompton, the inventor in 1799 of the spinning mule. Naturally, the hall has a replica of Crompton's mule on display.

Bolton's second grand house, **Smithills Hall**, stands on an easily defended hill and was built in the 1300s as a pele, or fortified dwelling. It was extended over the years and this superb Grade I listed building now displays some of the best examples of medieval, Tudor and Victorian Arts & Crafts architecture in

Turton Tower, Bolton

the region. The hall was bought by Bolton Corporation in the late 1930s and has been beautifully restored. In addition to the impressive collection of furniture and artifacts on display, the hall also hosts changing exhibitions throughout the year. As well as seeing one of the oldest and best preserved fortified manor houses in the county, visitors can also wander along the hall's wooded nature trail.

Close to Smithills Hall, in Moss Bank Park, is **Animal World & Butterfly House** (free) which provides a safe habitat for a variety of animals and birds ranging from farm animals to chipmunks, from wildfowl and tropical birds. In the tropical atmosphere of the Butterfly House, are free-flying butterflies and moths as well as insects, spiders, reptiles and tropical plants.

The centre of Bolton is a lasting tribute to the wealth and prosperity generated by the spinning of high quality yarn for which the town was famous. The monumental **Town Hall**, opened in 1873, is typical of the classical style of buildings that the Victorian town fathers favoured – tours are available. The hall is still the town's central point and it is now surrounded by the recently refurbished pedestrianised shopping malls, market hall, and the celebrated Octagon Theatre. The town's excellent **Museum, Art Gallery & Aquarium** (free) is one of the largest regional galleries in the northwest with excellent collections of fine and decorative art, including examples of British sculpture and contemporary ceramics. There are collections of natural history, geology, and Egyptian antiques here as well as some fine 18th and 19th century English watercolours and some contemporary British paintings and graphics.

Bolton's most recent major attraction is the state-of-the-art **Reebok Stadium**, home of Bolton Wanderers, one of the world's oldest football clubs. Visitors can take a look behind the scenes at one of Europe's finest stadiums, seeing everything from the players' changing rooms to the bird's eye vantage point of the Press Box.

On the northwestern edge of the town is **Barrow Bridge Village** (free), a small model village built during the Industrial Revolution to house workers at the two

6-storey mills that used to operate here. Small bridges cross a picturesque stream and a flight of 63 steps leads up the hillside to the moors. Barrow Bridge village was the inspiration for Benjamin Disraeli's famous novel *Coningsby*.

Around Bolton

Turton Bottoms
4 miles N of Bolton off the B6391

Turton Tower near Bolton was built both for defensive purposes and as a residence. In 1400, William Orrell erected his sturdy, four-square pele (fortified dwelling) in search of safety during those lawless and dangerous years. Some 200 years later, in more settled times, a lovely, half-timbered Elizabethan mansion was added. Successive owners made further additions in a charming motley of architectural styles. Quite apart from its enchanting appearance, Turton is well worth visiting to see its display of old weapons and a superb collection of vintage furniture, outstanding amongst which is the sumptuously carved Courtenay Bed of 1593.

Ramsbottom
6 miles NE of Bolton on the A676

One of the stops along the East Lancashire Railway, this picturesque village, overlooking the Irwell Valley, is well worth visiting. One of the best views of the village and, indeed, the surrounding area can be found from **Peel**

Tower which dominates the skyline. Erected in 1852 to commemorate the life of the area's most famous son, Sir Robert Peel, the tower is some 128 feet high. Now restored, the tower itself is occasionally open to the public.

Bury
6 miles E of Bolton on the A58

There was a settlement at Bury in Bronze Age times, but as late as 1770 it was still just a small market town, surrounded by green fields. That was the year a man named Robert Peel established his Ground Calico Printing Works, the first of many mills that would follow. The opening of the works along with the subsequent mills, print and bleach works so dominated this part of the Irwell Valley that not only did they transform the landscape but also heavily polluted the river. At the height of the valley's production it was said that anyone falling into the river would dissolve before they had a chance to drown. Today, thankfully, the valley towns are once again clean and the river clear and fast flowing.

With the family fortune gleaned from those prosperous mills, Robert Peel junior, born in the town in 1788, was able to fund his illustrious career in politics, rising to become Prime Minister in 1841. Famous for the repeal of the Corn Laws, Robert Peel was also at the forefront of the setting up of the modern police force – hence their nickname 'Bobbies'. A statue of Bury's most distinguished son stands in the Market

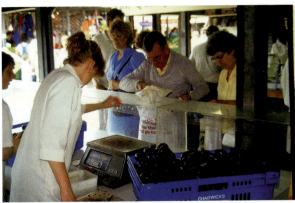

Black Pudding Stall, Bury Market

of paintings, including works by Turner, Constable and Landseer, and the outstanding Thomas Wrighley collection of Victorian oil paintings. Downstairs, visitors can stroll along "Paradise Street", a fascinating re-creation of Bury as it was in the 1950s.

Square and there's an even grander memorial near the village of Holcombe, a few miles to the north.

Another of Bury's famous sons was John Kay, inventor of the Flying Shuttle. Sadly, Kay neglected to patent his invention. He moved to France where he died a pauper and is buried in an unmarked grave. The people of Bury, however, remembered him. In his memory, they created the delightful Kay Gardens in the town centre and erected a splendidly ornate clock-house tower.

A short walk from Kay Gardens, **The Met** is a lively arts centre which puts on performances to suit all tastes, from theatre and children's shows to rock nights and world music. The Met also organises Bury's Streets Ahead Festival each May, a colourful street carnival which attracts artistes from around the world.

This part of town has become known as the "Culture Quarter", since Bury's **Art Gallery & Museum** is also located here. The Gallery has a fine collection

The town has a real treat for those who thrill to the sight, sound and smell of steam locomotives. Bolton Street Station is the southern terminus of the **East Lancashire Railway** which operates regular services along a 9 mile scenic route through the lovely Irwell Valley to Rawtenstall. Serious devotees of transport history will want to explore the **Bury Transport Museum**, just across the road from the station. The museum houses a wonderful collection of vintage road and rail vehicles, ranging from a 19th century steam road-roller to a "Stop Me and Buy One" ice-cream vendor's tricycle.

Another museum of interest is the **Lancashire Fusiliers Museum** which tells the story of Lancashire's famous regiment from its foundation in 1688 and has an outstanding collection of medals and period uniforms.

A major shopping centre for the northwest, Bury is also proud of its ancient **Market** which has been operating since 1440. It's now the largest market in the north with more than 370 stalls offering a huge choice of some 50,000 different product lines. Don't leave without purchasing one of Bury's famous black puddings!

Looking at Bury today it seems hard to imagine that at one time this typical Lancashire mill town had a castle. A settlement probably existed here in the Bronze Age and there is certainly evidence that the Romans passed through this area. By the 12th century the town was the manor of the Norman de Bury family and, in the mid-14th century, the land came under the ownership of the Pilkingtons. It was dismantled following the Battle of Bosworth in 1485 at which Henry VII defeated Richard III. Unlucky Thomas Pilkington had backed the wrong side. The foundations of the castle have recently been excavated and form the centerpiece of "Castle Square".

On the outskirts of the town lies **Burrs Country Park** which, as well as offering a wide range of activities, also has an interesting industrial trail around this historic mill site.

Walmersley
2 miles NE of Bolton on the A56

Hidden away in the village of Walmersley, just north of Bury, is **Hark to Dandler**, an attractive pub dating from the mid-19th century that is thought to have originally been a vicarage. During a recent refurbishment a very old child's coffin was found, full of early 19th century artifacts, behind the cellar walls and, along with the two resident ghosts, this certainly adds an air of mystery to the pub. The name though is more easily explained as it is named after a lead dog of the local hunt.

Tottington
4 miles N of Bolton on the B6213

Tottington's pub is also named after a dog. The **Hark to Towler**, in the centre of the town, is very much a local's pub that happily welcomes visitors. Dating back to the 1800s, this imposing red brick pub's unusual name means call - hark - to the lead dog of the hunt - towler.

An unspoilt farming town on the edge of moorland, Tottington escaped the industrialisation of many of its neighbours due to its, then, isolated position and it is still an attractive place to visit.

Rochdale
Lying in a shallow valley formed by the little River Roch, the town is surrounded, to the north and east, by the slopes of the Pennines that are often snow covered in winter. With its origins in medieval times, the town, like so many others in Lancashire, expanded with the booming cotton industry and its magnificent Victorian **Town Hall** (1871) rivals that of Manchester in style if not in size.

However, it is not textiles for which Rochdale is famous but for its role as the

ROCHDALE PIONEERS MUSEUM

31 Toad Lane, Rochdale OL12 0NU
Tel: 01706 524920
e-mail: museum@co-op.ac.uk
website: www.co-op.ac.uk/toad lane

The Rochdale Pioneers Museum is regarded as the home of the world wide co-operative movement. It's the perfect place to come and see how your ancestors did their shopping.

In Toad Lane on December 21 1844 the Rochdale Equitable Pioneers Society opened their store selling pure food at fair prices and honest weights and measures, starting a revolution in retailing.

See the recreation of the original shop with its rudimentary furniture and scales. Here the basic needs of daily life such as butter, sugar, flour and oatmeal first went on sale over 150 years ago.

Journey back in time with early advertising, packaging and retailing artifacts, Co-operative postage stamps, commemorative china and rare dividend coins and commodity tokens. See the development of 'dividend' and the Co-op's success.

birthplace of the Co-operative Movement. In carefully restored Toad Lane, to the north of the town centre, is the world's first Co-op shop, now the **Rochdale Pioneers Museum** (see panel above). Today, the Co-op movement represents a staggering 700 million members in 90 countries around the world and the celebration of its 150th anniversary in 1994 focused attention on Rochdale. The story of the Rochdale Pioneers and other aspects of the town's heritage are vividly displayed in the new Arts & Heritage Centre, **Touchstones**.

THE HARE & HOUNDS

865 Bury Road, Bamford, Rochdale,
Lancashire OL11 4AA
Tel: 01706 369189

Located about a mile from Rochdale town centre on the road to Bury, **The Hare & Hounds** is a handsome old building dating back to the early 1700s. Originally it was known as the Brew House since it brewed its own beer right up until the late 1940s. Today, this friendly and welcoming hostelry serves a wide range of beers, including two real ales ·

Thwaite's Cask and Lancaster Bomber. Mine hosts are Gail and Peter with Gail, an accomplished

cook, in charge of the kitchen and offering a tasty menu of home cooked food. The pub has a patio and beer garden enjoying lovely countryside views; pool and darts are available; there's a regular quiz on Wednesday evenings and occasional live entertainment.

THE BLUE BALL INN

539 Edenfield Road, Norden, Rochdale,
Lancashire OL11 5XH
Tel: 01706 642270 Fax: 01706 344248
e-mail: blueballnorden@ukonline.co.uk

Dating back to the early 1800s, the **Blue Ball Inn** was three storeys high until an explosion in a nearby coal mine meant the top storey had to be removed. Today, this fine old traditional inn is a popular social venue for the village, sustaining its own golf society (visitors welcome to join) and serving wholesome, appetising food every lunchtime and evening except on Mondays. One Wednesday each month, there's a themed food evening with a set price 4-course meal · bookings are essential. Landlord Simon Pattison has been here since 1995 and he keeps 3 real ales on tap along with all the popular brands. A lively pub quiz takes place each Tuesday and Sunday.

The restored Grade II listed building of 1889 was originally a library but now contains interactive high-tech exhibitions, 4 art galleries, the Tourist Information Centre, a local studies centre, café/bar, bookshop and performance studio.

As well as the Pioneers, Rochdale was home to several other famous sons and daughters, amongst them the 19th century political thinker, John Bright, the celebrated singer Gracie Fields, and Cyril Smith, Rochdale's former Liberal Member of Parliament.

The town's most distinctive church is **St John the Baptist Catholic Church** which has a beautiful dome modelled on the Byzantine Santa Sofya in Istanbul. The church is unique in England because of its huge mosaic of Italian marble depicting the Resurrection of Christ.

Running from the southeast corner of the town, the **Rochdale Canal** is a brave piece of early-19th century civil engineering that traversed the Pennines to link the River Mersey with the Calder and Hebble Navigation. Some 32 miles in length and with 91 locks, it must be one of toughest canals ever built and, though the towpath can still be walked, the last commercial boat passed through the locks in 1937. The canal was officially abandoned in 1952, but exactly

Rochdale Town Hall

half a century later the entire length has been re-opened to full navigation. Together with the newly restored Huddersfield Narrow Canal it allows a complete circuit of the South Pennine Ring.

Between Rochdale and Littleborough lies Hollingworth Lake, originally built as a supply reservoir for the canal, but for many years a popular area for recreation known colloquially as the 'Weavers' Seaport', as cotton workers unable to afford a trip to the seaside came here. Now part of the **Hollingworth Lake Country Park** (see page 143) and with a fine visitor centre, there are a number of pleasant walks around its shores.

North of Rochdale

Whitworth
3 miles N of Rochdale on the A671

This pleasant town, of cottages and farms, lies on Pennine moorland above Rochdale. Between here and Bacup, a distance of only seven miles, the railway line, another feat of Victorian engineering, climbs over 500 feet. Not surprisingly, there were many problems during its construction, such as frequent landslides, but once constructed this was a picturesque line with attractive station houses with neat well tended gardens along the route. The line, like so many, fell to the extensive railway cuts of the 1960s.

Healey
1 mile N of Rochdale on the A671

Lying in the valley of the River Spodden, this old village, now almost engulfed by the outer reaches of Rochdale, is an area rich in wildlife as well as folklore. Nearby is Robin Hood's Well, one of a number of springs feeding the river. Here, it is said, sometime in the 12th century the Earl of Huntingdon was lured to the well by a witch pretending to be his nursemaid. Once at the well, the witch told the young man that he would never inherit his earldom unless he had her magic ring as a means of identification. Gazing into the well, Robin got such a fright that he fainted and the witch took off on her broomstick. Emerging from the well the King of the Fairies gave the lad his own ring and told him to go up into Healey Dell and interrupt the witches whilst they were hatching their next spell. Doing as he was instructed Robin entered the coven and threw the ring into their cauldron whereupon there was a great flash of light and the witches were reduced to evil-looking fairies destined to live forever in the Fairy chapel.

Opened in 1972, **Healey Dell Nature Reserve** does not promise visitors sightings of either witches or fairies but there is a wealth of wildlife to be discovered along the nature trails. This is an ancient area which has only been invaded by the construction of the commercially non-viable Rochdale to Bacup railway in the late 19th century. The oak and birch woodland on the northern river bank is all that remains of a prehistoric forest and, whilst the owners of Healey Hall made some impact, little has changed here for centuries.

Littleborough

4 miles NE of Rochdale on the A58

This small town lies beside the River Roch and on the main route between Lancashire and Yorkshire first laid down by the Romans. Known as the Roman Causey, it was an impressive structure 16 feet 6 inches wide, cambered and with gutters at each side. In the middle of the road is a shallow groove which has been the subject of endless controversy – no-one has yet come up with a satisfactory explanation of its purpose. The road cuts across the bleak Pennine moors by way of **Blackstone Edge** where some of the best preserved parts of the Roman structure can still be seen. At the summit is a medieval cross, the **Aigin Stone**, which offers spectacular views over Lancashire right to the coast.

To the south of Littleborough, **Hollingworth Lake Water Activity Centre** (see panel opposite) offers sailing, canoeing, windsurfing, rowing and, during the summer months, lake trips on the *Lady Alice*.

THE MOORCOCK INN

Halifax Road, Blackstone Edge,
Littleborough, Rochdale,
Lancashire OL15 0LD
Tel: 01706 378156 Fax: 01706 838954
e-mail: moorcock@btinternet.com
website: www.themoorcockinn.com

Dating from 1641 **The Moorcock Inn** was originally Swainrod Farm and appears to have been first licensed in 1840 – all the landlords since then are listed in the bar. The inn enjoys a superb rural location, nestling at the foot of the Pennines and close to Hollingworth Lake with grand views over open countryside. This family-run hostelry is owned by Allan and Pauline Ashworth who will go out their way to ensure your visit is perfect – whether for an overnight stay, for a meal or just a drink. The inn's three top class chefs offer a wide choice of dishes, all freshly prepared using local produce and ranging from traditional favourites such as the Pan Fried Welsh Lamb Cutlets to Medallions of Ostrich Fillet with Armagnac and Peppercorn Sauce. Bar meals and snacks are also available.

To complement your meal there's an excellent choice of wines and an impressive list of cask-conditioned ales, amongst them Timothy Taylor Bitter, Marston's Bitter and Moorhouse's Bitter. A range of lagers, ciders, and Guinness is also available. The inn usually hosts live musical entertainment Friday evenings. Children are welcome and have their own play area in the spacious patio at the rear. The location makes this a delightful place to stay – the rooms all have en suite facilities, TV, phone/computer socket, hairdryer, and tea/coffee-making equipment.

Hollingworth Lake Country Park

Countryside Ranger Service, Visitor Centre,
Rakewood Road, Liftleborough,
Lancashire Oll 5 OAQ
Tel: 01706 373421
Fax: 01706 378753

Nestling on the edge of the Pennines, just 3 miles from Rochdale town centre, and junction 21on the M62, **Hollingworth Lake** provides a surprising haven for wildlife and excitement and entertainment for the young and the not so young.

Built to supply water to the recently re-opened Rochdale Canal, the Lake has always been a popular destination. In its heyday it boasted dance halls, a skating rink and steamboats. Today there is a nature reserve, visitor centre, and water sports facility.

Easy walking around the lake can be extended by following the trails into the surrounding countryside. The events programmes are packed full of ideas for the pleasure and enjoyment of everyone. Facilities in the area include caravan and camping sites, craft shops, and several pubs, cafes and restaurants.

Summit
5 miles NE of Rochdale off the A6033

At Summit, the Rochdale to Halifax railway line dives into a tunnel that runs for a mile and a half under the Summit Ridge of the Pennines before emerging in Yorkshire. This extraordinary feat of engineering was completed in 1844, as remarkable in its way as the Roman Causey which follows a similar route on top of the hills.

South of Rochdale

Milnrow
2 miles S of Rochdale on the A640

It was to this small industrial town in the foothills of the Pennines that John Collier came as the schoolmaster in

The Summit Inn

140 Todmorden Road, Summit,
Lancashire OL15 9QX
Tel: 01706 378011

The Summit Inn is a delightful traditional hostelry, splendidly situated with its rear garden sloping down to a stretch of the recently restored and re-opened Rochdale Canal. When Marshia Baldwin took over here in April 2002 the inn was "sad" but she has revived its fortunes amd made it a popular social centre. Attractions include two real ales, along with a wide range of well-known

brews, and excellent food available every lunchtime and evening · good pub grub in

hearty servings and very reasonably priced. There's a special menu for children who can also enjoy a safe play area in the rear garden. The inn hosts a Quiz on Thursday and Sunday evenings and live entertainment on Fridays.

1729. Then a woollen handloom weaving village, Collier is perhaps better known as Tim Bobbin, the first of the Lancashire dialect poets. Collier remained in Milnrow for the rest of his life and, drinking rather more than he should, he earned extra money by selling his verse and painting pub signs. The local pub which dates back to the early 1800s is, appropriately, named after him.

Shaw

3 miles SE of Rochdale on the A633

A typical mill town, founded on the wealth of the cotton trade, this was also a market town for the surrounding area. Closed since 1932, **Jubilee Colliery**, to the northeast of the town centre, has been reclaimed as a nature reserve and it is now an attractive haven for wildlife in the Beal Valley.

Delph

7 miles SE of Rochdale on the A6052

Taking its name from the old English for quarry, this is probably a reference to the bakestone quarries found to the north of the village. Also close by, high on a hill above the village, lies **Castleshaw**, one of a series of forts the Romans built on their military road between Chester and York. The banks and ditches give visitors an excellent indication of the scale of the fort and many of the items found

during recent excavations are on show in the Saddleworth Museum.

Dobcross

7 miles SE of Rochdale off the A6052

This attractive Pennine village, once the commercial heart of the district of Saddleworth, retains many of its original weavers' cottages, clothiers, and merchants' houses, and little has changed around the village square in the last 200 years. Used as the location for the film *Yanks*, Dobcross is also notable as the birthplace of the giant Platt Brothers Textile Machinery business which was, in the latter part of the 19th century, the largest such machine manufacturing firm in the world.

Uppermill

8 miles SE of Rochdale on the A62

Of the14 villages that make up Saddleworth parish, Uppermill is the most central. It is certainly home to the area's oldest building, **Saddleworth Parish Church** which was originally built in the 12th century by the Stapletons as their family chapel. Extended over the years, it has several interesting features including a gravestone to commemorate the Bill's o'Jack's murders. In 1832, the people of Saddleworth were stunned to learn that the landlord of the Bill's o'Jack's Inn and his son had been bludgeoned to death. Several thousand people turned out for

Saddleworth Moor

the funeral but the case was never solved. The tombstone relates the whole story.

Almost a century and a half later, the whole country was horrified by the "Moors Murderers", Ian Brady and Myra Hindley, who buried four of their victims on **Saddleworth Moor**.

The story of this once isolated area is illustrated at the **Saddleworth Museum,** housed in an old mill building on the banks of the Huddersfield Canal. There is a reconstruction of an 18th century weaver's cottage as well as a collection of textile machinery, local history gallery and local art exhibitions.

Also in Uppermill is the **Brownhill Visitor Centre**, which not only has information on the northern section of the Tame Valley but also exhibitions on local wildlife and the area's history.

Diggle

8 miles SE of Rochdale off the A62

Above the village, on **Diggle Moor** lies Brun Clough Farm where, it is said, the cries of child slaves who were ill treated in the early days of the textile mills can still be heard coming from the outhouses. Part of the **Oldham Way** footpath, a 30 mile scenic walk through the countryside on the edge of the Peak District National Park, crosses the moorland.

Much of the village itself is a conservation area, where the pre-industrial weaving community has been preserved along with some of the traditional skills. However, Diggle Mill, which used to operate the second largest waterwheel in the country, no longer exists.

THE GOLDEN FLEECE

41 Oldham Road, Denshaw, Lancashire
OL3 5SS
Tel: 01457 820851

The Golden Fleece sits high on a hill with exhilarating views from its terrace across the East Lancashire countryside. It stands beside the A640 Oldham to Huddersfield road and was originally built in the early 1800s to service the coaches that plied this route. Inside, the inn still has something of an olde worlde atmosphere and the landlords, Natasha and Steven Woodhouse, are local people with a real sense of Lancastrian hospitality. They have made the Golden Fleece a byword for good eating, offering a very extensive menu so varied that there is something here to suit every palate. Amongst

the starters for example you'll find Bury black pudding with fried onions and crispy bacon; Thai style Tom Yum prawns with citrus mayonnaise, and Chilli beef nachos served with guacamole and sour cream. For the main course, specialities of the house include handmade pork sausages served on a bed of mustard mash with a rich red wine and onion gravy, a 16oz leg of minted lamb, slow roasted to perfection, and Barbary duck breast flamed in Cointreau and finished with cream and cinnamon. The menu also offers a wide selection of steaks, fish, pasta and vegetarian dishes, as well as salads, home-made pies

and a roast of the day. To round off the meal, there's an enticing selection of desserts or a portion of mixed cheeses and biscuits.

To accompany your meal, the bar offers two real ales, Timothy Taylor Landlord and a rotating guest ale, along with John Smith's Smooth, Carling, Carling Extra Cold, Strongbow, regular Guinness and extra cold. Food is available from 6pm to 9.30pm, Monday to Thursday; between noon and 9pm, Friday and Saturday; and from noon until 7pm on Sunday. On Thursday evenings, a buffet style themed cuisine is available in additin to the main menu. Food is served either in the bar dining area or in the stylish downstairs restaurant which is non-smoking. At weekends and Bank Holidays, booking ahead is strongly recommended. In good weather, refreshments can be enjoyed in the delightful beer garden and patio area to the rear which command glorious panoramic views.

An additional service provided for people living within a 10-mile radius of the Golden Fleece is a courier service - this has to be booked in advance.

The Huddersfield Narrow Canal, completed in 1811, is one of the three canals that crossed the difficult terrain of the Pennines and linked Lancashire with Yorkshire. The entrance to the **Standedge Canal Tunnel**, the longest and highest canal tunnel in Britain, lies in the village. The last cargo boat passed through the tunnel in 1921 and following a long period of closure, it has now been re-opened.

Denshaw
5 miles SE of Rochdale on the A640

In the moorland above the village is the source of the River Tame which flows through the Saddleworth area and eventually joins the River Goyt at Stockport. A charming 18th century village, Denshaw's Scandinavian name would suggest that there has been a settlement here for many centuries.

Until 1974, the Saddleworth area was part of the West Riding of Yorkshire and residents of the parish are still eligible to play for the Yorkshire cricket team. Cricket has always been a passion here. One 19th century mill owner built 'Cricketers Row' near Denshaw to house his team and the terrace even includes one for the 12th man.

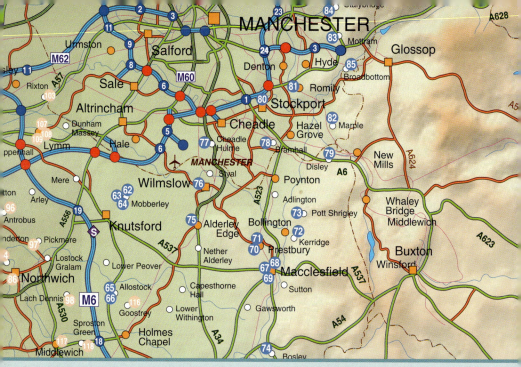

PLACES TO STAY, EAT AND DRINK

● Denotes entries in other chapters

8 North East Cheshire

Knutsford

Knutsford and its people were the heroes of one of the most durable of Victorian novels, Elizabeth Gaskell's *Cranford*. This gently humorous, sympathetic but sharply-observed portrait of the little Cheshire town, and the foibles and pre-occupations of its citizens, was first published in 1853 and is still delighting readers today. Elizabeth was scarcely a month old when she came to Knutsford. Her mother had died shortly after her birth: her father sent her here to be brought up by an aunt who lived in a road which has now been re-named Gaskell Avenue. The motherless child grew up to be both strikingly beautiful and exceptionally intelligent. Early on she evinced a lively interest in the town's characters and its history. (She was intrigued, for example, to find that in the house next door to her aunt's had once lived a notorious highwayman, Edward Higgins, hanged for his crimes in 1767. She wrote a story about him). Marriage to William Gaskell, a Unitarian pastor in Manchester, took her away from Knutsford, although she returned often and for long periods, and after her death in 1865 was buried in the grounds of the Unitarian Chapel here.

The Knutsford that Elizabeth Gaskell knew so well and wrote about so vividly has expanded a great deal since those days of course, but in its compact centre, now designated an "outstanding area of conservation", the narrow streets and cobbled alleys still evoke the intimacy of a small Victorian town. Two parallel roads, Toft Street and King Street, form a rectangle surrounding the

Shinto Temple, Tatton Park

old town. But Mrs Gaskell would surely be astonished by the building erected in King Street to her memory by Mr Richard Harding Watt in 1907. A gifted entrepreneur, Mr Watt had made a huge fortune in Manchester as a glove manufacturer, but what really aroused his enthusiasm was the flamboyant architecture he had seen during his travels through Spain, southern Italy and the Near East.

On his return, he spent lavishly on trying to transform Knutsford in Cheshire into Knutsford-on-the-Mediterranean. At the north end of the town, he built a laundry complete with Byzantine domes and a minaret. A vaguely Ottoman style of architecture welcomed serious-minded artisans to his Ruskin Reading Rooms. In Legh Road, he erected a series of villas whose south-facing frontages are clearly in need of a really hot sun. And in King Street, as homage to the town's most famous resident, Richard Watt spent thousands of Victorian pounds on the Gaskell Memorial Tower. This tall, blank-walled building seems a rather incongruous tribute to the author who was herself so open and so down-to-earth.

But it is eccentrics like Richard Watt who make English architecture as interesting as it is. He was so proud of his contribution to the town's new buildings that, travelling on his coach to the railway station, he would rise to his feet and raise his hat to salute them. As he did so, one day in 1913, his horse suddenly shied, the carriage overturned,

and Richard Watt was thrown out and killed. What other changes he might have made to this grand old town, had he lived, we can only imagine.

An unusual exhibition and well worth visiting is the **Penny Farthing Museum**, located in the Courtyard Coffee House off King Street. These bizarre machines were in fashion for barely twenty years before the last model was manufactured in 1892. The collection includes a replica of the famous "Starley Giant" with a front wheel 7ft in diameter and a sign outside the coffee house promises a free tea to anyone arriving on a penny-farthing.

Close by, in Tatton Street, is the **Knutsford Heritage Centre.** Knutsford is a town with a long history – Edward I granted the town a Charter in 1262, (on August 3rd of that year, to be precise); at the same time, the local landowner, William de Tabley, was given a money-making licence to control the market. The Heritage Centre is housed in a restored 17th century timber-framed building which in Victorian times was a smithy. During the restoration the old forge and bellows were found in a remarkable state of preservation. The wrought iron gate in front of the centre was specially created for the Centre and depicts dancing girls taking part in Knutsford's famous Royal May Day celebrations – Royal because in 1887 the Prince and Princess of Wales honoured the festivities with their presence. Every May Day the town centre streets are closed to all traffic except for the May

Queen's procession in which colourful characters such as "Jack in Green", "Highwayman Higgins", "Lord Chamberlain", Morris and Maypole dancers, and many others take part. One curious tradition whose origins are unknown is the practice of covering the streets

Tatton Hall Garden, Knutsford

and pavements with ordinary sand and then, using white sand, creating elaborate patterns on top.

Around Knutsford

Sweeping up to the very edge of Knutsford are the grounds of **Tatton Park**, 2000 acres of exquisite parkland landscaped in the 18th century by the celebrated Humphrey Repton. This lovely park, where herds of red and fallow deer roam at will, provides a worthy setting for the noble Georgian mansion designed by the equally celebrated architect Samuel Wyatt. The combination of the two men's talents created a house and park that have become one of the National Trust's most visited attractions. Tatton's opulent staterooms, containing paintings by artists such as Canaletto and Van Dyck along with superb collections of porcelain and furniture, provided the television series *Brideshead Revisited* with a sumptuous setting for Marchmain House.

More than 200 elegant pieces of furniture were commissioned from the celebrated cabinet-makers, Gillow of Lancaster.

Japanese Garden, Tatton Hall

Tatton Hall Gardens

gardens include a Victorian maze, an orangery and fernery, a serene Japanese garden, American redwoods, and a splendid Italian terraced garden. There's also a busy programme of educational activities for children, an adventure playground, shops, and a restaurant. You can even get married in the sumptuous mansion and hold your reception either in the house itself, in the recently refurbished Tenants Hall which can cater for parties of up to 430, or in a marquee in the magnificent grounds. With so much on offer no wonder Tatton Park has been described as the most complete historic estate in the country.

Particularly fine are the superb bookcases in the Library, constructed to house the Egerton family's collection of more than 8000 books. By contrast, the stark servants' rooms and cellars give a vivid idea of what life below stairs was really like. The Egerton family built Tatton Park to replace the much earlier **Tudor Old Hall** which nestles in a wood in the deer park and dates back to around 1520. Here, visitors are given a guided tour through time from the late Middle Ages up to the 1950s. Flickering light from candles reveals the ancient timber roof of the Great Hall, supported by ornate quatrefoils, while underfoot, the floor is strewn with rushes, providing a warm place for the medieval Lord of the Manor and his servants to sleep. There's much more: Home Farm is a working farm, but working as it did in the 1930s, complete with vintage machinery. Traditional crafts, (including pottery), stables and many farm animals provide a complete picture of rural life some sixty years ago. Tatton's famous

Just to the west of Knutsford, on the A5033, is **Tabley House,** home of the Leicester family from 1272 to 1975. Mrs Gaskell often came to picnic in the grounds of the last of their houses, a stately Georgian mansion designed by John Carr for the first Lord de Tabley in 1761. This Lord de Tabley loved paintings and it was his son's passion for art, and his hunger for others to share it, which led to the creation of London's National Gallery. His personal collection of English pictures, on display in Tabley House, includes works by Turner (who painted the house several times), Lely, Reynolds, Opie and Martin Danby, along with furniture by Chippendale, and fascinating family memorabilia spanning three centuries. The 17th century chapel next to the house looks perfectly in place but it was originally built on an island in Tabley Mere and only moved to its present site in 1927.

Also in Tabley, at the Old School, is the Tabley Cuckoo Clock Collection. Brothers Roman and Maz Piekarski are well-known horologists and clock restorers and over the last 25 years they have sought out and renovated some of the rarest and most notable examples of this 300-year-old craft. Also on display are some mid 19th century cuckoo clocks which included complex musical movements to reproduce popular tunes of the day. For opening times, call 01565 633039.

Mere

3 miles NW of Knutsford on the A50/A556

One of the **Kilton Inn**'s more notorious guests, back in the 18th century, was Dick Turpin. The intrepid highwayman made this historic old inn the base from which he plundered travellers along the Knutsford to Warrington road (now the comparatively safe A50). After one such robbery (and murder) Turpin, on his famous horse Black Bess, "galloped to the Kilton and, altering the clock, strolled on to the bowling green and proved an alibi by the short time he took to cover the four miles".

Mobberley

2 miles E of Knutsford on the B5085

Mobberley village is scattered along the B5085, with its notable church set slightly apart. The main glory here is the spectacular woodwork inside: massive roof beams with striking winged figures and one of the finest rood screens in the country, dated 1500. The screen is covered with a rich tracery of leaves and fruit, coats-of-arms, and religious symbols. Two generations of the Mallory family held the rectorship here, one of them for 53 years. He is commemorated in the east window. Another window honours his grandson, George Mallory, the mountaineer who perished while making his third attempt to climb Mt Everest in 1924.

THE BULL'S HEAD

Mill Lane, off Town Lane, Mobberley,
Cheshire WA16 7HX
Tel: 01565 873134

Situated off the old main road through the scattered village of Mobberley, **The Bull's Head** started life in the middle of the 18th century as three cottages. Inside, it is splendidly olde-worlde and cosy, with a large log fire burning on chilly days and evenings, and leaseholders Jenny and Ted guarantee a smiling welcome and the best of hospitality.

Looking after the appetites of locals and visitors is the excellent cook, Carole, whose menus are available at all sessions except for Sunday, Monday and Tuesday evenings. On these evenings you can, if you wish, order from 3 local takeaways who will deliver to the inn, enabling you to enjoy a meal and the inn's ale in comfort. Lunch is served between

blackberry pie or treacle tart.

Children are welcome here up until 9pm and have their own menu. On Sundays there's always a choice of beautifully cooked roasts, The 40 seats fill up quickly so it's best to book, particularly on Friday and Saturday nights.

Thirsts are quenched by an excellent selection of ales, including five real ales · Tetley's, Boddingtons, and three regularly changing guest brews. Lord Ted's Ripping Good Quiz, which is free to enter, starts at 9 o'clock on Thursday, and other diversions include a games room with pool, cards, dominoes and an excellent bowling green which costs just £1 per person to hire, And if you want to bring your own food for a summer's day party, the inn also has a

noon and 2pm; evening meals from 6pm to 9pm and on Sundays, food is available from noon until 4pm.

You can choose from the printed menu or the specials board and there's always a choice of light snacks for fillers. But it's best to go for one of Carole's hearty main course specialities, a curry perhaps or a hotpot, braised liver or the famed Bull's Head Steak and Ale Pie. Room should definitely be left for one of her super sweets such as apple &

barbecue to hire.

An attraction hosted at the pub, that should not be missed, is the Annual Mobberley Steam Party, held on Whitsun Bank Holiday. Steam engine owners bring their wonderful machines and their friends to the inn to enjoy a weekend of delights that includes live music, pub games and a mini real ale festival.

Diners, Mastercard and Visa credit cards are welcome and the pub has ample parking.

COPPOCK HOUSE

Faulkners Lane, Mobberley,
Cheshire WA16 7AL
Tel: 01565 873312 Mobile: 07860 425636

Amidst 34 acres of grazing and pasture land, **Coppock House** offers quality bed & breakfast or self-catering accommodation in a peaceful, rural setting. The main house, home to Malcolm and Dorothy Dennison, dates from 1650 and is Grade I listed. Two rooms in this house, both doubles, are available for bed & breakfast guests. The adjoining former farm buildings have been restored and turned into top quality modern living space with top of the range décor and furnishings. There are 1, 2 or 3-bedroom apartments and each property can be taken on either a bed & breakfast or self-catering basis. All are en suite and the largest can sleep up to 6 guests. Short or long term rentals are available; children are welcome, but no pets.

At the Whitsun Bank Holiday each year steam traction enthusiasts from all across the country descend on the village for the **Mobberley Steam Party** hosted by the Bull's Head Inn.

Lower Peover

4 miles S of Knutsford on the B5081

The village of Lower Peover (pronounced Peever) is effectively made up of two hamlets. One is grouped around the village green on the B5081, the other is at the end of a cobbled lane. It's a picturesque little group. There's a charming old coaching inn, The Bells of Peover, which numbers amongst its former customers Generals Patton and Eisenhower during World War II. The American flag still flies here alongside the Union Jack. Nearby are a handsome village school founded in 1710, and a lovely black and white timbered church, more than 700 years old. St Oswald's is notable as one of the few timber-framed churches in the country still standing. Inside, there is a wealth of carved wood

– pews and screens, pulpit and lectern, and a massive medieval chest made from a single log of bog oak. At one time local girls who wished to marry a farmer were required to raise its lid with one hand to demonstrate they had the strength to cope with farm life.

About 3 miles east of Lower Peover is **Peover Hall**, very much hidden away at the end of a winding country road but well worth tracking down. During World War II, General George Patton lived for a while at the Hall which was conveniently close to his then headquarters at Knutsford. There's a memorial to him in the church nearby, but many many more to the Mainwaring family whose fine monuments crowd beside each other in both the north and south chapels. (Please note that the Hall is only open to the public on Monday afternoons between April and October).

Macclesfield

Nestling below the hills of the High Peak, Macclesfield was once an important silk manufacturing town.

COTTAGE RESTAURANT AND LODGE

London Road, Allostock, Knutsford,
Cheshire WA16 9LU
Tel: 01565 722470 Fax: 01565 722749
website: www.thecottageknutsford.co.uk

The village of Allostock lies in the heart of rural Cheshire on the A50 road between Knutsford and Holmes Chapel. Set slightly back from the main road you will find the **Cottage Restaurant and Lodge** which is owned and personally run by the Marr family. The Cottage is well known throughout the area for serving a superb menu of modern British food from both an à la carte and table d'hôte menu each lunch time (noon

are 12 en suite guest rooms, (4 doubles and 8 twins), with 8 of the rooms dedicated as non-smoking. If necessary, the twins which have "zip and link" beds can be used as doubles. The accommodation is also available on a room only basis. The tariff, which includes a full English breakfast, remains static throughout the year and special discounts are given for longer stays. All major credit cards apart from Diners are welcome.

The Cottage Restaurant is a member of the Hi-Life Diners Club which was established some 18 years ago and now has more than 500 member restaurants in the North West. In return for an annual fee, participating diners receive two meals for the price of one. When paying the bill, just present your membership card and the charges for the second meal will be deleted.

until 2pm) and evening (6pm to 10pm) with the exception of Sunday evenings. Up to 60 diners can be accommodated in the waitress-served, non-smoking restaurant and children are welcome. It is also worth noting that you can simply enjoy a drink should you wish, although once you have a look at the menu you will almost certainly be tempted to try a bite to eat.   The menu offers a good choice of steaks, fish dishes and vegetarian options, as well as some enticing desserts such as Blackberry Cheese Cake.

In addition to offering fine food the Cottage also has comfortable bed and breakfast accommodation. There

THE DROVERS ARMS

1 London Road, Allostock, nr Knutsford,
Cheshire WA16 9JD
Tel: 01565 723535 Fax: 01565 723682
e-mail: leemax@cs.com

The Drovers Arms is a wonderful public house with real warmth and atmosphere. It boasts an excellent beer garden and one of the best bowling greens in Cheshire, and the interior is traditional in style and feel, with stone floors and lots of memorabilia on display.

Mine hosts, Katrina and Lee Russell, have many years experience in the trade and have been here since 1997. Open all day, seven days a week, The Drovers serves excellent food Monday to Friday, from noon until 9.30pm; weekends from midday to 10pm. There's a non-smoking dining area as well of plenty of room in the bar and outdoors. Booking is advised, particularly from Thursday to Sunday.

The food here is a major attraction. The extensive menu features home-made pasta, sirloin steak, liver and onions, mixed grill, salmon, plaice and mushroom stroganoff. One speciality is the Cheese and Pâté board; there are also daily specials. The list of desserts is truly impressive so guests should be sure to leave room for delicacies such as summer fruit pudding, caramel and banana antillais, or hand-made fruit pie of the day.

All food is fresh and cooked to order, There's a good choice of wines by the glass, especially the range of superb Spanish wines. The full range of quality real ales includes local brews.

Charles Roe built the first silk mill here, beside the River Bollin, in 1743 and for more than a century and a half, Macclesfield was known as *the* silk town. It's appropriate then that Macclesfield can boast the country's only **Silk Museum** (see panel on page 158) where visitors are given a lively introduction to all aspects of the silk industry, from cocoon to loom. The museum has an award-winning audio-visual presentation, there are fascinating exhibitions on the Silk Road across Asia, on silk cultivation, fashion and other uses of silk. A shop dedicated to silk offers a range of attractive and unusual gifts – scarves, ties, silk cards and woven pictures along with inexpensive gifts for children.

The silk theme continues at nearby **Paradise Mill**. Built in the 1820s, it is now a working museum demonstrating silk weaving on 26 jacquard hand looms. Exhibitions and restored workshops and living rooms capture the working conditions and lives of mill workers in the 1930s. It is also possible to buy locally-made silk products here. The Silk Museum is housed in what used to be the Macclesfield Sunday School, erected in 1813. The school finally closed in 1970 and the Silk Museum now shares this rather grand building with the town's **Heritage Centre** which has some interesting displays on Macclesfield's rich and exciting past, (the town was occupied for five days by Scottish troops during the Jacobite

JASPERS

71 Park Lane, Macclesfield,
Cheshire SK11 6TX
Tel/Fax: 01625 421514

A short walk from the town centre, **Jaspers** is a friendly eating place offering wholesome and appetising fare at very reasonable prices. The owner, Mark Capper, has more than 23 years in the catering trade and opened Jaspers in January 2002. Customers can choose from the main menu or from the daily specials listed on the blackboards. A favourite with regulars is the hearty home-made Steak and Ale Pie but there's also a wide range of other dishes including poultry, fish, pasta and vegetarian, as well as an All Day Breakfast. Non-smoking, Jaspers seats 36 and is open 7 days a week from 8am to 3pm, (from 9am on Sundays). Children are welcome; cash and cheques only are accepted. Mark will also take bookings in the evening for private parties.

Rebellion of 1745, for example), and on the Sunday School itself.

In pre-Saxon times, Macclesfield was known as "Hameston" – the homestead on the rock, and on that rock is set the church founded by King Edward I and Queen Eleanor. From the modern town, a walk to the church involves climbing a gruelling flight of 108 steps. **St Michael and All Angels** was extended in the 1890s but its 14th century core remains, notably the Legh Chapel built in 1422 to receive the body of Piers Legh who had fought at Agincourt and died at the Siege of Meaux. Another chapel contains the famous Legh Pardon brass, which recalls the medieval practice of selling pardons for sins past, and even for those not yet committed. The inscription on the brass records that, in

MACCLESFIELD SILK MUSEUMS

Silk Museum, Park Lane, Macclesfield,
Cheshire SK11 6TJ
Tel: 01625 612045 Fax No: 01625 612048
e-mail: postmaster@silk-macc.u-net.com
website: www.silk-macclesfield.org

Macclesfield Silk Museums, based on 3 listed sites, tells the story of silk with particular reference to Macclesfield, once known as the silk capital of England and associated with silk for 400 years.

The Silk Museum is housed within the Heritage Centre, a former Sunday School built in 1814 to educate the children who worked in the mills. There is an award winning audio visual programme whilst silk costume and textiles illustrate the importance of silk to fashion and its use for special occasions. The Mulberry Tree coffee shop offers light snacks and a fuller menu. Just a short walk away new displays have been developed for 2002 in the former School of Art and Design exploring the properties of silk, design education and

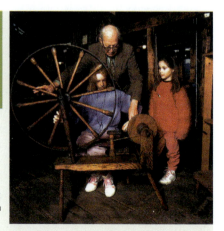

Macclesfield's diverse textile industries. Archive footage accompany displays of historic textile machinery. Experience what life was like in a typical silk mill by taking a guided tour with one of the Museum's knowledgeable and entertaining guides. Exhibitions and room sets illustrate life in the 1930s.

THE NAGS HEAD

60 Watergreen, Macclesfield,
Cheshire SK11 6JT
Tel: 01625 423786

A handsome and imposing building, **The Nags Head** was in poor shape when Sandra and Stephen Hulse took over here in January 2002. Much hard work later, it has been restored to its Victorian state of grace and the atmosphere is again that of a traditional inn. On Friday and Saturday evenings there is entertainment by live bands. The Nags Head is open all day, every day, with three real ales available – as well as a wide range of other popular brews. Good food is served every lunchtime (noon until 3pm; 4pm on Sunday) and on Thursday, Friday and Saturday evenings from 5pm until 7pm – anything from a sandwich to a steak! Children are welcome until 7.30pm; there are designated non-smoking areas; and currently only cash or cheques are accepted.

return for saying five Paternosters and five Aves, the Legh family received a pardon for 26,000 years and 26 days.

One of the Macclesfield area's most famous sons is Charles Frederick Tunnicliffe, the celebrated bird and wild-life artist, who was born at the nearby village of Langley in 1901. He studied at the Macclesfield School of Art and first came to public attention with his illustrations for Henry Williamson's *Tarka the Otter* in 1927. A collection of Tunnicliffe's striking paintings can be seen at the **West Park Museum** on the northwest edge of the town. This purpose-built museum, founded in 1898 by the Brocklehurst family, also includes exhibits of ancient Egyptian artifacts, fine and decorative arts.

Much less well-known is William Buckley who was born in Macclesfield around 1780 and later became a soldier. He took part in a mutiny at Gibraltar against the Rock's commanding officer, the Duke of York, father-to-be of Queen Victoria. The mutiny failed and Buckley was transported to Australia. There he escaped into the outback and became the leader of an aboriginal tribe who took this giant of a man, some 6 feet 6 inches tall, as the reincarnation of a dead chief. For 32 years Buckley never saw a white man or heard a word of English. When the explorer John Bateman, on his way to found what is now Melbourne, discovered him, Buckley had virtually forgotten his mother tongue. He was pardoned, given a pension and died at Hobart at the age of 76.

Canal, Macclesfield

Ye Olde Admiral Rodney

New Road, Prestbury, Cheshire SK10 4HP
Tel: 01625 829484
Tel/Fax: 01625 828078
website: www.yeoldeadmiralrodney.com

Ye Olde Admiral Rodney inn stands on Prestbury's main street, close to the River Bollin. The charming old building dates back to the late 17th century and before becoming an inn was part of a row of cottages, and then a brewhouse. Full of character and atmosphere, befitting a building of such great age, Ye Olde Admiral Rodney is a traditional English village inn where you can be sure of finding good ale, good food and good company. The olde worlde atmosphere

is enhanced by a magnificent display of vintage ceramic Pirate Pots, a striking collection of commemorative plaques from old boats and regiments, and a lovely old ship's wheel.

An interesting feature is a history of Admiral Rodney, the distinguished naval commander whose most famous exploit was his victory over the French at the Battle of Cape St Vincent in 1780. Also on display is a history of the inn and a fascinating list of past licensees going right back to 1730.

The present licensees are Gail and Peter Brady who have been in the licensed trade since 1978

and here for the past 9 years. Both of them cook and they have made the Admiral Rodney a popular eating place, serving a good range of bar snacks and main meals. A speciality of the house is the choice of tasty curries on offer – usually five of them ranging from mild to red hot. The inn serves meals from noon until 2.30pm, Monday to Sunday, and well-behaved children are welcome to come and eat here.

To complement the food, there's a choice of 2 real ales – Robinson's Best and Hatter's Mild, as well as a wide selection of draught ciders, lagers and stout and a well-chosen wine list. If you're lucky with the weather there's a pleasant and secluded sitting area outside at the rear of the inn. Please note that cash and cheques only are accepted.

Once visited, Ye Olde Admiral Rodney with its well-kept ales and wonderful atmosphere, is the kind of pub you will want to return to time and time again.

Around Macclesfield

Prestbury

3 miles N of Macclesfield via the A523/A538

A regular winner of the Best Kept Village title, Prestbury is a charming village where a tree-lined High Street runs down to a bridge over the River Bollin, ancient stocks stand against the church wall, old coaching inns and black and white buildings mingle with the mellow red brick work of later Georgian houses. The Church of St Peter, dating from the 13th century, still maintains a tradition which began in 1577. Every autumn and winter evening at 8pm a curfew bell is rung, with the number of chimes corresponding to the date of the month. Close by is a building known as the **Norman Chapel** with a striking frontage carved with the characteristic Norman zig-zags and beaked heads. Even older are the carved fragments of an 8th century Saxon cross preserved under glass in the graveyard. Opposite the church is a remarkable magpie timber-framed house which is now a bank but used to be the Vicarage. During the Commonwealth, the rightful incumbent was debarred from preaching in the church by the Puritans. Undaunted, the priest addressed his parishioners from the tiny balcony of his Vicarage.

THE BRIDGE HOTEL & BENEDICT'S RESTAURANT

Prestbury, Cheshire SK10 4DQ
Tel: 01625 829326 Fax: 01625 827557
e-mail: reception@bridge-hotel.co.uk
website: www.bridge-hotel.co.uk

In 2002 the outstanding **Bridge Hotel** celebrated its 50th anniversary and for the whole of that half-century it has been owned and run by the Grange family – Norman, Elaine and their son Fraser. When the family acquired the property it was a row of timbered cottages dating back to 1626, one of which had provided Bonnie Prince Charlie with a night's lodging during the course of his march southwards in 1745. Today, the hotel has 23 guest bedrooms, some in the older, half-timbered part of the hotel; the remainder in the new wing which overlooks the River Bollin. There's a choice of single, double and twin-bedded rooms, all with en suite facilities, television, ISDN telephone points, iron and ironing board, hair dryer, and hospitality tray.

The award-winning Benedict's Restaurant offers superb modern European cuisine in a charming Elizabethan galleried dining room with live music every Friday and Saturday evening. Private dining facilities for up to 22 guests are available in the Elizabeth Suite overlooking the main dining room while the Whiteside Suite, opening onto a riverside terrace, can accommodate up to 105 people. For larger parties, a marquee can be erected on the terrace. The hotel holds a licence to conduct civil marriage ceremonies and what could be better for the wedding photographs than the hotel's lovely riverside setting?

Adlington

4 miles N of Macclesfield off the A523

Adlington boasts a fine old house, **Adlington Hall,** which has been the home of the Legh family since 1315 and is now one of the county's most popular attractions. Quadrangular in shape, this magnificent manor house has two distinctive styles of architecture: black and white half-timbered buildings on two sides, later Georgian additions in warm red brick on the others. There is much to see as you tour the hall, with beautifully polished wooden floors and lovely antique furnishings enhancing the air of elegance and grandeur. The Great Hall is a breathtaking sight, a vast room of lofty proportions that set off perfectly the exquisitely painted walls. The beautifully preserved 17th century organ here has responded to the touch of many maestros, none more famous than George Frederick Handel who visited the Hall in the 1740s.

It wasn't long after Handel's visit to Cheshire that the county was gripped by a mania for building canals, a passion that has left Cheshire with a uniquely complex network of these environmentally friendly waterways.

Bollington

4 miles NE of Macclesfield on the B5091

In its 19th century heyday, there were 13 cotton mills working away at Bollington, a little town perched on the foothills of the High Peak. Two of the largest mills, the Clarence and the Adelphi, still stand, although now adapted to other purposes. The Victorian shops and cottages around Water Street and the High Street recall those busy days. A striking feature of the town is the splendid 20-arched viaduct which once carried the railway over the River Dean. It is now part of the **Middlewood Way** a ten mile, traffic-free country trail which follows a scenic route from Macclesfield to Marple. The Way is open to walkers, cyclists and horse riders and during the season cycles are available for hire, complete with child seats if required. Just as remarkable as the viaduct, although in a different way, is **White Nancy.** This sugar-loaf shaped,

---

THE LORD CLYDE INN

Clarke Lane, Kerridge, Cheshire SK10 5AH
Tel: 01625 573202 Fax: 01625 576139
website: joy@clyde.com

Originally two weavers' cottages, the **Lord Clyde Inn** dates back to 1843. Now listed as a building of special architectural and historic interest it is full of character and charm. Landlady of this hospitable free house with its cosy fire, Joy Murphy, offers her customers a good choice of fine ales, including 4 real ales – Greenalls, Bass and two guest ales, and excellent home cooked food with Lamb Henry and Mixed Grills as the specialities of the house. Food is served every lunchtime (noon until 3pm) and evening (6pm to 9pm), except Monday and Tuesday evenings. Children are welcome and all major credit cards apart from American Express and Diners are accepted.

THE COFFEE TAVERN

Shrigley Road, Pott Shrigley,
Cheshire SK10 5SE
Tel: 01625 576370

The Coffee Tavern was built in 1887 as a Reading Room and Library for staff on the nearby Lowther estate. Interest had waned by the end of World War I and it was converted into a tea room. That venture also failed but this characterful old building is now, once again, in business. The Buffey family who have run the Coffee Tavern since 1992 offer a menu that includes everything from a cup of tea, to home-baked treats and 3-course meals. The regular menu, available every day except Tuesday from 10am to 6pm, is supplemented by at least 6 daily specials. There is also a remarkable selection of paintings, jewellery, pottery, dried flowers and much more, all created by artists who live and work nearby.

whitewashed round tower stands on Kerridge Hill, more than 900ft above sea level. It was erected in 1817 to commemorate the Battle of Waterloo and offers sweeping views in all directions.

Sutton

2 miles S of Macclesfield on minor road off the A523

This small village, close to the Macclesfield Canal, is honoured by scholars as the birthplace of Raphael Holinshed whose famous *Chronicles of England, Scotland & Ireland* (1577) provided the source material for no fewer than 14 of Shakespeare's plays. As well as drawing heavily on the facts in the Chronicles, the Immortal Bard wasn't above plagiarising some of Holinshed's happier turns of phrase.

Bosley

6 miles S of Macclesfield on the A523

To the east of Bosley town centre runs the **Macclesfield Canal,** one of the highest waterways in England, running for much of its length at more than 500 feet above sea level. Thomas Telford was the surveyor of the 26-mile long route, opened in 1831, which links the Trent & Mersey and the Peak Forest canals. Between Macclesfield and Congleton, the canal descends over a hundred feet in a spectacular series of 12 locks at Bosley, before crossing the River Dane via Telford's handsome iron viaduct.

THE HARRINGTON ARMS

Leek Road, Bosley, Macclesfield,
Cheshire SK11 0PH
Tel: 01260 223224

Named after the former Lord of the Manor, **The Harrington Arms** is a former coaching inn with a welcoming traditional atmosphere. The friendly landlords, Ian and Michaela Biggar, have turned the inn's fortunes around since they arrived here in the summer of 2001. They now offer excellent food (created by Ian who is a gifted and experienced chef) and top quality ales with Robinsons Best real ale always on tap. The dining area seats 40, the Snug another 20, and there's plenty of room to sit out in the beer garden. There's a children's play area outside while inside customers have the use of a separate pool room as well as all the traditional pub games.

Other unusual features of this superbly engineered canal are the two "roving bridges" south of Congleton. These swing from one bank to the other where the towpath changes sides and so enabled horses to cross over without having to unhitch the tow-rope.

Gawsworth
3 miles SW of Macclesfield off the A536

Gawsworth Hall is a captivating sight with its dazzling black and white half-timbered walls and lofty three-decker Tudor windows. The Hall was built in 1480 by the Fitton family, one of whose descendants, the celebrated beauty, Mary Fitton is believed to be the "Dark Lady" of Shakespeare's sonnets. The Bard would no doubt approve of Gawsworth's famous open-air theatre where performances range from his own plays to Gilbert and Sullivan operas with the Hall serving as a lovely backdrop. Surrounded by a huge park, Gawsworth, to quote its owner Timothy Richards, "is the epitome of a lived-in historic house". Every room that visitors see (which is virtually every room in the house) is in daily use by him and his family. And what wonderful rooms they are. Myriad windows bathe the rooms in light, the low ceilings and modest dimensions radiate calm, and even the richly-carved main staircase is conceived on a human scale. The beautifully sited church, and the lake nearby, add still more to the appeal of this magical place. The Hall is open every afternoon during the season, at other times by appointment. Tel: 01260 223456.

Capesthorne Hall
5 miles W of Macclesfield off the A34

The home of the Bromley-Davenport family for generations, **Capesthorne Hall** dates back to 1730 but, following a fire in 1861, was remodelled and extended by the celebrated architects Blore and Salvin. The present building presents a magnificent medley of Elizabethan style turrets and towers, domes and cupolas while inside the house there is a wealth of portraits and artifacts collected by family members during the course of their Grand Tours. In medieval times the head of the Bromley-Davenport family held the post of Chief Forester of Macclesfield Forest which gave him authority to mete out summary justice to anyone who transgressed the savage forestry laws. As a reminder of their power, the family crest includes the severed head of a felon. One of these crests, on the main staircase built in the 1860s, was commissioned by the staunchly Conservative Bromley-Davenport of the day and the felon's head is instantly recognisable as the Liberal leader of the day, W.E. Gladstone.

Nether Alderley
6 miles NW of Macclesfield on the A34

The village of Nether Alderley lies on the A34 and here you will find **Nether**

Alderley Mill, a delightful 15th century watermill that has been restored by the National Trust. The red sandstone walls are almost hidden under the huge sweep of its stone tiled roof. Inside is the original Elizabethan woodwork and Victorian mill machinery which is still in working order, with two tandem overshot wheels powering the mill. Nether Alderley Mill is open to the public on Wednesday and Sunday afternoons in April, May & October, and every afternoon except Monday from June to September. If you have time, visit the 14th century church of St Mary which is almost a private mausoleum for the Alderley branch of the Stanley family: monuments to dead Stanleys are everywhere. Living members of the family were provided with an unusual richly carved pew, set up on the wall like an opera box and reached by a flight of steps outside. Tel: 01625 523012

Alderley Edge
6 miles NW of Macclesfield on the A34

Alderley Edge takes its name from the long, wooded escarpment, nearly two miles long, that rises 600ft above sea level and culminates in sandy crags overlooking the Cheshire Plain. In Victorian times, this spectacular area was the private preserve of the Stanley family and it was only under great pressure that they grudgingly allowed the "Cottentots" of Manchester access on

THE DRUM & MONKEY AT MOSS ROSE

off Heyes Lane, Alderley Edge, Cheshire SK9 7LD
Tel: 01625 584747 Fax: 01625 584975
e-mail: jlavininndrum@supernet.com

Looking out across its own beautifully tended bowling green, The Drum & Monkey at Moss Rose is well-known for its real ales – Robinson's Bitter, Cumbrian Way, Hatters Stockport Mild and a guest brew – and even more so for the excellent cuisine on offer. Classically trained, James Lavin has been chef here for some time and since March 2002 he is also the landlord. The fare on offer ranges from tasty quick snacks, like the pork pie platters, which are available all day, to main meals served every lunchtime and evening except Sunday and Monday evenings. Everything is fresh and appetising and the pub's popularity means that booking is recommended for Friday and Saturday evenings, and Sunday lunchtime (ask if you want a table in the non-smoking area). Children are welcome until 8pm; all major credit cards are accepted apart from American Express. The food's good, the drink's good, the company's good, and on most nights of the week there's even more on offer: karaoke on Monday, a quiz on Tuesday, live performances on Wednesday, an Irish band every other Thursday, after-dinner entertainment on Saturday. Pool, darts and skittles add to the entertainment options and that immaculate bowling green is also available for the use of patrons.

Alderley Edge

Wilmslow

9 miles NW of Macclesfield off the A34

The oldest building in Wilmslow is St Bartholomew's Church, built between 1517 and 1537, and notable for its magnificent ceiling, some striking effigies, and for the fact that Prime Minister-to-be W.E. Gladstone worshipped here as a boy. A hamlet in medieval times, Wilmslow mushroomed as a mill town in the 18th and 19th centuries, and is now a busy commuter town offering a good choice of inns, hotels and restaurants.

occasional summer weekends. It was the Stanley daughters who took great umbrage when the Wizard Inn hung up a new sign. They demanded its removal. The Merlin-like figure depicted could, they claimed, be taken as a representation of their father, Lord Stanley, at that time a virtual recluse and more than a little eccentric. Nowadays, however, walkers can roam freely along the many footpaths through the woods, one of which will take them to **Hare Hill Gardens**, a little known National Trust property. These Victorian gardens include fine woodland, a walled garden themed in blue, white and yellow flowers, and huge banks of rhododendrons. There is access by way of gravel paths for the less able.

Styal

1 mile N of Wilmslow, on a minor road off the B5166

Cared for by the National Trust, **Styal Country Park** is set in 250 acres of the beautifully wooded valley of the River Bollin and offers many woodland and riverside walks. The Park is open to the public from dawn to dusk throughout the year and is a wonderful place for picnics. Lying within the Park is **Quarry Bank Mill**, a grand old building erected in 1784 and one of the first generation of cotton mills. It was powered by a huge

DINKS WINE BAR & RESTAURANT

5-6 Warham Street, Wilmslow Green,
Cheshire SK9 1BT
Tel: 01625 548223 Fax: 01625 528967

In the two and a half years that Cathy Plant and her son James have been running **Dinks Bar & Restaurant** it has established a fine reputation for serving an outstanding range of quality wines and excellent food. The elegant restaurant with its crisp linen tablecloths and napkins offers both a regular menu that changes frequently as well as daily specials. Fish dishes such as King Prawn Thermidor or seafood pancakes are the specialities of the house but there's also a good choice of meat dishes - Pan-fried Rib-eye Steak served with Lyonnaise potatoes, local asparagus and sun-blush tomatoes for example - along with vegetarian offerings like Portobello Mushroom & Asparagus Risotto finished with Parmesan shavings and truffle oil.

From Monday to Friday, Dinks is open from noon until 2.30pm, from 5pm for drinks with food served between 6pm and 10pm. On Saturday, it's open from 6pm until last orders. At present Dinks is not open on Sundays but such is its popularity Cathy and James are planning to start opening in the not too distant future. The 40 seater Restaurant is non smoking, but guests are encouraged to retire to the bar area, where there are large smoke extractors, if they would like to smoke. They are sympathetic to both smokers and non smokers. Dinks has a charming patio area that can seat another 20. There's also a private dining room that can accommodate up to 20 guests.

---

iron waterwheel fed by the River Bollin. Visitors follow the history of the mill through various galleries and displays within the museum, including weaving and spinning demonstrations, and can experience for themselves, with the help of guides dressed in period costume, what life was like for the hundred girls and boys who once lived in the Apprentice House. The Mill has a shop and a restaurant and is open every day from April to September from 11am to 6pm, and from October to March every day except Monday from 11am to 5pm (last entries 90 minutes before closing time). Also within the park is the delightful **Styal Village** which was established by the mill's original owner, Samuel Greg, a philanthropist and pioneer of the factory system. He took children from the slums of Manchester to work in his mill, and in return for their labour provided them with food, clothing, housing, education and a place of worship.

Altrincham

7 miles NW of Wilmslow on the A560

The writer Thomas de Quincey visited Altrincham in the early 1800s and thought its bustling market "the gayest scene he ever saw". The market is still very active although the old houses that

THE CHURCH INN

90 Ravenoak Road, Cheadle Hulme,
Cheshire SK8 7EG
Tel: 0161 485 1897

Well known for its excellent cuisine **The Church Inn** is also believed to be the oldest hostelry in the area. Mine hosts Simon Bromley and his sister Carol Sumner have been here since 1988 and have firmly established the inn's reputation for warm hospitality. Much larger inside than you would expect from the exterior, the inn has charm and character in abundance. Edward's Restaurant offers an extensive menu with fresh fish dishes as the

speciality of the house. The fish is purchased daily from the fish market so there could always be a surprise on the specials board. On Sundays a traditional Sunday roast is also available. Food is served every lunchtime and evenings (except Sunday).

de Quincey also noted have sadly gone. A modern bustling town, Altrincham nevertheless has a long history with a charter granted in 1290 and clear evidence that there was a settlement beside the River Bollin some 6,000 years ago. Even older than that is the prehistoric body preserved in peat discovered on Lindow Common nearby. From Victorian times, Altrincham has been a favoured retreat for Manchester businessmen and the town is well-supplied with inns and restaurants.

Cheadle Hulme

7 miles NE of Wilmslow off the A34

Developed in Victorian times as a commuter town for better-off workers in Manchester, Cheadle Hulme is a busy place with a fine park on its eastern edge in which stands one of the grandest old "magpie" houses in Cheshire, **Bramall Hall.** This eye-catching, rambling perfection of black and white timbered buildings overlooks some 62 acres of exquisitely landscaped woods, lakes and formal gardens. The oldest parts of the Hall date from the 14th century: for five of the next six centuries it was owned by the same family, the Davenports. Over the years, the Davenport family continually altered and extended the originally quite modest manor house. But whenever they added a new Banqueting Hall, "Withdrawing Room", or even a Chapel, they took pains to ensure that its design harmonised

THE SHADY OAK

Redford Drive, Bramhall, Cheshire SK7 3PG
Tel: 0161 439 1070

Very much a Hidden Place, **The Shady Oak** is well worth tracking down. Purpose-built some 16 years ago, this attractive pub is run by Karen and Martin Davis, a friendly and welcoming couple. At present, food is only available at Sunday lunchtimes, when Karen cooks the traditional meal with a choice of roasts, and on Saturday evening when the inn hosts a Curryoke – that is, a selection of curries to enjoy along with a karaoke session. There's also a karaoke on Wednesday evening; a

quiz on Thursday and live entertainment on Friday. Beers on offer include 3 real ales – Tetley's, Old Speckled Hen and a guest ale; opening times are from 4pm, Monday to Thursday, and from 1pm, Friday to Sunday.

happily with its more ancient neighbours. Along with Little Moreton Hall and Gawsworth Hall, Bramall represents the fullest flowering of a lovely architectural style whose most distinctive examples are all to be found in Cheshire.

Lyme Hall, Disley

Disley

8 miles SE of Stockport on the A6

The small town of Disley lies close to the Macclesfield Canal and little more than half a mile from **Lyme Park Country Park**. At the heart of the 1400 acre park where red and fallow deer roam freely stands Lyme Park (National Trust), home of the Legh family for more than 600 years. The elegant Palladian exterior of this great house encloses a superb Elizabethan mansion. Amongst the many treasures on show are carvings by Grinling Gibbons, tapestries from Mortlake, and a unique collection of English clocks. The house featured many times in the BBC's 1995 production of *Pride and Prejudice* when it represented the exterior of Pemberley, the home of Elizabeth Bennett's curmudgeonly lover, Mr Darcy. The "Pemberley Trail" guides visitors to the bridge from which Elizabeth (Jennifer Ehle) first sees the imposing building; on through the courtyard and garden to the pool in which Mr Darcy (Colin Firth) takes a sexy dip – a scene which was definitely not included in Jane Austen's original novel. Don't expect the interior of Lyme

THE WHITE LION

135 Buxton Road, Disley, Stockport, Cheshire SK12 2HA
Tel: 01663 765290
e-mail: whiteliondisley@hotmail.com

A former coaching inn dating back to the 1800s, **The White Lion** stands just yards from the Derbyshire border and the Peak District National Park. Newcomers are attracted by the pub sign which depicts a zebra – a device by an earlier landlord to create interest. Present landlord John Hinchcliffe, aided by daughters Gemma and Joanne, have made the The White Lion renowned for its excellent traditional pub food, as well as specialities such as Jambalaya. Food is served every day from noon until 7pm and the wide selection of beverages on offer includes one or two real ales. Monday night is Quiz Night; karaoke on Fridays, and live bands on Saturday evening.

THE ROYAL OAK

Buxton Road, High Lane, Stockport SK6 8AY
Tel: 01663 762380

Only a short walk from the famous Lyme Park and the Peak District National Park, **The Royal Oak** was originally built as miners' cottages in the early 1800s and has been dispensing hospitality for some 120 years. Mine hosts, Peter and Susan Abell, with 20 years in the trade locally have been here since 1992. Susan is a superb cook whose specialties include home-made pies, curries and delicious fresh

fish dishes. Children's meals and sandwiches are also available. (No food on Monday and Tuesday evenings unless it's a Bank Holiday). Beverages on offer include two real ales. Children love the picturesque beer garden at the rear with its bouncy castle and there's fun for adults too with the Tuesday Fun Quiz and live music on Friday evening.

Park to match the rooms shown in the series – all the "Pemberley" interiors were filmed at Sudbury Hall in Derbyshire.

The Panhandle

The narrow finger of land pointing up to West Yorkshire was chopped off from Cheshire in the 1974 Local Government redrawing of boundaries, but a quarter of a century later most of its population still consider themselves Cheshire folk. At its northern end lie Longdendale and Featherbed Moss, Pennine scenery quite unlike anywhere else in the county. Visitors to Cheshire tend to overlook this orphaned quarter: we strongly

recommend that you seek it out.

Marple

4 miles SE of Stockport on the A626

Marple's most famous son is probably the poet and novelist Christopher Isherwood who was born at Marple Hall in 1904 and could have inherited it from his grandfather had he so wished. Instead, the author of *Mr Norris Changes Trains* and *Sally Bowles* (the source material for the musical *Cabaret*) renounced the life of a country squire for the more sybaritic attractions of California. But Marple made a great impression on him as is evident from his book *Kathleen and*

THE DUKE OF YORK

Stockport Road, Romiley, Stockport SK6 3AN
Tel: 0161 430 2806 Fax: 0161 406 9445
e-mail: duke.of.york.@quista.net

A delightful country pub on the Peak Forest Canal, **The Duke of York** was originally built as a coaching inn and the archway still stands through which horses passed to the stables behind. Painted in traditional black and white, the pub still retains much of the character and charm of those bygone days. Landlord Jim Grindrod has been here since 1992 and is also the chef, offering an appetizing selection

of traditional food and daily specials every lunchtime (noon to 2.30pm) and evening (5pm to 10pm), except Sunday evening. Open all day, every day, the inn has four real ales on tap along with a wide choice of other brews and wines. There's a pleasant beer garden and on Monday evenings you can join in the regular pub quiz.

DOLCE VITA RESTAURANT

27 Stockport Road, Marple,
Cheshire SK6 6BD
Tel: 0161 449 0648

Superb Italian cuisine served in stylish surroundings is the secret of the **Dolce Vita Restaurant's** popularity. Giovanni Lacava and his manager Franco Amatulli have been here since 1987 and started the restaurant on the first floor. Then in 1990 they took over the ground floor, a former laundry. Everything on the menu is Italian and the extensive menu is supplemented by a daily specials board.

Giovanni is the chef and his cooking is out of this world – booking at weekends is essential. The restaurant is licensed for diners; there are non-smoking areas, and all major credit cards except Diners are welcome. La Dolce Vita is open Monday to Thursday from noon until 2pm, and from 6pm to 10.30pm; Friday and Saturday from noon until 2pm and from 6pm to 11.00pm.

Frank, based on the letters and diaries of his parents. Isherwood revels in the wildness of the Goyt Valley, not just its scenery but also its weather. This is the wettest part of Cheshire – "it never really dries out" says Isherwood – and winters are often punctuated with ferocious storms.

Marple is also famous for its flight of 16 locks on the Peak Forest Canal and the mighty three-arched aqueduct that carries the canal over the River Goyt. At Marple, the Peak Forest Canal is joined by the Macclesfield Canal and there are some attractive towpath walks in both directions.

Stalybridge

6 miles E of Manchester on the A57

Set beside the River Tame and with the North Pennine moors stretching for miles to the east, Stalybridge was one of the earliest cotton towns and its mill workers amongst the most radical and militant during the Chartist troubles of the 1840s. Oddly, one of their leaders was a former Methodist minister, the Rev. Joseph Rayner Stephens, who had broken away from the Wesleyan ministry and established his own "Stephensite" chapels – one in King Street,

THE TRAVELLERS CALL

26 Wakefield Road, Stalybridge,
Cheshire SK13 1AJ
Tel/Fax: 0161 338 3087

The first things to catch your eye in the bar of **The Travellers Call** are a magnificent old range (c.1880) and a fascinating collection of clocks of varying shapes, sizes and designs. Mine hosts, John and Rachel Cichowicz, have been here for around 5 years and their pub's reputation for good food and well-maintained ales is firmly established. John is the chef and

offers a full range of dishes with steaks as his speciality, and at Sunday lunchtime a traditional roast is also served. The upstairs restaurant is non-smoking and children are welcome until 8.30pm. On Saturday evenings the inn hosts live entertainment. The Travellers Call is open evenings only, Monday to Friday; all day on Saturday and Sunday.

The White Hart & Restaurante El Cuba Libre

91 Market Street, Mottram, Cheshire
SK14 6JQ
Tel: 01457 766953 Fax: 01457 767437
e-mail: geoff.cangui@btopenworld.com

Standing opposite the village green and its ancient stocks, **The White Hart & Restaurante El Cuba Libre** is a wonderful combination of a traditional hostelry and an innovative restaurant. The enterprise is owned and run by Geoff and Cangui Oliver, welcoming hosts who took over here in early 2000. The atmospheric old pub on the ground floor is open all day, every day, and real ale devotees will be delighted to find a choice of 7 or 8 real ales always on offer. The brews permanently on offer are Timothy

Taylor Landlord, Plassey Bitter, Phoenix Bantam, Black Cat Mild, and JW Lees Bitter, and they are supplemented by other rotating guest ales. There's also a fine range of differing draught lagers, Guinness and an ever-changing farmhouse cider. Sandwiches are available throughout the day.

Geoff and Cangui opened their first-floor restaurant in November 2001 and it has proved to be a great success, so much so that booking is strongly recommended. The menu is extremely varied, offering a full range of Cuban cuisine, Spanish tapas and many vegetarian options. Diners are presented with a huge choice of hot and cold tapas.

Amongst the former, how about *Papas Rellenas A La Cubana* · "mashed potato balls stuffed with cheese, onion, garlic and fried in breadcrumbs", or a *Chorizo al Vino* · Chorizo (Spanish) sausage cooked in red wine? The cold varieties include an Embutidos Salteados, chorizo, salchichón, Serrano ham, salami and spicy cheese, and a vegetarian *Ensalada de Inglaterra* · English Cheddar and/or red Leicester cheese salad. Many of the tapas are vegetarian and some are suitable for Vegans also. In addition to the extensive menu, daily specials are also listed on the blackboard.

Beverages include the most comprehensive choice of cocktails available locally · no fewer than 66 different varieties. Coffee is served the traditional Cuban way, · a small serving but very strong, and the roasted freshly brewed coffee is usually Cuban, depending on availability.

This outstanding restaurant is open Thursday to Saturday from 6pm with last orders at 10.30pm and the licence for diners continues until 12.30am. Children are welcome in the restaurant.

THE HAREWOOD ARMS

2 Market Street, Broadbottom,
Cheshire SK14 6AX
Tel/Fax: 01457 763383

Built in 1849, **The Harewood Arms** was known as The Griffin until May 2002, when Adam and Sue Waters took over. As well as changing the name, they have also completely refurbished, using quality furniture, furnishings and décor. The Harewood has quickly gained a reputation for quality food, served every lunchtime and evening except Sunday and Monday evenings. Bar food is available from 5.30pm to 7pm; the non-smoking restaurant serves from 7pm to 9.45pm. Children are welcome until 7.45pm, later if eating. Three real ales are on tap – Boddington's, Timothy Taylor Landlord and a guest brew. In good weather, patrons can enjoy their refreshments in the safe and secluded beer garden at the rear.

Stalybridge, the other in the sister town across the Tame, Ashton under Lyme. He campaigned tirelessly against the long hours worked in the factories and the policy, introduced in 1834, of refusing poor relief outside the workhouse.

When in 1842 the mill-owners tried to impose reductions in pay, the workers' embryo trade union closed all the mills in north Cheshire and south Lancashire. Stephens was tried and sentenced to 18 months in Chester gaol. On his release, he continued his efforts to improve the workers' pay and conditions for another 38 years. His funeral was attended by thousands and the workers erected a granite obelisk to his memory in Stalybridge's attractive Stamford Park. On it is inscribed a quotation from the speech he delivered at his trial: "The only true foundation of Society is the safety, the security and the happiness of the poor, from whom all other orders of Society arise".

Mottram

4 miles NE of Hyde on the A628

Mottram village is set on a breezy hillside on the edge of the Pennines. According to the 1930s guide-book writer Arthur Mee, the off-Atlantic gusts that scour the village are known locally as Captain Whitle's Wind. In the 16th century, so the story goes, coffin bearers carrying the late Captain were struggling up the steep hill to the church when gale force winds swept the coffin from their shoulders and back down the hill.

PLACES TO STAY, EAT AND DRINK

Denotes entries in other chapters

9 North West Cheshire

The north-western part of the county contains the pleasant rural area known as the Vale Royal, and the more industrial environs of Warrington, Widnes and Runcorn. The Vale Royal is a pretty name for a very attractive part of the county. It was Prince Edward, later Edward I, who named it so and who founded the great Abbey of Vale Royal in fulfilment of a solemn vow made in dramatic circumstances. He was returning from the Crusades when his ship was struck by a violent storm. The Prince made a pledge to the Virgin that if his life were spared he would found an Abbey for one hundred monks. Lo! the ship was tossed ashore, the Prince and his companions waded through the surf to safety. In 1277, Edward, now King and with his young wife Eleanor of Castile by his side, honoured his vow by placing the first stone of Vale Royal Abbey. "No monastery" he decreed "shall be more royal than this one in liberties, wealth and honour, throughout the whole world". Vale Royal Abbey, about 3 miles south of Northwich, indeed became the largest and most powerful Cistercian Abbey in England, a building reputedly even more glorious than Tintern or Fountains. Unlike those Abbeys, however, barely a stone of Vale Royal now remains in place. The abuse by the medieval Abbots of their vast wealth, and of their unfettered power of life and death over the inhabitants of the Vale, may partly explain why their magnificent building was so quickly and completely destroyed after Henry VIII's closure of the monasteries. Over the centuries, the county has lost many fine buildings unnecessarily but the deliberate destruction of Vale Royal Abbey must take prime place in the litany of crimes against sublime architecture.

Northwich

The Vale Royal is now a district borough centred on the old salt town of Northwich. Even before the Romans arrived, Cheshire salt was well known and highly valued. But production on a major scale at Northwich began in 1670 when rock salt was discovered in nearby Marston. Salt may seem an inoffensive sort of product, but its extraction from the Keuper marl of the Cheshire Plain

THE BOWLING GREEN

London Road, Northwich,
Cheshire CW9 8AA
Tel: 01606 42333

Just five minutes walk from the centre of
Northwich, **The Bowling Green** is one of
those lovely old black and white buildings so
typical of the county. It appears even more
appealing in summer when the colourful
window-boxes and hanging baskets are in full
bloom. The pub, incidentally, takes its name
from the bowling green which, until about 20
years ago, lay right alongside and is now an
attractive children's play area. The pub also
boasts a very spacious and lovely rear garden

overlooking the River Weaver and the railway
viaduct.

This ancient hostlery dates back to 1650
and the interior is much more spacious than
you would imagine from outside.
Here you'll find a wealth of eye-
catching features - old beams,
floors of wood or quarry tiles, and
lots of interesting bygones and
memorabilia strewn around the
rooms.

Landlord Bruce Notman took
over here in April 2001, bringing
some 18 years experience in the
hospitality business with him.
Open all day, every day, The
Bowling Green is noted for its
wholesome, value-for-money food
which is available every lunchtime
(noon to 2.30pm) and evening

(5pm to 8pm), apart from Sunday when food
is served from noon until 4pm. The choice
includes a hearty All Day Breakfast, Sizzling
Platters and a good selection of lighter meals
- baguettes, jacket potatoes, salads and light
bites. In addition to the regular
menu, daily specials are also
available and kids eat free from
their own menu when an adult
meal is purchased from the
Sizzling Platters, Main Course or
Baguette menus.

Tuesday nights at The Bowling
Green are especially popular.
This is Steak Night when,
between 5pm and 8pm,
customers can enjoy an 8oz
rump steak and chips for an
incredible £1.99. Later the same
evening, there's a regular quiz
with a cash prize for the winning
team and a rollover cash jackpot.
The pub has a pool table and
Bruce also lays on live entertainment on
Friday and Saturday evening which varies
between a singer, disco or karaoke.

All major credit cards are welcome.

has produced some quite spectacular side-effects. In Elizabethan times, John Leland, recorded that a hill at Combermere suddenly disappeared into underground workings, and Northwich later became notorious for the number of its buildings leaning at crazy angles because of subsidence. Even today, the White Lion Inn in Witton Street lies a complete storey lower than its original height. The arrival in the 19th century of new processes of extraction brought different problems. In 1873, John Brunner and Ludwig Mond set up their salt works at Winnington on the northern edge of the town to manufacture alkali products based on brine. The ammonia process involved cast an appalling stench over the town and devastated vegetation for miles around. On the other hand, Brunner and Mond were model employers. They paid their workforce well, built houses for them and were amongst the first firms in the country to give their employees annual holidays with pay.

The long involvement of Northwich and Cheshire with salt production is vividly recorded at the **Salt Museum**, the only one of its kind in Britain. It stands in London Road and occupies what used to be the Northwich Workhouse which, like so many of those dreaded institutions, is an exceptionally

CHAPELS WINE BAR

15/17 High Street, Weaverham, Cheshire
CW8 3HA
Tel: 01606 854485

Located on the main street of this pleasant village a few miles from Northwich, **Chapels Wine Bar** boasts a smart black and white frontage and is entered between small paned bow windows. Although named a wine bar, it is actually a cosy, traditionally furnished pub with wooden tables and chairs and oak beams. It also doubles as a friendly guest house.

Local couple Gillian and John Payne took over here early in 2002 and have quickly established a reputation for well-maintained ales and excellent bar food which is available from opening time right through until about 7pm. Choose from the printed menu – and children are welcome.

Opening times for the pub are from 11.30am until 11pm, Monday to Saturday; noon until 10.30pm on Sunday. A good array of draught ales are available including John Smiths, John Smiths Smooth, Tetley Smooth, Carling, Carlsberg and Carlsberg Export, Strongbow, Tetley Mild and Guinness.

There's a secluded beer garden to the rear and during the afternoon the pub has happy hours for draught beers and lagers. If you are planning to stay in the area, Chapels has four attractively furnished and decorated guest bedrooms with family, double and twin rooms available. A hearty breakfast is included in the tariff.

THE BEECH TREE

Runcorn Road, Barnton, Northwich,
Cheshire CW8 4HS
Tel: 01606 77292 Fax: 01606 782671

The Beech Tree is a handsome redbrick building set back from the main A533 Northwich to Runcorn road. Built in 1940 to replace the original which stood opposite, the inn wins top marks not only for the quality of the décor and furnishings but also for the warmth of the welcome provided by leaseholders Stuart and Mary Piper and their son William. In the three and a half years they have been here, their hard work and friendly personalities have turned the Beech

Tree into a real success.

One of the inn's attractions is its quality food, prepared by Stuart and Mary. Excellent bar snacks and a wide choice of meals are always available – choose from the printed menu or the specials board. Food is served lunchtime (noon until 2.30pm) and evening (5pm to 9pm), Monday to Saturday, and from noon until 6pm on Sundays and Bank Holiday Mondays. Drinks on offer include one rotating guest real ale plus a good selection of draught keg bitters, mild, lagers, cider and stout.

From Tuesday to Thursday there are special lunchtime deals for senior citizens.

Wednesday is also the day of the weekly quiz with cash

prizes and live entertainment every Thursday evening from about 9pm. During the summer months, a super bouncy castle is provided for kids (who are welcome at all times), and the inn also boasts a rather special amenity in its bowling green at the rear. The green is available for hire.

The Beech Tree is open every lunchtime and evening and all day Friday, Saturday and Sunday. Its location on the main Northwich to Runcorn road provides easy access to those two important towns, and the minor roads in the vicinity lead to numerous places to visit, amongst them the Anderton Boat Lift, Marbury Country Park, and Arley Hall & Gardens.

The Beech Tree is an excellent base for exploring these attractions and its accommodation offers 5 well-appointed guest bedrooms, (3 family; 2 twins). A full English breakfast is included in the tariff. Currently, only cash and cheques are accepted but Stuart and Mary expect to accept credit cards in the near future.

handsome late-Georgian building, designed by George Latham, the architect of Arley Hall. With its unique collection of traditional working tools, and lively displays which include working models and videos, the Salt Museum recounts the fascinating story of the county's oldest industry. Not only can ancient remains such as Roman evaporating pans and medieval salt rakes be seen, but there is also much to remind visitors of the vital part that salt plays in the modern chemical industry.

Around Northwich

Anderton

1 mile N of Northwich on minor road off the A533

One of the most stupendous engineering feats of the canal age was the **Anderton Boat Lift**, built in 1875 and recently restored. This extraordinary construction was designed to transfer boats from the Trent & Mersey Canal to the Weaver Navigation 50ft below. Two barges would enter the upper tank, two the lower, and

by pumping water out of the lower tank, the boats would exchange places. Thousands of visitors come every year to marvel at this impressive structure which was conceived and designed by Edward Leader Williams who later went on to engineer the Manchester Ship Canal.

About a mile north of Anderton, **Marbury Country Park** was formerly part of a large country estate but the area is now managed by Cheshire County Council whose wardens have created a variety of habitats for plants, trees and animals. The Park lies at the edge of Budworth Mere and there are attractive walks and bridleways around the site where you'll also find an arboretum, picnic area and garden centre.

Cuddington

5 miles SW of Northwich off the A49

Cuddington is at the western end of the **Whitegate Way**, a pleasant rural walk of about 5 miles which follows the trackbed

---

THE STANLEY ARMS HOTEL

Old Road, Anderton, nr Northwich,
Cheshire CW9 6AG
Tel: 01606 75059

Standing right next to the famous Anderton Boat Lift, the **Stanley Arms Hotel** is known locally as "The Tip" because in the old days salt was tipped here down chutes into the canal barges. Dating back to 1753 this welcoming hostelry serves excellent home-cooked food from noon until 9pm (7pm, Sunday) and offers an absolutely enormous

choice of main dishes, baked potatoes, hot baguettes, sandwiches and toasties. To accompany your meal

there's a good selection of ales, including 3 real ales, and wine is available by the bottle and small, medium and large glasses. Outside there's a beer garden and patio overlooking the canal where boat trips are available all year round on the *Canal Explorer*.

THE CARRIERS INN

Delamere Road, Hatchmere, Norley,
Cheshire WA6 6NL
Tel: 01928 788255

Only a short walk from Delamere Forest Park, **The Carriers Inn** dates back to 1637 and was once home to the village smithy. Landlords Karen and Paul Ashton, with the assistance of Chef Anne Rothwell, have made this friendly traditional inn well-known locally for its excellent restaurant and bar food and its well-maintained ales – including 3 real ales. The

freshly-prepared food is served every lunchtime and evening except Monday evening and at weekends booking for the restaurant is strongly advised. On weekdays, Pensioner Specials are available at lunchtime. The inn has a spacious beer garden and other attractions include a Quiz on Tuesday evenings and entertainment on Thursday and Saturday evenings.

of the old railway that used to carry salt from the Winsford mines. There is a picnic site and car park at the former Whitegate Station.

Hatchmere

8 miles W of Northwich on the B5152

In medieval times the village of Hatchmere was surrounded by the Forest of Delamere, the largest of Cheshire's three woodlands. It stretched from the Mersey to Nantwich and although there were small areas of pasture and arable land, its status as a royal forest meant that the prime duty of those in charge of it was the preservation of the "beasts of the chase". It was not until 1812 that Delamere was officially "disafforested" and today Delamere Forest covers little more than an area about two miles long and one mile deep. From Hatchmere there are attractive trails through the woods and around Hatch Mere, the sizeable lake that gives the village its name.

Crowton

4 miles W of Northwich on the B5153

Crowton has many times been voted the Best Kept Village in Cheshire and its 18th century hostelry, The Hare & Hounds (see separate entry), enjoys a

THE POPLARS

Norley Lane, Crowton, Northwich,
Cheshire CW8 2RR
Tel: 01928 788083
e-mail: thepoplarsbandb@aol.com

Whether you are touring with a caravan or looking for quality bed & breakfast accommodation you'll find both available at **The Poplars** in the little village of Crowton. Barbara Holloway has been welcoming guests here for more than 12 years and many return again and again to this charming old house,

parts of which date back more than a hundred years. The Poplars has a spacious, beautifully maintained garden with tables and chairs for guests to relax in. The 2 double and 1 twin are pleasantly furnished bedrooms and all have en-suite facilities. The house is non-smoking; children are welcome; cash and cheques only are accepted. For caravanners there are 5 soft standings with electric hook-ups and the 1-acre site has toilets and running water.

HARE AND HOUNDS

Station Road, Crowton, Cheshire CW8 2RN
Tel: 01928 788851 Fax: 01928 788244

Hailed by the Chester Chronicle as one of the six best eating establishments in the county, the **Hare and Hounds** is a delightful 19th century hostelry run by Joe and Pamela Nicholson. Joe is the chef and although his repertoire includes an excellent selection of meat, poultry and vegetarian meals, he's even more famous for his fish dishes. Dover and lemon sole, sea bream and sea bass, crab, salmon, hake – all delivered fresh each day and transformed into memorable meals. The main restaurant is a stylish 1993 addition overlooking the garden and its sparkling stream. If you want to eat here, booking is strongly advised. The full menu is served throughout the inn at lunchtime but only in the restaurant in the evening.

particularly scenic position in this appealing village. A sparkling stream runs through its gardens and here you'll also find a pleasant patio area and two popular pet goats, Honeysuckle and Parsley. Joe and Pamela Nicholson run this charming pub which the *Chester Chronicle* hailed as one of the six best eating establishments in Cheshire.

Acton Bridge
4 miles W of Northwich off the A49

The bridge here crosses the River Weaver, a waterway whose scenic merits have been largely unsung. The Vale Royal Council has developed the **Weaver Valley Way** which allows walkers to enjoy some lovely stretches,

THE MAYPOLE INN

Hilltop Road, Acton Bridge, nr Northwich, Cheshire CW8 3RA
Tel: 01606 853114

For many years a popular place in the local community, **The Maypole Inn has** excellent leaseholders in Brenda and Keith Morris. They've been in the trade for more than 30 years and here for more than a decade and there's no doubting the warmth of the welcome that awaits visitors. Outside, floral displays provide a lovely blaze of colour and recent additions are a patio area and children's play area. Inside, the low-beamed ceilings, open log fires and an assortment of ornaments and memorabilia add to the cosy, intimate atmosphere.

Excellent ales and traditional home-cooked food keep the inner man happy but booking ahead is recommended, particularly at the weekend. Blackboard and vegetarian specials supplement the main menu which is available lunchtime and evening every day. Long-time favourites include steak pie, braised steak in onion and mushroom gravy, and chicken breast in a creamy leek and Stilton sauce; traditional roasts offer pork, beef, ham and lamb with lemon and mint seasoning; there's a choice of ten salads; and a fish menu with the likes of salmon with prawn sauce, or sea bass with a Mediterranean sauce.

Also available is a lighter menu of closed, open and toasted sandwiches, filled jacket potatoes and hot snacks, followed perhaps by a dessert from the trolley and a speciality coffee. To complement your meal, there's a good selection of wines, ales and liqueurs.

THE SALT BARGE

Ollershaw Lane, Marston,
Cheshire CW9 6ES
Tel: 01606 43064

Standing directly opposite the Lion Salt Works Museum, **The Salt Barge** is right beside bridge 193 over the Trent & Mersey Canal and a popular resort for canal travellers and towpath walkers. The inn is much larger than it appears from outside, offering visitors no fewer than eight different areas in which to drink and dine as well as a large patio area to the rear. Weather permitting there is a bouncy castle for the under 10's. One of the rooms, a tap room and public bar named the Engine Room is

dedicated to the people of Marston and nearby Wincham who worked in the salt industry or on the canal. Evocative old photographs and other memorabilia bring those long-gone days vividly to life. There is a games room with a pool table and darts for the over 10's but children must be accompanied by a parent at all times.

Mine hosts at this delightful old hostelry are Susan and Trevor Prince, a friendly and welcoming couple who have established the inn's reputation for excellent food and well-maintained ales. There are 3 real ales on tap – Tetley, Burtonwood and a rotating guest ale – along with a good range of brews that includes Carlsberg, Carling, Stella, Guinness, Guinness Extra Cold, Tetley Smooth, Burtonwood Dark Mild and Strongbow on draught.

Trevor and the Salt Barge's chefs offer an extensive menu with a maritime theme. *Anchors Away!* lists the starters,

including a tasty Pâté de Maison, Soup of the Day, Garlic Mushrooms, Chicken Goujons and more, then *Sailing on to the Main Course*, offers a *Bounty of Meat* – Choicest Cheshire Gammon, for example, or a Big Barge Grill that will satiate the most ravenous appetite. *Fresh from the Net* lists some delicious fish dishes, while *Tastes of the World* includes authentic dishes from India, Mexico and Italy. A variety of chef's salads, daily specials and *Veggie Castaways* extend the choice even further.

Children have their own Young Sailors Menu and those looking for a lighter meal can choose between Piping Jackets, hot tortilla wraps, hot grannies pies, and tasty sandwiches and baguettes. Food is available every lunchtime and evening and the inn is open all day on Friday, Saturday and Sunday. On Sundays, lunch is served from noon throughout the day and offers a choice of 2 roasts at very competitive prices. Booking is advisable and essential for parties of more than 10 people. Pocket menus are available.

The Salt Barge hosts a pub quiz every Thursday and there's live music about once a month; the inn has good disabled access and special areas for non-smokers. All major credit cards are welcome.

THE HORNS INN

Warrington Road, Acton Bridge, Little Leigh,
Cheshire CW8 4QT
Tel: 01606 852192

The Horns Inn stands close to the Trent &
Mersey Canal which provides some peaceful
towpath walks along the Cheshire Ring Canal
Walk. Mine hosts, Barry and Diane, took over
this friendly traditional pub in September
2001 and have made it a popular social
venue.

There's a pleasant beer garden with,
rather unusually, outdoor table tennis and a
pool table. Monday evening is Quiz Night and
Barry and Diane also arrange
occasional karaoke sessions.
The inn has its own bus so if
you book a party here they'll
pick you up and drop you back
home.

A major attraction at The
Horns is the quality food on
offer. The regular menu is
supplemented by daily specials
and also a Pensioners Special
board. Children are welcome
and there are smoking and

non-smoking areas available, together
seating 45.

It is advisable to book ahead at weekends
at this is a very popular place! Open all day
every day, there are 3 real ales to choose
from · Speckled Hen, Theakstons Best and
Tetley Imperial, as well as a variety of other
beers and lagers such as Greenalls Mild,
Carling, Carlsberg Export, Kronenberg,
Strongbow and Guinness. And if you are
looking for somewhere to stay in the area,
The Horns has 4 guest bedrooms available,
three doubles and one single, with breakfast
included in the price. Credit cards are
accepted except for American Express and
Diners.

particularly those between Weaver
Bridge and Saltersford Locks, and the 6-
mile route from Northwich to Winsford
Marina.

During World War I, Acton Bridge
made an unusual contribution to the war
effort. Near the village was a plantation
of hazel pear trees whose fruit is quite
inedible but whose juice provided the
khaki dye for soldiers' uniforms.

Marston

*1 mile NE of Northwich on a minor
road*

In Victorian times, the Old Salt Mine at
Marston was a huge tourist attraction.
About 360 ft deep and covering 35
acres, it even brought the Tsar of Russia
here in 1844. Ten thousand lamps
illuminated the huge cavern as the
Emperor sat down to dinner here with
eminent members of the Royal Society.
By the end of the century, however,
subsidence caused by the mine had made
some 40 houses in the village
uninhabitable, and one day in 1933 a
hole 50ft wide and 300ft deep suddenly
appeared close to the Trent & Mersey
Canal. Happily, the village has now
stabilised itself, and at the **Lion Salt
Works Museum** on most afternoons you
will find volunteer workers keeping alive
the only surviving open pan salt works
in Britain.

THE ANTROBUS ARMS

Warrington Road, Antrobus, Northwich,
Cheshire CW9 6JD
Tel: 01606 891333
e-mail: andywilson@tinyworld.co.uk

Set in one and a half acres, **The Antrobus Arms** was first licensed in 1760 and has been providing good food and fine ales ever since. Mine hosts, Anne and John, took over here in October of 2002 and are putting the final touches to a complete makeover of the interior. Good food is served daily with both bar menus and specials. There is also a function room for hire and tourers and campers are welcome on a space at the rear of the inn. They plan to create a beer garden with a kids activity area and establish regular entertainment with professional musicians and singers.

Antrobus

5 miles N of Northwich on minor road off the A559

Just a couple of miles from the magnificent Arley Hall and its world-famous gardens, is the pleasing little village of Antrobus, the only place in Britain to bear this name. Even the *Oxford Dictionary of English Place Names* is baffled by Antrobus: "Unexplained" it says curtly, adding as its excuse, "Hardly English". But what could be more English than The Antrobus Arms? (see separate entry). Set in one and a half acres of land and surrounded by scenic countryside, this impressive building was first licensed in 1760 and ever since has been providing good food and fine ales for both locals and for travellers along the main A559 between Warrington and Northwich.

Arley

From Junction 19 of the M6, take the A556 towards Northwich, then follow the signs for Arley Hall

There are many grand houses in Cheshire, and many fine gardens, but at **Arley Hall and Gardens** you will find one of the grandest houses and one of

Arley Hall

the finest gardens in perfect harmony. The present Hall was completed in 1845, a few years after Rowland Egerton-Warburton arrived at Arley with his new bride, Mary Brooke. The newly-married couple took possession of a dilapidated old mansion, infested with rats and with antiquated drains from which an unbearable stench drifted through the house. Understandably, Rowland and Mary soon demolished the old hall and in its place rose a sumptuous early-Victorian stately home complete with (bearing in mind those drains) such state-of-the-art innovations as "Howden's Patent Atmospheric Air Dispensers". Rowland and Mary were both ardent gardeners and it was they who master-minded the magnificent panoramas of today's Arley Gardens. Rowland is credited with creating what is believed to be the first herbaceous border in England; his descendant, the present Viscount Ashbrook, has continued that tradition by cultivating "The Grove", an informal woodland garden planted with spring bulbs,

flowering shrubs and exotic trees, a pleasing contrast to the more formal design of the main gardens.

Other attractions at Arley include a tea room housed in a beautifully converted 16th century barn and a plant nursery offering a wide selection of herbaceous and other plants.

Also within the Arley estate, **Stockley Farm** is a 400 acre organic dairy farm that provides a great family day out. A visit begins with a tractor and trailer ride to the farm where there are always baby animals for children to handle and feed. Adult animals include an 18-hand shire horse, Star, a lovely big pig called Olive, and Kate, the Highland cow. There are miniature tractors to ride, pony rides, an adventure play area, a souvenir shop and a Country Café.

Great Budworth
3 miles NE of Northwich off the A559

A charming small village nowadays, "Great" Budworth was accorded that designation at a time when it was the

THE ELMS COUNTRY INN

Park Lane, Pickmere, Cheshire WA16 0JX
Tel: 01565 733395

In the two years or so since they arrived at **The Elms Country Inn**, David and Janet Flint have made their hostelry the social hub of the village with a 4-fold promise of "Events – Food – Music – Real Ales". The latter includes regulars Tetley, Greene KingGPA and Webster's Yorkshire Bitter along with two rotating guest ales. The excellent food prepared by David the chef is available throughout the day and one of David's specialities is curry – he offers no fewer than 16 varieties. On Friday and Saturday evenings

(sometimes Sunday as well) the inn hosts live entertainment and there's also a large screen TV for major sporting events. Other amenities include an attractive patio to one side and good off road parking.

largest ecclesiastical parish in all Cheshire, the administrative centre for some 35 individual communities. The imposing church on the hill, built in the 14th and 15th centuries, reflects its importance during those years. **St Mary & All Saints** attracts many visitors to its host of quaint carvings and odd faces that peer out at unexpected corners: some with staring eyes, others with their tongues poking out. There's a man near the pulpit who appears to be drowsing through some interminable sermon. Under the roof of the nave you'll find a man with a serpent, another in mid-somersault, and a minstrel playing bagpipes. The distinguished 17th century historian, Sir Peter Leycester, is buried in the Lady Chapel, and in the Warburton Chapel there is a finely carved Tudor ceiling and 13th century oak stalls – the oldest in Cheshire. During the 19th century, Great Budworth was part of the Arley Hall estate and it is largely due to the energetic Squire Egerton-Warburton, a "conservationist" well ahead of his time, that so many of the attractive old cottages in the village are still in place.

Pickmere
6 miles NE of Northwich on the B5391

The delightful village of Pickmere commands superb views of the Cheshire Plain, extending from the Dee estuary to the Pennine hills. The nearby **Pick Mere,** from which the village takes its name, is popular with wind surfers and yachtsmen, and boats are available for hire.

Lostock Gralam
2 miles E of Northwich on the A559

What a wonderful name for a relaxing pub: **The Slow and Easy.** It could be referring to the bowls players on the manicured green that lies alongside. If you bowl yourself, you are welcome to use the green, free of charge, unless one of those very English, courteously lethal matches happens to be under way. In fact the inn's name, like that of so many Cheshire pubs, comes from a racehorse who presumably wouldn't have been quite so famous if he had really lived up to his name.

THE DUKE OF PORTLAND

Holmes Chapel Road, Lach Dennis, Northwich, Cheshire, CW9 7SY
Tel: 01606 46264

The little village of Lach Dennis may be small but it boasts a great pub, **The Duke of Portland.** Anthony and Helen Ryan took over this traditional old hostelry in May 2002 and Anthony's 27 years of experience as a professional chef quickly established the inn as one of the best eating places in the area. He and his team of cooks believe in using only fresh ingredients from local suppliers. The regular menu is supplemented by a wide choice of daily specials and

home-made vegetarian meals. During the week there's a good value 2-course lunch on offer and children's portions are available. An extensive range of traditional and bottled beers is stocked along with a fine selection of wines from around the world. Booking is advised at weekends.

Lach Dennis

4 miles SE of Northwich on the B5082

The small village of Lach Dennis derives its name from the Old English *laecc*, meaning a bog, and the Dennis family which once had an estate here. A mile or so to the east, **Shakerley Mere Nature Reserve** is host to a diverse range of wildlife with Canada Geese, herons, mute swans and mallards a common sight. Cormorants fly here from their breeding grounds on the coast to feast on the fish and more exotic species arrive at different times of the year. There's a pleasant 1.5 mile walk around the mere.

Winsford

6 miles S of Northwich on the A54

Winsford is another of the Cheshire salt towns which expanded greatly during the 19th century, swallowing up the old villages of Over and Wharton on opposite banks of the River Weaver. Two legacies of those boom years should be mentioned. One is Christ Church which was specifically designed so that it could be jacked up in the event of subsidence. The other is Botton Flash, a sizeable lake caused by subsidence but now a popular water recreation area for the town.

Little Budworth

7 miles SW of Northwich on minor road off the A49 or A54

Little Budworth Common Country Park is a pleasant area of heathland and woods, ideal for picnics and walking. The nearby village enjoys splendid views over Budworth Pool but will be better known to motor racing enthusiasts for the Oulton Park racing circuit a mile or so to the south.

Tarporley

12 miles SW of Northwich on the A51/A49

In the days when most of this area was part of Delamere Forest, Tarporley was the headquarters of the verderers or forest wardens. It was from Tarporley in the early 17th century that John Done, Chief Forester and Hereditary Bow-bearer of Delamere entertained King James to a hunt. The chase was, he

SHREWSBURY ARMS

Chester Road, Little Budworth,
Cheshire CW6 9EY
Tel: 01829 760240

Dating back to the mid-1800s the **Shrewsbury Arms** is conveniently located on the main A54 not far from Oulton Park Racing Circuit. This attractive old inn is run by Tim and Margaret Gandy whose aim it is to maintain a traditional country pub atmosphere whilst offering a wide selection of freshly prepared food in comfortable surroundings. The regular menu contains mouth-watering meat, fish and vegetarian dishes which cater for all appetites, home-made Steak & Kidney Pie and fresh haddock being particular favourites. A Light-Bite menu is also available Monday to Friday lunchtimes. The inn has a large beer garden and on Wednesday evening, there is a popular Pub Quiz.

ROYAL OAK HOTEL

Chester Road, Kelsall, nr Tarporley,
Cheshire CW6 0RR
Tel: 01829 751208

The **Royal Oak Hotel** is a large and impressive Victorian building and hosts Andrew and Karen Grant offer their customers a good choice of wholesome and appetising food right through the day until 8.30pm (except on Mondays). The bar is open all day, every day and stocks a wide selection of beers including 3 real ales and a guest ale.

There's a weekly quiz on Sunday evening and occasional live entertainment. Other amenities include a 50-seat function room, an excellent beer garden, a children's room, disabled toilets, and ample parking. The Royal Oak also welcomes bed & breakfast guests with 5 letting rooms available all year round – 1 double and 4 family rooms.

reported, a great success: *"deer, both red and fallow, fish and fowl, abounded in the meres"*. A gratified King rewarded his host with a knighthood.

The village boasts an impressive survivor in the Tarporley Hunt Club which is primarily a dining club for hunting people and still holds an annual banquet in the town. Founded in 1762, it is now the oldest Hunt Club in the country.

Tiverton

2 miles S of Tarporley on the A49

Set around a delightful village green, Tiverton lies almost in the shadow of Beeston Castle, with the Shropshire

Union Canal running nearby. Enjoying an excellent position alongside the bank of the canal, The Shady Oak pub is a popular watering hole for canal travellers.

Utkinton

10 miles SW of Northwich off the A49 or A51

During the Middle Ages, the verderers had their own courts in which they meted out rough justice to offenders against the forest laws. One such court was at Utkinton, just north of the town, and in an old farmhouse there stands a column formed by an ancient forest tree, its roots still in the ground. When the

YEW TREE FARM

Fishers Green, Utkinton, Tarporley,
Cheshire CW6 0JB
Tel: 01829 732441

In the picturesque village of Utkinton, **Yew Tree Farm** stands on a 120-acre working arable and beef farm, surrounded by hundreds more acres of scenic countryside. Edward Williamson, who was born here, and his wife Sheila have been welcoming bed and breakfast guests for 10 years and visitors are quickly made to feel at home. Open all year except over Christmas and the New Year, Yew

Tree Farm has 3 guest bedrooms, all very attractively furnished and decorated, and all non-smoking. The rooms either overlook the beautifully maintained gardens or look out to unspoilt countryside. A full English breakfast is included in the tariff and packed lunches are available on request. Children are welcome and the tariff is on a sliding scale – the longer you stay, the lower the rate.

court was in session, the wardens would place on this tree the symbol of their authority, the Hunting Horn of Delamere. The farmhouse is not open to the public but the horn, dating from around 1120, has survived and can be seen at the Grosvenor Museum in Chester.

Ashton

8 miles E of Chester on the B5393

A couple of miles to the northeast of Ashton stretch the 4000 acres of **Delamere Forest,** a rambler's delight with a wealth of lovely walks and many picnic sites, ideal for a peaceful family day out. In Norman times, a "forest" was a part-wooded, part-open area, reserved as a hunting ground exclusively for royalty or the nobility. There were savage penalties for anyone harming the deer, even if the deer were destroying crops, and household dogs within the forest had to be deliberately lamed to ensure that they could not harass the beasts. James I was the last king to hunt deer here, in August 1617, and enjoyed the day's sport so much that he made his Chief Forester a knight on the spot. Even at that date, many of the great oaks in the forest had already been felled to provide timber for ship-building – as well as for Cheshire's familiar black and white half-timbered houses. Since the early 1900s, Delamere Forest has been maintained by the Forestry Commission which has undertaken an intensive programme of tree planting and

THE GOLDEN LION

Kelsall Road, Ashton Hayes, Cheshire CH3 8BH
Tel: 01829 751508 Fax: 01829 752337
e-mail: edgebee@madasafish.co.uk

Just a short distance off the main A54 road, Ashton village is worth seeking out for the pleasure of visiting **The Golden Lion.** These 300-year-old premises, run by Andrew and Claire Edgeley, are an absolute picture. Cosy, characterful rooms and open fires – every detail of the decorations, furnishings, even the crockery and cutlery, is just as one would wish it. Food is available every lunchtime (noon until 2.30pm) and evening (6pm to 9pm), except Monday evening, with different menus for each session.

The inn's talented chef, Taku Hunt, offers a good choice of freshly prepared and appetising dishes such as Chef's Pie of the Day, Thai chicken with noodles, Linguini Gamberoni and a vegetarian Arrabiatta. The no-smoking restaurant seats 50 but at weekends booking is strongly recommended.

From time to time, Andrew and Claire arrange themed food nights. To accompany your meal there are two real ales on tap, Theakston's Best and Cains, along with a wide range of other beverages that includes Tetley Smooth, Cains Mild, Carling, Fosters, Kronenburg, Scrumpy Jock, Guinness and Guinness Extra Cold.

Children are welcome and major credit cards, apart from American Express and Diners are accepted. Wednesday is Quiz Night and for summer days there's an attractive, secluded beer garden to the rear of the inn.

THE BLACK SWAN

550 Manchester Road, Rixton, Warrington,
Cheshire WA3 6LA
Tel: 0161 777 9673 Fax: 0161 776 9897

Once an important refreshment stop on the Liverpool to Manchester coaching run, **The Black Swan** has been dispensing hospitality for more than 300 years. It was originally called the Old Swan and acquired its name when black swans, native to Australia, first appeared on the nearby Mersey and Glaze rivers. The tradition of serving good ale and good food is being carried on in fine style by Liz and Mike Morrison who took over the lease in October 1999.

accompanied by the diner's choice from a mouth-watering list of sauces: pepper, Diane, creamy Stilton, honey & cider, redcurrant and red wine, and bosceolla – capers, peppers, onions, olives, mushrooms, cream, wine. Special deals are available for senior citizens during the week. It's advisable to book at the weekend to be sure of a table in the 50-cover non-smoking restaurant. Children are welcome if eating. Diners, Mastercard and Visa credit cards are accepted.

On the social side, there seems to be something gong on every night of the week at the Black Swan: a Quiz on Monday and Wednesday at 9.15pm; fun bingo on Tuesday at 9.30pm; Open Tie Box Game on Friday from 9.30pm; and Play Your Cards Right game on Sunday at 9.30pm.

The Morrisons have many plans to broaden still further the amenities of their very attractive pub, including the creation of a beer garden and the bringing on stream of 6 guest bedrooms, all upstairs and all with en suite facilities.

The inn has all the charm and character you'd hope for in such a venerable hostelry – beams and gleaming brasses, and a host of decorative memorabilia. Real ale devotees will be delighted to find a choice of three regularly changing real ales and those in search of tasty, satisfying food will also not be disappointed. The freshly prepared food for a wide-ranging menu, is served every lunchtime (noon to 2.30pm) and evening (5pm to 9pm), Monday to Thursday, and all day Friday and Saturday (noon to 9pm) and Sunday (noon to 8pm). Snacks include sandwiches, jacket potatoes, burger on a barm cake, and hot roast beef baguette with onions and gravy, while main dishes run from jumbo battered cod to lasagne and an excellent steak & ale pie. Steaks and chicken fillets can be

woodland management. Delamere is now both an attractive recreational area and a working forest with 90% of the trees eventually destined for the saw mills.

Warrington

Lying on an important bridging point of the River Mersey, Warrington claims to enjoy Britain's most convenient location. It stands midway between the huge conurbations and ports of Manchester and Liverpool and on a nodal point of communications close to where the M6, M62 and M56 motorways intersect, and where the electrified West Coast main line links London and Scotland.

Warrington is North Cheshire's largest town – an important industrial centre since Georgian and Victorian times and with substantial buildings of those days to prove it. Its imposing **Town Hall** was formerly Lord Winmarleigh's country residence, built in 1750 with all the appropriate grandeur: windows framed in painfully expensive copper, and elaborately designed entrance gates 25ft high and 54ft wide. Along with its park, it provides a dignified focus for the town centre. A major Victorian contribution to the town is its excellent **Museum and Art Gallery** in Bold Street, one of the earliest municipal museums dating from 1857. The exhibits are remarkably varied: amongst them are shrunken heads, a unique china teapot collection, a scold's bridle, Egyptian mummies, a Roman actor's mask and other Roman artifacts discovered in nearby Wilderspool. There are some fine paintings as well, most of which are Victorian watercolours and oils, and a rare Vanous still life.

Also worth visiting is **St Elphin's Church** with its 14th century chancel and memorials celebrating the Butler and Patten families.

An interesting curiosity at Bridge Foot nearby is a combined telephone kiosk and letter box. These were quite common in the early 1900s, but Warrington's is one of the few survivors. Also associated with the town are two prominent entertainers: the television

THE RAMS HEAD

Church Lane, Grappenhall, Cheshire WA4 3EP
Tel: 01925 262814 Fax: 07092 347359
e-mail: davidcross1@leneone.net

Occupying a lovely position in the picture postcard village of Grappenhall, **The Rams Head** is a striking stone building dating back to 1893. It enjoys a reputation for outstanding food, prepared by landlord Michael Whalley who is a qualified chef. Amongst his specialities are a memorable Lamb Henry, home-made Steak & Ale Pie and some delicious fresh salmon dishes. Food is served Monday to Saturday from noon until 2pm, and from 6pm to 9pm; on Sundays between noon and 8pm. To accompany your meal there's a wide choice of beverages, including no fewer than 5 real ales. If you are planning to stay in this delightful village, The Rams Head has 3 quality en suite guest rooms available all year round.

presenter Chris Evans was born here, and the durable comedian and ukelele player George Formby is buried in the town's cemetery.

Around Warrington

Winwick

3 miles N of Warrington on the A49

An unusual feature on Winwick's church tower is the carving of a pig with a bell round its neck. Various explanations for its presence here have been mooted. According to one theory, it was the mason's cryptic way of recording the initials of St Oswald's, Winwick (SOW). An old legend asserts that a pig was employed to move stones here during the building, but the most likely reason is that a pig was the mascot of St Anthony whose carved figure stands in a niche next to it.

Widnes

6 miles SW of Warrington on the A557

Described in the 1860s as a "quiet industrial village", Widnes now has a population of around 60,000. It stands on the north shore of the Mersey, linked to Runcorn by a remarkably elegant road bridge. A popular attraction is **Spike Island** which has recently had a makeover by the local council and now provides a landscaped walk from which

THE RING O' BELLS INN

Northwich Road, Lower Stretton, Cheshire WA4 4NZ
Tel: 01925 730556 Fax: 01925 730326

The Ring O'Bells Inn is just the place for discerning ale drinkers since there are always 3 real ales on tap – Greenalls Bitter, Tetley's Dark Mild plus a rotating guest ale – along with a wide range of other popular brews. Stuart and Susan Hindes are mine hosts at this appealing old hostelry with its many beams, gleaming horse brasses and lots of memorabilia on display in the small cosy rooms. Outside, there's a terraced garden and a boules pitch, and

other entertainment includes a folk evening on the first Tuesday of each month and fortnightly Quizzes between October and March.

the superstructures of ships passing along the Manchester Ship Canal can be seen gliding past.

Runcorn

7 miles SW of Warrington on the A557

Runcorn is one of Britain's best known post-war new towns, developed around a much older town bearing the same name. Here, **Norton Priory** is always a delightful and intriguing place for a family outing, whatever the weather. Despite being situated close to Junction 11 of the M56, it lies in a peaceful oasis with 16 acres of beautiful woodland gardens running down to the Bridgewater Canal. The Augustinian priory was built in 1134 as a retreat for just 12 "black canons", so named because they wore a cape of black woollen cloth over a white linen surplice. Recent work by the Norton Priory Museum Trust has uncovered the remains of the church, chapter house, cloisters and dormitory, and these finds are informatively explained in an audio-visual presentation. The Museum is open every afternoon, all year; the Gardens, which include a charming walled garden, are open from March to October.

Lymm

During the stage coach era, Eagle Brow was notorious, a dangerously steep road that dropped precipitously down the hillside into the village of Lymm. To

LYMM BISTRO

16 Bridgewater Street, Lymm, Cheshire WA13 0AB
Tel: 01925 754852
website: www.lymmbistro.com

For lovers of fine food the place to seek out in this attractive little town is the **Lymm Bistro,** housed in a delightful 200-year-old building. Since they opened the bistro in 1988 Jo Shenton and Michael Venning have earned themselves an excellent reputation for providing first class food and fine wines. Michael is the chef and goes to great lengths to ensure that his customers receive only the very best and freshest of produce.

Michael's speciality is fish and this can be anything from a simple but exquisite whole Dover Sole to really exotic and exciting dishes – amongst the daily specials you might well find Australian Snow Crab or Parrot Fish on offer.

The menus are always changing but starters could include King Prawns Thai Style with coriander, ginger, lemon grass and kaffir

lime, while amongst the main courses fresh Marlin fish sautéed with various shellfish and served with a cream sauce might be one of the options. The bistro seats 75 but such is its popularity that booking is strongly advised at all times.

Opening hours are from 7pm, Tuesday to Saturday, with last orders at 10pm in the week, 1030pm on Friday and Saturday. Non-smoking areas are available; all major credit cards except Diners are welcome.

BARN OWL INN

Agden Wharf, Warrington Lane, Lymm,
Cheshire WA13 0SW
Tel: 01925 752020 Fax: 01925 758272
e-mail:
carl.warburton@thebarnowlinn.co.uk
website: www.thebarnowlinn.co.uk

Just 5 minutes drive from the centre of Lymm **The Barn Owl Inn** enjoys a picturesque position beside the Bridgewater Canal with open countryside in all directions. The premises were purpose built in 1994 and has top quality décor and furnishings throughout. Since 1998 the inn has been owned and personally run by Carl and Teresa Warburton who have established the Barn Owl's reputation for good, wholesome food

in the bar or in the non-smoking conservatory and children are welcome. If you are planning to eat at the Barn Owl over the weekend or at one of the special food-themed evenings, booking is essential.

The inn is a free house so there's an excellent range of ales, including 4 real ales – Marston's Bitter, Marston's Pedigree and two rotating guest ales. Also on offer are Mansfield Smooth, Strongbow, Guinness and Guinness Extra Cold. There's live entertainment on Saturday evenings from 9.15pm; all major credit cards are welcome.

You might like to combine a visit to the Barn Owl Inn with a walk along the Bridgewater Canal. The inn has its own ferry. Alternatively, you could follow part of Cheshire Ring Canal Walk which passes right by the inn.

and well-maintained ales. The inn is open all day, every day, with food served every weekday lunchtime (noon to 2.30pm) and evening (6pm to 8.30pm), and from noon until 8pm on Saturday and Sunday. The extensive menu offers a wide choice of dishes with steak and salmon as specialities. An All Day Breakfast and vegetarian options are available, while for those with lighter appetites there's a selection of jacket potatoes, sandwiches, batons and large barms. In addition to the regular menu, daily specials are listed on the board and the inn also offers a Senior Citizens Menu with the option of 2 or 3 courses at value for money prices. Customers can eat either

THE STAR INN

Star Lane, Statham, Lymm,
Cheshire WA13 9LN
Tel: 01925 753715

The Star Inn is very much the social centre of the tiny hamlet of Statham near Lymm. There's a regular weekly quiz night on Thursday; a piano and sing-along on Sunday evening from 8.30pm; occasional race nights and in the spacious beer garden at the rear a marquee is often raised for special events and parties.

The inn itself is a Listed Building dating back to the early 1800s and has a warm and welcoming atmosphere with lots of old beams, a feature fireplace and attractive prints of old Statham and Lymm around the walls. In its early days, the premises were used as a fustian cutters workplace and when it became an inn was named The Cutters Arms. One of the displays records the history of the fustian cutters.

Mine hosts at The Star are David Gleave, who has been in the business since 1986 and before moving here in October 2001 with his business partner, Lois Martin, had been Steward at Warrington Town Football Club for many years. Open all day, every day, The Star offers excellent food ranging from bar snacks to substantial meals from noon until 8pm.

Real ale fans will be pleased to find three rotating ales always available as well as Carling, Stella, Carlsberg, Fosters, Strongbow and Guinness on draught. Children are welcome; cash payment only.

bypass this hazard, a turnpike was built (now the A56), so preserving the heart of this ancient village with its half-timbered houses and well preserved village stocks. The Bridgewater Canal flows past nearby and the church is reflected in the waters of Lymm Dam. Popular with anglers and bird-watchers, the dam is a large man-made lake, part of a lovely woodland centre which is linked to the surrounding countryside and the canal towpath by a network of footpaths and bridleways. The village became an important centre for the fustian cloth (corduroy) trade in the 19th century but is now best known simply as a delightful place to visit.

Lymm stands on the sides of a ravine and its streets have actually been carved out of the sandstone rock. The same rock was used to construct Lymm's best-known landmark, the ancient cross crowned with a huge cupola that stands at the top of the High Street.

Dunham Massey
4 miles E of Lymm on B5160

Dunham Massey Hall and Park (National Trust) has 250 acres of parkland where fallow deer roam freely and noble trees planted in the late 1700s still flourish. There's a restored water mill which is usually in operation every Wednesday, and there are splendid walks in every direction. The Hall, once the home of the Earls of Stamford and

THE RED BULL INN

The Brow, Kingsley, Cheshire WA6 8AN
Tel: 01928 788097
e-mail: theredbullinn@aol.com

The Red Bull Inn has just about everything you'd expect in a typical country inn. From the leaded bay windows, open log fires and decorative hops displays to the fine selection of excellent homemade food, quality wine, real ales and classic malt whiskies. Since taking over 12 months ago, Landlords Richard and Clare West set about offering their customers a good range of freshly made food and now employ two talented chefs.Outside, there are attractive well-stocked gardens bordered by a small lively stream.A Boules court provides a welcome and alternative source of entertainment for individuals and groups alike. The pub also provides hugely successful themed food evenings, regular quizzes and folk music nights

Warrington, is a grand Georgian mansion of 1732 which boasts an outstanding collection of furniture, paintings and Huguenot silver. The Hall is open most days from April to October: the Park is open every day.

Daresbury

5 miles SW of Warrington on the A558

All Saints' Church in Daresbury has an absolutely unique stained glass window. There are panels depicting a Gryphon and a Cheshire Cat, others show a Mock Turtle, a March Hare and a Mad Hatter. This is of course the **Lewis Carroll Memorial Window**, commemorating the author of *Alice in Wonderland*. Carroll himself is shown at one side, dressed in clerical garb and kneeling. His father was Vicar of Daresbury when Carroll was born here in 1832 and baptised as Charles Lutwidge Dodgson. The boy enjoyed an apparently idyllic childhood at Daresbury until his father moved to another parish when Charles/Lewis was eleven years old.

Helsby

8 miles NE of Chester on the A56

There are seven Iron Age forts scattered across Cheshire, but only the one at Helsby, maintained by the National Trust, is open to the public. The climb out of the village along pretty woodland paths to the red sandstone summit is quite steep but the views across the marshes to the Mersey Estuary and Liverpool repay the effort.

Frodsham

10 miles NE of Chester on the A56

This is an attractive town with a broad High Street lined with thatched cottages and spacious Georgian and Victorian houses. During the 18th and early 19th centuries, Frodsham was an important coaching town and there are several fine coaching inns. Built in 1632, The Bear's Paw with its three stone gables recalls the bear-baiting that once took place nearby. Of the Earl of Chester's Norman castle only fragments remain, but the **Church of St Laurence** (an earlier

THE TRAVELLERS REST

Kingsley Road, Frodsham, Cheshire WA6 6SL
Tel/Fax: 01928 735125

Family-run since 1999 by Ann and David Lamb together with their daughter Nicola, **The Travellers Rest** is a distinctive redbrick building standing alongside the road that runs south from Frodsham through Delamere Forest. Aptly named, it's one of the most popular places in the area to pause for refreshment and a warm and friendly welcome. Inside, the scene is pleasingly traditional with tiled floor, handsome wooden panelling and photographs of the area in days gone by.

A very pleasant setting in which to enjoy a glass of real ale or keg bitter and also strongly recommended for its food which ranges from hearty meals such as traditionally home cooked pies or vegetable lasagne to jacket potatoes and sandwiches. The regular menu is supplemented by daily specials. And it's certainly worth leaving space for one of the superb desserts. The pub is open all day, seven days a week; children are always welcome and there's plenty of off-road parking.

Frodsham itself is well worth taking time to visit with its handsome Georgian and Victorian houses and the exceptional Church of St Lawrence. Ramblers can head south to explore the 4000 acres of Delamere Forest, once a royal hunting ground and now both an attractive recreational area and a working forest maintained by the Forestry Commission.

church here was recorded in the *Domesday Book*) is noted for the fine 17th century panelling in its exquisite north chapel. The Vicar here from 1740 to 1756 was Francis Gastrell, a name that is anathema to all lovers of Shakespeare. Gastrell bought the poet's house, New Place, at Stratford and first incensed the townspeople by cutting down the famous mulberry tree. Then, in order to avoid paying the Corporation poor rate, he pulled the house itself down. The outraged citizens of Stratford hounded him from the town and he returned to the parish at Frodsham that he had neglected for years.

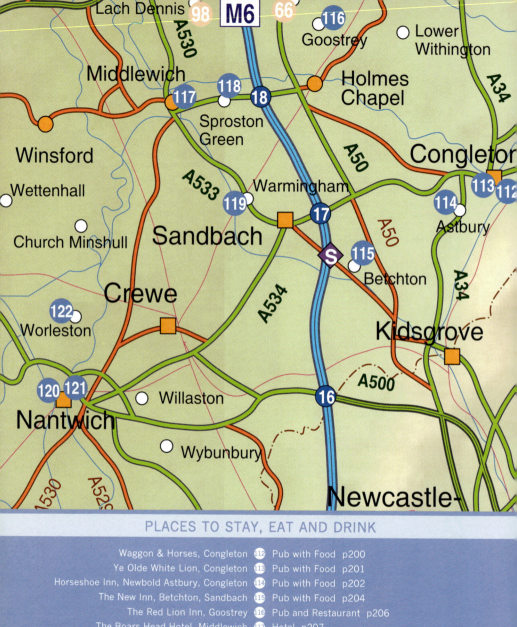

PLACES TO STAY, EAT AND DRINK

● Denotes entries in other chapters

10 Cheshire Peaks and Plains

To the east rise the Peak District hills, westwards gently undulating pastures and woods drop down to the Cheshire Plain. This is an area of sudden and striking contrasts. Within half a mile you can find yourself travelling out of lowland Cheshire into some of the highest and wildest countryside - acres of lonely uplands with rugged gritstone crags, steep valleys watered by moorland streams. Here too is the old salt town of Middlewich, and Sandbach with its famous Saxon crosses, along with a host of quiet, attractive villages. The busy M6 cuts through the area, north to south, but you have only to drive a few miles off the motorway to find yourself wandering along winding country lanes between fertile fields. The two major towns of South Cheshire are Nantwich, with a history stretching back beyond Roman times, and Crewe, with no history at all until 1837. That was when the Grand Junction Railway arrived and five years later moved all its construction and repair workshops to what had been a green field site. We begin our survey of this varied region at Congleton, set amongst the foothills of the Pennines.

Congleton

Some residents have dubbed this thriving old market town the "Venice of the North" because of the number of nearby man-made lakes such as Astbury Mere and Brereton Country Park which both offer a wide range of recreational activities. Set in the foothills of the Pennines, Congleton was an inhabited place as long ago as the Stone

Canal Barges, Ellesmere Port

WAGGON & HORSES,

West Road, Congleton,
Cheshire CW12 4HB
Tel: 01260 274366
Fax: 01260 271202
e-mail: onatthewaggon@aol.com

Occupying a prime corner site at the junction of the A534 and the A54, the **Waggon & Horses** stands on the site of an earlier pub of 1860. Before that a farmhouse and an alehouse with rooms stood here. The traditional black and white exterior you see today conceals a more updated interior which is cosy yet with a great deal of character. Popular with locals as well as visitors to the area, is the entertainment provided in the form of fruit machines, pool, darts and a large screen TV showing major sporting events. Other entertainment includes a quiz on Sunday evening starting at 8.30pm and a

Marston's Pedigree, Banks's Bitter and a fourth, rotating guest brew. Other draught ales available include Mansfield Smooth Bitter, Heineken, Fosters, Stella and Kronenbourg lagers, Strongbow cider and Guinness. There is also a wide choice of spirits and soft drinks.

Food is served each lunch time, Tuesday to Sunday, and Friday evenings, with the selection being offered from a regular printed menu supplemented by blackboard specials. There are a number of bar snacks and hot dishes to choose from with the home-made pies a speciality of the house. Children are welcome and there are designated non-smoking areas available during the times when food is being served.

The "early doors" special on Friday evenings can be very popular so it is worth arriving in good time if you want to take advantage of this value-for-money offering. The manager is Ron Dalton who has been here for eight years and together with loyal staff such as right hand man Ant (better known as "Turks") has created the faithful following that the Waggon & Horses presently enjoys. Ron is also happy to

karaoke/disco once a month on a Saturday.

The pub is well-liked for the good range of beers that are stocked behind the bar, with the real ales including Marston's Bitter,

offer a full package of food, drinks and entertainment for outside catering.

The inn is open all day, every day from noon; cash and cheques only are accepted.

YE OLDE WHITE LION

22 High Street, Congleton,
Cheshire CW12 1BD
Tel: 01260 272702
e-mail: thewhitelion@talk21.com

Amanda Roberts is the leaseholder of the historic **Ye Olde White Lion**. It dates back some 500 years and was the office of John Bradshaw, who signed the death warrant of Charles I. The bars are cosy and inviting, with a wealth of ornaments hanging from the beams and walls. Amanda does the cooking, producing a good variety of dishes for the printed menu and the daily specials board. Food is served Tuesday to Sunday lunchtimes and it's best to book at weekends. Three or four real ales are always on tap, including Abbot and guest ales. A live band performs every other Sunday evening and the pub holds occasional quiz nights. At the back is a little gem of a garden.

Age. The remains of a 5000-year-old chambered tomb known as **The Bridestones** can be seen beside the hill road running eastwards from the town to the A523 road to Leek.

In Elizabethan times, the townspeople of Congleton seem to have had a passion for bear baiting. On one occasion, when the town bear died they handed 16 shillings (80p) to the Bear Warden to acquire another beast. The money had originally been collected to buy a town bible: the disgraceful misappropriation of funds gave rise to the ditty: *"Congleton rare, Congleton rare, sold the bible to buy a bear"*. Known locally as the "Bear Town", Congleton was the very last town in England to outlaw the cruel practice of bear baiting but the town's emblem is still an upright chained bear. A more attractive distinction is the fact that it is also one of only four towns in Cheshire where the medieval street pattern has remained intact and the only town where the curfew bell is still rung each night at 8pm.

One of the oldest buildings in Congleton is **The Lion & Swan Hotel**, a 16th century coaching inn on the old Manchester to London route. This grand old building with its superb black and white half-timbered frontage has been fully restored to its Tudor glory, with a wealth of exposed, dark oak beams and elaborately carved fireplaces, as well as the oldest window in town, dating from 1596. Another ancient hostelry is Ye Olde Kings Arms whose pink-washed half-timbered frontage leans picturesquely to the left as if exhausted with the weight of years.

Congleton's impressive Venetian Gothic style **Town Hall**, built in 1864, contains some interesting exhibits recalling the town's long history, including some fine civic regalia. There are displays recording the work of such ancient civic officials as the swine-catcher, the chimney-looker and the ale-taster, and aids to domestic harmony like the "brank" – a bridle for nagging wives which used to be fastened to a wall in the market place. Other exhibits include a prehistoric log boat, coin hoards from the Civil War, and more recent acquisitions covering the

Industrial Revolution and the Second World War.

During the 18th century Congleton developed as an important textile town with many of its mills involved in silk manufacture, cotton spinning and ribbon weaving. In Mill Green near the River Dane, you can still see part of the very first silk mill to operate here.

Little Moreton Hall, Astbury

Around Congleton

Astbury

2 miles SW of Congleton on the A34

The pretty little village of Astbury, set around a triangular village green, was once more important than neighbouring Congleton which is why it has a much older church, built between 1350 and 1540. Arguably the finest parish church in the county, **St Mary's** is famous for its lofty recessed spire (which rises from a tower almost detached from the nave), and the superb timber work inside: a richly carved ceiling, intricate tracery on the rood screen, and a lovely Jacobean font cover.

But just three miles down the A34 is an even more remarkable building. Black and white half-timbered houses have almost become a symbol for the county of Cheshire and the most

HORSESHOE INN

Fence Lane, Newbold, Astbury, Congleton, Cheshire CW12 3NL
Tel: 01260 272205

Set within 11 acres of grounds the **Horseshoe Inn** dates back to 1774. It presents an attractive white-painted façade whilst inside, the look is very traditional with a wealth of horse brasses and other ornaments on the walls and beams. Mervyn and Siobhan White have been tenants here since 1995 and they have a warm welcome for all – including children who will find a very well-equipped adventure playground in the garden. Food is served every

lunchtime and evening, a mainly traditional choice with gammon steaks and mixed grills among the most popular items. To go with the good food is an excellent selection of ales – the pub is CAMRA-listed. A fun quiz starts at 9pm on the last Wednesday of each month.

stunning example is undoubtedly **Little Moreton Hall** (National Trust), a "wibbly wobbly" house which provided a memorable location for Granada TV's adaptation of *The Adventures of Moll Flanders*. The only bricks to be seen are in the chimneys, and

Mow Cop

the hall's huge overhanging gables, slanting walls, and great stretches of leaded windows, create wonderfully complex patterns, all magically reflected in the still flooded moat. Ralph Moreton began construction in 1480 and the fabric of this magnificent house has changed little since the 16th century. A richly panelled Great Hall, parlour and chapel show off superb Elizabethan plaster and wood work. Free guided tours give visitors a fascinating insight into Tudor life, and there's also a beautifully reconstructed Elizabethan knot garden with clipped box hedges, a period herb garden and a Yew Tunnel.

About a mile south of Little Moreton Hall is the Rode Hall estate. It was an 18th century owner of the estate, Randle Wilbraham, who built the famous folly of **Mow Cop** (National Trust) to enhance the view from his mansion. This mock ruin stands atop a rocky hill 1100 feet above sea level, just yards from the Staffordshire border. On a clear day, the views are fantastic: Alderley Edge to the north, the Pennines to the north-east, south to Cannock Chase and Shropshire, and westwards across Cheshire. **Rode Hall** itself, home of the Wilbraham family since 1669, is a fine early 18th century mansion standing within a park landscaped by Humphry Repton. The extensive gardens include a formal rose garden of 1860, a large walled kitchen garden, a terraced rock garden with a grotto, and an ice house. The Hall and gardens are open from 2pm to 5pm on Wednesdays and Bank Holiday Mondays from April to September; the gardens on Tuesdays, Wednesdays, Thursdays and Bank Holiday Mondays.

Biddulph
5 miles SE of Congleton on the A527

The 10-year restoration of **Biddulph Grange Gardens** has recently been completed and visitors can now enjoy the full beauty of this unique project. The gardens are imaginatively divided

THE NEW INN

Newcastle Road, Betchton, Sandbach,
Cheshire CW11 2TG
Tel: 01477 500237

The superb **New Inn** stands in the hamlet of Betchton on the A533, a mile or so south of Sandbach and a few minutes drive from Junction 17 of the M6. The building dates back to the mid 1800s and was once a coaching inn and part of the vast Betchton Estate. Paul and Claire Beresford took over here in 2000 and have made the New Inn one of the places to be visited in Cheshire. Paul has some 20 years experience in the catering and licensed trade, Clare is a professional chef, and together they have put that knowledge to good use in the creation of their popular menu. Indeed, such is the inn's popularity, booking ahead is advisable at all times. Everything is prepared using the

of options – grills, poultry, pasta, chicken and fish dishes (a speciality of the house), as well as vegetarian and salad dishes such as home-made vegetarian Balti and a Warm Chicken and Smoked Bacon Salad. Extending the choice even further, the daily specials board lists a selection of enticing dishes with a seasonal flavour. The delicious desserts change every day. (Incidentally, if you have any special occasion coming up, Paul and Claire are very happy to cater for any kind of large party).

freshest of local produce with another professional chef working alongside Claire.

The printed menu offers an extensive choice of wholesome and appetising food – amongst the starters for example you'll find a home-made soup of the day, home-made pâté and a tasty Creamy Stilton with Guinness. The main courses offer a full range

To accompany your meal there are always a minimum of 2 real ales on tap – Marston's Bitter and Marston's Pedigree amongst them – along with Banks's Smooth, Hanson's Mild, Carlsberg, Stella, Strongbow and Guinness.

Food is available every lunchtime (noon until 2.30pm) and evening (6pm to 9.30pm) with a traditional lunch on Sundays when there's a choice of 3 roasts and the option of either a 2- or 3-course meal. Children under 10 have their very own menu and they also have their own play area in the pub's beer garden. The New Inn has its own car park and there's another large car park just across the road.

Cyclists on the Cheshire Cycle Route, which passes the front door, enjoy a pit stop at the New Inn, as do users of the nearby Trent and Mersey Canal and walkers along the Cheshire Ring Canal Walk.

into a series of enclosed areas bounded by massive rock structures, hedges, stumps, roots and moulded banks. A trail leads through a superb Chinese garden to an enchanting Scottish glen while other areas reproduce the magic of Egypt or the tranquillity of rural America. The shop is packed with gardening books, Victorian plants, cards and quality souvenirs, and there's also a pleasant tearoom offering local specialities and home-made cakes.

Sandbach

1 mile SW from Junction 17 of the M6

Sandbach's former importance as a stopping place for coaches (both stage and motor) is evident in the attractive old half-timbered inns and houses, some of them thatched, which line the main street. Sandbach's handsome market square is dominated by its two famous stone crosses, 16 and 11 feet tall. These superbly carved crosses (actually only the shafts have survived) were created some time in the 9th century, and the striking scenes are believed to represent the conversion of Mercia to Christianity during the reign of King Penda. A plaque at their base notes that they were restored in 1816 "after destruction by iconoclasts" – i.e. the Puritans. The restorers had to recover fragments from here and there: some had been used as street paving, cottage steps or in the walls of a well. Somehow they fitted the broken stones together, like pieces of a jigsaw, and the result is immensely impressive.

Holmes Chapel

5 miles N of Sandbach on the A50/A54

In the mid 18th century, the little village of Holmes Chapel was stirred by two important events. In 1738, John Wesley came and preached outside St Luke's Church. Fifteen years later, on July 10th 1753, a disastrous fire swept through the village. When the flames were finally quenched, only two buildings had survived the blaze: St Luke's Church and The Old Red Lion alongside.

About 3 miles southeast of Holmes Chapel, **Brereton Heath Country Park** is a popular beauty spot where the heath land and flower meadows are criss-crossed by a network

Sandbach

of many footpaths. The former sand quarry provides a congenial habitat for a range of species, details of which can be obtained from the park ranger at the Visitor Centre. The lake here is used for angling, canoeing and windsurfing.

Goostrey

6 miles NE of Middlewich on minor road off A50

The village of Goostrey is a quiet little place on a minor road just north of Holmes Chapel but famous for its annual gooseberry shows where competitors vie to produce the plumpest berries. The name of the village has nothing to do with gooseberries but derives from a personal name, Godhere, and the Saxon word for tree.

Lower Withington

7 miles NE of Middlewich on the B5392

Visible from miles around, the huge white dish of the world famous **Jodrell Bank** radio telescope has a good claim to being the most distinctive building in the county. The Observatory came into service in 1957 and was used by both Americans and the Soviets in their exploration of space. In November 2002, following an upgrading, the radio telescope re-entered service with a capacity 30 times that of the original. Jodrell Bank's Science Centre offers visitors a wonderful array of hands-on exhibits, including a 25ft telescope, while its Planetarium travels through

THE RED LION INN

3 Station Road, Goostrey, Cheshire CW4 8PJ
Tel: 01477 532033

Since taking over here in August 2001, Mike and Karen Garnett, both locally born, have made **The Red Lion Inn** a focal centre for the social life of this picturesque village.

Pool and darts are available, there's Sky-TV Premier on the box with a pay-for-view facility, and on Friday evenings a free juke box. Mike and Karen also organise occasional events such as a Tarot reading evening.

A major attraction is definitely the food, prepared by chef Wayne Doyle and offering a wide choice of home-made dishes, all at very reasonable prices.

Apart from Monday when the kitchen is closed, food is available every lunchtime, between noon and 3pm, and from 6.30pm to 9pm in the evenings. On Sundays, the

hours are noon until 3pm or so. The non-smoking restaurant seats 50 and it's strongly recommended that you book for the evenings and on Sunday.

Throughout the week, the Red Lion is open all day, every day, for ale. There are always at least two real ales on tap – Tetley's and a guest brew – and an extensive choice of all the popular brands.

In good weather, customers can take advantage of the picnic tables at the front while to the rear there's a children's play area and ample parking.

Jodrell Bank

the heavens, explaining the secrets of Rocky Dwarfs and Gassy Giants along the way. The dynamic duo of Albert Einstein and Isaac Newton are at hand to guide visitors on this fascinating exploration of the Universe. Outside, there's a superb 35-acre Arboretum planted with 2000 species of trees and shrubs, each one helpfully labelled, and an Environment Discovery Centre which explains the importance of trees to the natural environment. The site also contains a picnic area, play area, café and shop.

In the nearby village of Lower Withington, old farm buildings have been sympathetically converted to provide an attractive setting for **Welltrough Dried Flowers** (free) which boasts one of the largest selections of

THE BOARS HEAD HOTEL

Kinderton Street, Middlewich, Cheshire CW10 0JE
Tel: 01606 833191 Fax: 01606 833198

The Boars Head Hotel began life as a coaching inn and has been dispensing hospitality for some 200 years. Mine hosts, Pat and Liz, continue the tradition, offering well-maintained draught ales, good food and comfortable accommodation. The inn is open all day, every day, with Robinson's Best, Three Shires Mild, Carling, Strongbow and Guinness all available on draught. Lunches are available (between noon and 2.30pm) but by the time you read this

the 42-seater restaurant will also be offering evening meals from 6pm to 9pm. The hotel has 5 guest bedrooms – 2 family rooms, 2 twins and 1 single. Evening meals are available for residents if required and the tariff includes an excellent breakfast.

dried and silk flowers in the North. There are literally hundreds of different kinds and shapes, and the seven separate showrooms include a permanent Christmas Room, a Dickensian Street and a demonstration room where Day Workshops are held.

Middlewich
2 miles W of Junction 18 of the M6

The Romans called their settlement here Salinae, meaning saltworks. Excavations have revealed outlines of their long, narrow, timber workshops, brine pits and even a jar with the word AMYRCA scratched on it. (Amurca was the Latin name for brine waste which was used throughout the Empire as a cleansing agent). Middlewich Town Council

publishes an informative leaflet detailing the **Roman Middlewich Trail,** a one mile circular walk that reveals the history and layout of the Roman town and shows how Middlewich would have looked in those days.

In modern times, it was the need for Cheshire's salt manufacturers to get their cumbersome product to markets in the Midlands and the south which gave a great impetus to the building of canals in the county. Middlewich was particularly well-provided for with its own Middlewich Branch Canal linking the town to both the Shropshire Union and the Trent & Mersey canals. Today, most of the canal traffic comprises traditional narrow boats which can also be hired for holiday trips.

THE FOX & HOUNDS INN

Holmes Chapel Road, Sproston Green, Middlewich, Cheshire CW4 7LW
Tel: 01606 832303

Motorists driving along the M6 need only the briefest of diversions to find this excellent place of refreshment. **The Fox & Hounds Inn**, a handsome old black-and-white building, stands less than a mile from Junction 18 and its motto "happiness is a drink and good food" is well chosen.

Run for the past five years by the French family, it has a history going back almost 300 years and the traditional bar and restaurant are cosy and inviting.

Food is served every lunchtime and evening (except Mondays unless it's a Bank Holiday) with the choice of either à la carte, the daily specials board and, at lunchtimes, a snack menu. The daily fish specials are always worth looking out for but everything is good and fresh and such is the inn's popularity booking is strongly recommended from Thursday to Saturday.

Also very well attended are the special occasion themed evenings which are held from time to time. Three real ales – Greenalls, Bass and a guest ale – are always available along with the usual range of popular brews.

The inn has a large off-road car park and a beer garden with a former bowling green that is now used as a children's play area (kids also have their own menu). Other amenities include a toilet with facilities for disabled visitors.

During the Civil War, Middlewich witnessed two of the bloodiest battles fought in the county. In March 1644, Royalists trapped Cromwell's men in the narrow lanes and alleys of the town and slaughtered 200 of them. A few managed to find refuge in **St Michael's Church.** The church has changed greatly since those days but still has some notable old carvings and a curiosity in the form of a carved coat of arms of the Kinderton family of nearby Kinderton Hall. Their crest shows a dragon eating a child, a reference to the occasion on which Baron Kinderton killed a local dragon as it was devouring a child. The incident apparently took place at Moston, near Sandbach, and a lane there is still called Dragon Lane.

South Cheshire

Crewe

5 miles NE of Nantwich on the A534

The two major towns of South Cheshire are Nantwich, with a history stretching back beyond Roman times, and Crewe,

with no history at all until 1837. That was when the Grand Junction Railway arrived and five years later moved all its construction and repair workshops to this green field site. A workforce of nine hundred had to be housed so the company rapidly built cottages, each one shared by four of the lowest paid workers, and detached "mansions" which accommodated four families of the more highly skilled. At one time, seven out of every ten men in Crewe worked on the railways.

Later, in 1887, the railway company also provided the town with one of the most splendid parks in the north of England, **Queens Park,** some 40 acres of lawns and flowerbeds together with an ornamental lake. Rolls Royce's engineering works brought further prosperity to the town, but it is as a railway centre that Crewe is best known. Even today, the station offers a choice of six different routes to all points of the compass. The **Railway Age** museum offers a fascinating insight into Crewe's place in railway history with hands-on exhibits, steam locomotive rides, model

---

THE BEAR'S PAW

School Lane, Warmingham, Crewe, Cheshire CW11 3QN
Tel: 01270 526317 Fax: 01270 526465
e-mail: enquiries@thebearspaw.co.uk
website: www.thebearspaw.co.uk

The picturesque village of Warmingham has an excellent place to stay, wine, dine – and even get married! **The Bear's Paw** is licensed for civil weddings and the Warmingham Suite is ideal for receptions, private parties, seminars and conferences. Experienced staff will organise every kind of event. The inn has a fine restaurant offering superb food created by imaginative chefs and there is a well-stocked bar. The accommodation maintains the same high standards with sumptuously furnished en suite rooms with satellite TV, hair dryer, trouser press, direct dial telephone and hospitality tray.

railway displays and a children's playground. Also worth a visit is the **Lyceum Theatre**, built in 1902 and with its glorious Edwardian opulence undimmed.

A couple of miles north of Crewe, **Lakemore Country Park Animal Kingdom** is home to a wide variety of animals – wallabies, llamas, miniature donkeys, owls and many other unusual and rare breeds. Children can feed the farm animals, visit the pets corner and enjoy both the indoor and outdoor play areas. Within the 36 acre site are five fishing lakes and there's also a log cabin coffee shop.

Nantwich

4 miles SW of Crewe on the A51

The most disastrous event in the long history of Nantwich was the Great Fire of 1583 which consumed some 600 of its thatched and timber-framed buildings. The blaze raged for 20 days and the townspeople's terror was compounded when some bears kept behind the Crown Hotel escaped. (Four bears from Nantwich are mentioned in

Shakespeare's comedy *The Merry Wives of Windsor*). Queen Elizabeth contributed the huge sum of £2000 and also donated quantities of timber from Delamere Forest to assist in the town's rebuilding. A grateful citizen, Thomas Cleese, commemorated this royal largesse with a plaque on his new house at No. 41, High Street. The plaque is still in place and reads: "God grant our ryal Queen in England longe to raign / For she hath put her helping hand to bild this towne again".

The most striking of the buildings to survive the conflagration, perhaps because it was surrounded by a moat, is the lovely black and white house in Hospital Street, known as **Churche's Mansion** after the merchant Richard Churche who built it in 1577. Astonishingly, when the house was up for sale in 1930, no buyer showed any interest and the building was on the point of being transported brick by brick to America when a public-spirited local doctor stepped in and rescued it. The ground floor is now a restaurant, but the upper floor has been furnished in

HILTONS TEA ROOMS

27 Beam Street, Nantwich, Cheshire CW5 5NA
Tel: 01270 611488

Located in the heart of historic Nantwich, **Hiltons Tea Rooms** are where you'll find a tasty selection of home-baked goods including scones, teacakes, fruit pies and delicious cakes. Owners Karen and Morag share the cooking and their menu also offers main meals such as home-made quiches, lasagne, macaroni cheese and a selection of salads. All day breakfasts are available as well as home-

made soup, sandwiches and a children's menu – everything is freshly prepared to order. The Tea Rooms have smoking and non-smoking areas and are open Monday to Saturday from 9.30am until 4.30pm. Karen and Morag will open in the evenings for parties of 12 or more and they are also happy to provide outside catering.

Elizabethan style and is open to the public during the summer.

The Great Fire also spared the stone-built 14th century church. This fine building, with an unusual octagonal tower, is sometimes called the **"Cathedral of South Cheshire"** and dates from the period of the town's greatest prosperity as a salt town and trading centre. Of exceptional interest is the magnificent chancel and the wonderful carvings in the choir. On the misericords (tip-up seats) are mermaids, foxes (some dressed as monks in a sharp dig at priests), pigs, and the legendary Wyvern, half-dragon, half-bird, whose name is linked with the River Weaver, 'wyvern' being an old pronunciation of Weaver. An old tale about the building of the church tells of an old woman who brought ale and food each day from a local inn to the masons working on the site. The masons discovered that the woman was cheating them by keeping back some of the money they put "in the pot" for their refreshment. They dismissed her and took revenge by making a stone carving showing the old woman being carried away by Old Nick himself, her hand still stuck in a pot.

During the Civil War, Nantwich was the only town in Cheshire to support Cromwell's Parliamentary army. After several weeks of fighting, the Royalist forces were finally defeated on 25th January, 1644 and the people of Nantwich celebrated by wearing sprigs of holly in their hair. As a result, the day became known as "Holly Holy Day" and every year, on the Saturday closest to January 25th, the town welcomes Cromwellian pikemen and battle scenes are re-enacted by members of the Sealed Knot. There are records of the Civil War in the **Nantwich Museum** (free) in Pillory Street which also has exhibitions about the town and its dairy and cheese-making industries.

But it was salt that had once made Nantwich second only in importance to Chester in the county. The Romans had mined salt here for their garrisons at Chester and Stoke where the soldiers received part of their wages in "sal", or salt. The payment was called a "salarium", hence the modern word

---

THE ODDFELLOWS ARMS

97 Welsh Row, Nantwich, Cheshire CW5 5ET
Tel: 01270 624758

Despite being close to the heart of historic Nantwich, **The Oddfellows Arms**, dating back to the 1600's, has a lovely, spacious beer garden at the rear. The present licensees, Roger and Kay Drinkwater, have recently redesigned and redecorated the old building, taking care to retain its old world charm and character. Kay is an accomplished cook and offers quality food every lunchtime from noon until 2.30pm except Mondays (unless Bank Holiday), and every evening from 7pm until 9pm. Kay's home-made pies  are especially popular as is the traditional Sunday lunch. The last Saturday of each month is Piano Night and there are occasional jazz duo performances on Thursday evenings. Children are welcome up to 9pm; credit cards are not accepted.

THE ROYAL OAK

Main Road, Worleston, Nantwich, Cheshire
Tel: 01270 624138 Fax: 01270 611663

The Royal Oak is the social hub of the village of Worleston which lies on the B5074 a short distance from Nantwich. Built in the mid-1800s on the site of a much earlier hostelry, the pub is spacious and stylish with plenty of comfortable seating, a restaurant area and a pool table. Robert and Rachel Hollinshead have held the lease here for 13 years and Rachel, who was born in Worleston, knows everything there is to know about the village and the locality. Chef Tom looks after the cooking with an extensive restaurant menu and hot or cold bar snacks all available every lunchtime and evening except Sunday evening. Meals are rounded off in fine style with a delicious selection of mouth-watering home-made desserts. Booking is advisable for Tuesday and Saturday evenings, and for Sunday lunch.

Robert and Rachel also offer an excellent bar service for outside events. Boddington's and John Smith's real ales are among the brews which also include Worthington Smooth. There are designated non-smoking areas in the newly decorated, smartly furnished bars, and children have their own play area in the beer garden. Country music is played from 8.45pm on Tuesday evenings. The River Weaver and the Shropshire Union Canal are both a short walk from the pub, while a few miles drive will bring you to the important towns of Nantwich and Crewe, the former with a splendid 14th century church, the latter not to be missed by anyone interested in the history of the railways.

"salary". Nantwich remained a salt producing town right up to the 18th century but then it was overtaken by towns like Northwich which enjoyed better communications on the canal system. But a brine spring still supplies Nantwich's outdoor swimming pool!

Within a few miles of the town are two notable gardens. A major attraction, a mile south of the town off the A51, is **Stapeley Water Gardens** which attracts nearly 1.5 million visitors each year. The 64-acre site includes the National Collection of Nymphaea – more than 350 varieties of water lilies, a Tropical Oasis with exotic flowers and pools stocked with piranhas and huge catfish, and a comprehensively equipped garden centre. Other attractions within the attractively landscaped grounds include a restaurant, two cafes and a gift shop.

About 6 miles further south along the A51 and straddling the Staffordshire border, **Bridgemere Garden World** provides the location for BBC TV's Gardeners' Diary. This is just one of 22 different gardens, amongst them a French rose garden, a woodland setting, a cottage garden and a rock and water area. The extensive glasshouses contain houseplants of every description and the garden centre is stocked with everything a gardener could possibly need. There's also an aquatics house with some splendid fish, a specialist food hall, a flower arrangers' centre, a bookshop, restaurant and coffee shop.

Beeston

8 miles NW of Nantwich on minor road off the A49

A craggy cliff suddenly rising 500ft from the Cheshire Plain, its summit crowned by the ruins of **Beeston Castle** (English Heritage), Beeston Hill is one of the most dramatic sights in the county. The castle was built around 1220 but didn't see any military action until the Civil War. On one rather ignominious occasion during that conflict, a Royalist captain and just eight musketeers managed to capture the mighty fortress and its garrison of 60 soldiers without firing a shot. A few years later, Cromwell ordered that the castle be

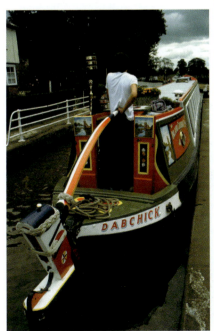

Beeston Locks

"slighted", or partially destroyed, but this "Castle in the Air" is still very imposing with walls 30ft high and a well 366ft deep. An old legend asserts that Richard II tipped a hoard of coins, gold and jewels down the well, but no treasure has yet been discovered. The castle hill is a popular place for picnics, and it's worth climbing it just to enjoy the spectacular views which extend across seven counties and over to a "twin" castle. **Peckforton Castle** looks just as medieval as Beeston but was, in fact, built in 1844 for the first Lord Tollemache who spared no expense in re-creating features such as a vast Great Hall and a keep with towers 60ft tall. The architect Gilbert Scott later praised Peckforton as "the very height of masquerading". Its authentic medieval appearance has made the castle a favourite location for film and television companies, and on Sundays and Bank Holidays during the season the Middle Ages are brought to life here with mock battles and tournaments. The castle also offers guided tours, refreshments and a speciality shop.

Church Minshull

7 miles N of Nantwich on the B5074

This picturesque little village is known to a few people as the home of Elizabeth Minshull before she became the third wife of the poet John Milton in 1660. There's a fine old hostelry here, The Badger Inn, which has been designated as a Building of Historic and Architectural Interest and is attractively located close to the River Weaver. Built in 1760, the inn was originally known as the Brookes Arms, named after the family who were great landowners in the Mere and Tatton area. In a play of words on their name, the Brookes coat of arms bears two brocks, the old English name for badgers, (brocks/Brookes), and so led to the inn's present name.

Wettenhall
8 miles N of Nantwich on minor road off the B5074

Wettenhall is a pretty little village surrounded by open countryside. Records show that it has enjoyed the amenity of a public house since 1651. The hostelry used to be called The Little John and was located on the very spot where The Little Man Inn now stands. The change of name came about in the 19th century when local licensees decided to pay

tribute to a real life "little man". Sammy Grice, less than four feet tall, was much valued for his skill in providing vent pegs for them, and skewers for the butchers of Chester.

Willaston
2 miles E of Nantwich between the A534 and A500

It was in the village of Willaston that one of the most unusual world records was established in 1994. Some 200 competitors had gathered at the Primary School here for the annual **World Worm Charming Championships**. The prize goes to whoever induces the greatest number of worms to poke their heads above a 9-square metre patch of playing field aided only by a garden fork. Each contestant is allowed half an hour and the current world champion charmed 511 out of the ground – a rate of more than 17 wrigglies a minute. The secret of his wonderful way with worms has not been revealed.

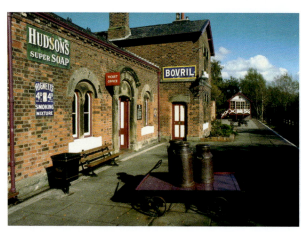

Willaston Station

Wybunbury
5 miles S of Crewe on the B5071

South Cheshire's answer to the Leaning Tower of Pisa is the 100ft high tower of **St Chad's Church** in Wybunbury. It was built in 1470 above an unsuspected ancient salt bed. Subsidence has been the reason for the tower's long history of leaning sideways by as much as four feet and then being straightened up, most recently in 1989. It now rests on a reinforced concrete bed and is unlikely to deviate from the vertical again. The tower stands alone: the body of the church, once capable of holding a congregation of 1600, collapsed on no fewer than five occasions. In 1972, the villagers finally decided to abandon it and build a new church on firmer ground.

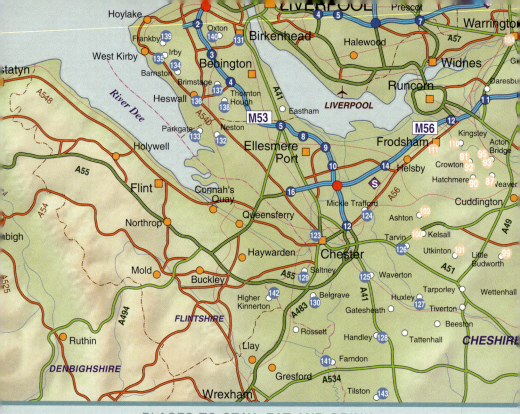

PLACES TO STAY, EAT AND DRINK

● Denotes entries in other chapters

11 Chester & West Cheshire

Around the 1890s, guide-book writers took a fancy to describing the topography of various counties by comparing their outlines to some appropriate emblem. The hunting county of Leicestershire, for example, clearly resembled a fox's head with its ears pricked up. In Cheshire's county boundaries however they were unable to discern anything more imaginative than the shape of a teapot. Its base is the Staffordshire border, its handle the strip of land running from Stockport up to the Yorkshire border, with the Wirral providing the spout. And, tucked away in the crook of the spout, is the capital of the county, the City of Chester.

The city's actual position, a strategic site on the River Dee close to the Welsh border, was important even before the Romans arrived in AD70. They based a large camp, or *caster*, here and called it Deva after the Celtic name for the river. It was during this period that the splendid city walls were originally built – two miles round, and still the most complete in the country.

In Saxon times "Ceastre" became the administrative centre of a shire, and was the last major town in England to fall to William the Conqueror during his dreadful Harrowing of the North. William pulled down half of Chester's houses and re-inforced the message of Norman domination by building a castle overlooking the Dee.

Chester Visitor Centre and Amphitheatre

Subsequent Earls of Chester (the present Prince of Wales is the current one, incidentally) were given a free, and very firm hand, in dealing with the local Saxons and with the still-rebellious Welsh who continued to make a nuisance of themselves right through the Middle Ages. In return for its no-nonsense dealing with these problems Chester received a number of royal privileges: borough status, a licence for a market and, around 1120, the first commission in England for a Sheriff, ~ long before his more famous colleague in Nottingham received his. And the Mayor of Chester can still claim the medieval title of "Admiral of the Dee".

The problem with the Welsh was finally resolved in 1485 when a Welsh-based family, the Tudors, defeated Richard III at Bosworth Field and Owen Tudor claimed the throne as Henry VII. For more than 150 years Chester enjoyed an unprecedented period of peace and prosperity. Then came the Civil War. Chester supported the King but Charles I had the galling experience of watching from the city walls as his troops were defeated at nearby Rowton Moor. For two long years after that rout, the city was under seige until starvation finally forced its capitulation. **The King Charles Tower** on the wall is now a small museum with displays telling the story of that siege.

Seventy years later, in the course of his "Tour through the Whole Island of Great Britain", Daniel Defoe came to Chester by the ferry over the River Dee.

He liked the city streets, "very broad and fair"; admired the "very pleasant walk round the city, upon the walls", disliked its cathedral, "built of red, sandy, ill looking stone", but had nothing but praise for its "excellent cheese". Cheshire cheese had been famous for generations. John Speed, the famous Elizabethan map-maker and a Cheshire man himself, noted: "The soil is fat fruitful and rich....the Pastures make the Kine's udders to strout to the pail, from whom the best Cheese of all Europe is made". Later, some enthusiasts even promoted the idea that the name Cheshire was actually short for cheese-shire.

The county's other major industry was salt, mined here even before the Romans arrived. By the time of the *Domesday Book*, the salt towns, or "wiches" – Nantwich, Northwich, Middlewich, were firmly established. The process then involved pumping the salt brine to the surface and boiling it to produce granular salt. In 1670, huge deposits of rock salt were discovered and these are still being mined, mostly for use in keeping the country's roads free from ice.

Both these historic industries have been overtaken in the 20th century by tourism. Chester, with its long history, varied and fascinating "magpie" architecture, and huge range of shops, restaurants and inns, is now the fourth most visited location in England after the "golden triangle" of London, Stratford and Oxford. One small disappointment, though: visitors don't get to see the county's best known character, the grinning Cheshire Cat. The phrase "To grin like a Cheshire cat" was in use long before Lewis Carroll adopted it in *Alice in Wonderland*. Carroll spent his childhood in the Cheshire village of Daresbury and would have regularly seen the local cheeses moulded into various animal shapes, one of which was a grinning cat.

Chester

James Boswell, Dr Johnson's biographer, visited Chester in the 1770s and wrote "I was quite enchanted at Chester, so that I could with difficulty quit it". He was to return again, declaring that "Chester pleases my fancy more than any town I ever saw". Modern visitors will almost certainly share his enthusiasm.

Probably the best introduction to this compact little city is to join one of the frequent sightseeing tours conducted by

a Blue Badge guide. These take place every day, even Christmas Day, and leave from the **Chester Visitor Centre.** The Centre can also provide you with a wealth of information about the city, including a full calendar of events that range from the **Chester Regatta,** the oldest rowing races in the world and Chester Races, the oldest in Britain, to the Lord Mayor's Show in May and the Festival of Transport, featuring an amazing parade of vintage cars, in August.

Towering above the city centre is **Chester Cathedral**, a majestic building of weathered pink stone which in 1992 celebrated its 900th birthday. It was originally an Abbey and is one of very few to survive Henry VIII's closure of the monasteries in the 1540s. The cloisters are regarded as the finest in England and the monks' refectory is still serving food although nowadays it is refreshments and lunches for visitors.

The Rows, Chester

There's a fine 14th century shrine to St Werbergh, the princess/abbess who founded the first church on this site in Saxon times, and some intricately carved Quire stalls almost 800 years old which are reckoned to be the finest in Britain. It was at Chester

THE CROSS KEYS

Lower Bridge Street, Chester CH1 1RP
Tel: 01244 344460

Centrally situated in the heart of Chester, close to the city walls and the River Dee, is **The Cross Keys** public house. The prominent location makes this a popular haunt for city workers and is particularly convenient for shoppers and tourists. In a city full of attractive, historic buildings this striking red

brick and stone building was originally a number of cottages dating back to the early 18th century. A new frontage was added in the last century in an attempt to give the pub a more modern appearance. The result is an impressive feature of the street, especially when decorated with colourful hanging baskets through the summer.

Here visitors can enjoy a refreshing drink with the bar stocking a good range of beers and lagers, including two real ales. Food is also served daily, at lunch time and in the evening, from a regular printed menu supplemented by a specials board. The selection includes a classic range of bar meals and snacks with the home-made Hot Pot being a popular choice.

The meals are reasonably priced with no dish costing more than £4.95. There are dedicated non-smoking areas and children are welcome.

Your hosts are Angela and Graham who arrived at the Cross Keys in 1999 bringing with them several years experience in the catering trade. They are usually to be found serving behind the bar or preparing meals together with the chef, Natalie.

Cathedral, in 1742, that George Frederick Handel personally conducted rehearsals of his oratorio *"The Messiah"* before its first performance in Dublin: a copy of the score with annotations in his own hand remains on display.

Chester is famous for its outstanding range of museums. At the **Dewa Roman Experience** you can re-live the sights, sounds and even the smells of daily life in Roman Chester. A superb display of artifacts from Chester and elsewhere in the Roman Empire are on display and kids love dressing up in replica suits of Roman armour. "Dewa" incidentally is not a mis-spelling of the Roman name for Chester but is how Romans of the time pronounced "Deva". The **Grosvenor Museum** (free) has furnished period rooms, a Timeline gallery travelling back through the city's history, a gallery of paintings by local contemporary artists, crafts and other artifacts connected with Chester. The **Chester Heritage Centre** tells the city's story from the Civil War siege to the present day. **On The Air** broadcasting museum chronicles the world of radio and television from the pioneering days of BBC radio to satellite and digital TV, while the **Chester Toy & Doll Museum** is a nostalgic treasure-house of antique playthings. Recently re-opened after a major redevelopment, the Cheshire Military Museum which recounts the story of the county's military history using computers, tableaux and hands-on exhibits to present the soldier's life through the last 300 years.

Quite apart from its historical attractions, Chester is also one of the major shopping centres for the north west and north Wales. All the familiar High Street names are here, often housed in much more appealing buildings than they usually inhabit, along with a great number of specialist and antique shops. For a unique shopping experience, you must visit the world-famous, two-tiered galleries of shops under covered walkways known as **The Rows** which line both sides of Bridge Street. The Rows are an architectural one-off: no other medieval town has anything like them. Many

The Groves, Chester

THE SHREWSBURY ARMS

Warrington Road, Mickle Trafford,
Chester CH2 4EB
Tel: 01244 300309

A fine, traditional hostelry, **The Shrewsbury Arms** is located on the A56 Chester to Warrington road. In the 18th century this route was a notorious haunt of highwaymen, and in the spring of 1796, James Price and Thomas Brown held up and robbed a 15-year-old mail boy by the name of Peter Yoxall. The highwaymen were apprehended in Birmingham, were tried and condemned to death in Chester, and their corpses hung on gibbets in Mickle Trafford in a field which to

this day is known as 'Gibbets Field'.

By the time of the First World War, the inn formed part of the Earl of Shrewsbury's estate and on the break-up of the estate in 1917, it was sold to the West Cheshire Brewery as Lot 68, which also comprised land measuring in area "21 acres, 2 rods and 26 perches". Today, 'the Shrew' as it has fondly become known, is a picturesque pub, lovingly restored and closely resembling the traditional Cheshire Inn of yesteryear, with oak beams, flagstone floors, attractive rugs and comfy sofas, complementing a real log fire and making this the ideal place in which to enjoy a choice of 4 cask ales, 3 rotating guest ales and Boddingtons Bitter.

Outside, there is a spacious paved area with ample seating which provides views over open countryside, where patrons can enjoy the excellent food provided by mine hosts, Ron and Pam Crellin. They have been in the hospitality business locally for many

years and their philosophy is summed up by a note on the menu which promises "generous platefuls of delicious, home-cooked food complemented by old-fashioned service and values, and the attentiveness which will take you back to days when hospitality really meant something".

The extensive menu has something for everyone. There are snacks, sandwiches, filled jacket potatoes and light bites (such as Stir Fry Vegetables in a plum sauce served with rice) for those with smaller appetites. The enticing selection of main meals includes grills, fish, poultry, and traditional favourites such as Steak & Mushroom Pie. In addition, favourite specialities comprise mouthwatering dishes such as the famous home-made Lasagne, Seasonal Salads and "Shrew Wraps" such as Thai Chicken or Italian Vegetable. Whatever else you do, don't miss out on the superb desserts · mouthwatering Apple Pie or one of the Seasonal Desserts from the specials board.

On Mondays (except on Bank Holidays) and Tuesdays, customers are offered a special 3-course meal at an outstanding price. To enhance your meal, you will find a well-chosen selection of wines, with the added attraction of a special wine of the month, and you will appreciate the competitive prices.

Abbey Square, Chester

of the black and white, half-timbered frontages of The Rows, so typical of Chester and Cheshire, are actually Victorian restorations, but crafted so beautifully and faithfully that even experts can have difficulty distinguishing them from their 13th century originals.

Close by is the **Eastgate Clock**. It was erected in 1897 to celebrate Queen Victoria's Diamond Jubilee, a beautifully ornate construction which is probably the most photographed timepiece in the world. If *your* timing is right and you arrive hereabouts at 12 noon in the summer, you should see, and certainly hear, the **Town Crier** delivering some stentorian civic message.

A few steps bring you to Chester's famous City Walls which were originally built by the Romans to protect the fortress of Deva from attacks by pesky Celtic tribes. Nowadays, the two-mile long circuit – an easy, level promenade, provides thousands of visitors with some splendid views of the River Dee, of the

city's many glorious buildings and of the distant Welsh mountains. Here, during the summer months, you may come across Caius Julius Quartus, a Roman Legionary Officer in shining armour conducting a patrol around the fortress walls and helping to re-create the life and times of a front-line defender of the Empire. At one point, the wall runs alongside St John Street, which has a curious history. In Roman times it was the main thoroughfare between the fortress and the **Amphitheatre**, the largest ever uncovered in Britain, capable of seating 7000 spectators. During the Middle Ages however this highway was excavated and turned into a defensive ditch. Over the years, the ditch gradually filled up and by Elizabethan times St John Street was a proper street once again.

No visit to Chester would be complete without a trip to **Chester Zoo** on the northern edge of the city. Set in 110 acres of landscaped gardens, it's the largest zoo in Britain, caring for more than 5000 animals from some 500 different species. The Zoo also provides a refuge for many rare and endangered animals which breed freely in near-natural enclosures. What's more, it has the UK's largest elephant facility and is

THE BLACK DOG

Whitchurch Road, Waverton,
Chester CH3 7PB
Tel: 01244 335020 Fax: 01244 333030

Dating back to the early 1700s, **The Black Dog** is a delightful black and white building with an interior just as traditional as one could hope. Mine hosts, Linda and Philip Jeffreys, took over here in 2000 and have made the inn well-known for its excellent food and quality ales, including two regularly changing real ales. Food is available every lunchtime and evening and the huge menu offers an appetising choice of main meals, grills, dishes for smaller appetites, vegetarian options, salads, jacket potatoes, sandwiches and baguettes. A speciality of the house is a delicious oven roasted Lamb Henry and on Sundays there's a choice of home-made curries as an alternative to the Sunday roast. On Tuesdays the inn hosts a quiz to which all are welcome.

the only successful breeder of Asiatic elephants in this country – to date four youngsters have been born here. The Zoo has more than a mile of overhead railway providing a splendid bird's-eye view of the animals and the Roman Garden. Other attractions include the Rare Penguin Breeding Centre with windows enabling visitors to see the birds "flying" underwater; a Forest Zone with spacious homes for Buffy Headed Capuchin monkeys; and special enclosures for the black rhinos and red pandas. Offering more than enough interest for a full day out, the Zoo is open every day of the year except Christmas Day.

Around Chester

Tarvin

5 miles E of Chester off the A54 or A51

In the *Domesday Book* Tarvin is recorded as one of the larger manors in Cheshire and by the 1300s was the centre of an extensive parish. The present church was begun at this time and boasts the oldest surviving timber roof in Cheshire. The village came to prominence in the Civil War when Gen. Sir William Brereton made it his headquarters during the siege of Chester. In August 1644 there was fighting around the church and bullet marks can still be seen around

THE GEORGE & DRAGON

62 High Street, Tarvin, Cheshire CH3 8EE
Tel: 01829 741446
e-mail: melcorrall@aol.com

The George and Dragon is a fine Georgian building with a black-and-white exterior and an interior that is full of character. A unique feature is a huge, brightly painted mural depicting the village as it was in the 1800s. Five years ago the inn passed into the care of Mel and Karen Corrall. Regulars sing the praises of Karen's cooking which offers a choice of light snacks to 3-course meals and is served every lunchtime except Tuesday from 11.30am to 2pm, (Sundays, noon until 7pm). To accompany the appetising food there are 3 real ales, including a guest brew, and a wide choice of other thirst-quenchers. The inn hosts a karaoke session on the first Saturday of the month; with live music on the other Saturdays.

its west door. One of them even penetrated a brass by the chancel in memory of a former mayor of Chester and remained there for many years until a Victorian sightseer prised it out and made off with it. Just over a century after that skirmish, a major fire in 1752 destroyed much of Tarvin but one fortunate result of the conflagration was that the rebuilding of the village left it with an abundance of handsome Georgian buildings.

Gatesheath

8 miles SE of Chester off the A41

Occupying a Victorian farmhouse in Gatesheath, the **Country Centre** at New Russia Hall is a quite unique attraction. To begin with, there's the Orchard Paddock, a magnet for children with its appealing collection of farm animals and pets, swings and crazy golf. Anyone interested in flower arranging can watch the staff of the Dried Flower Workshop creating unique arrangements which can be bought, or you can buy all the materials to make your own. You can also see them creating painted plant pots, boxes and small pieces of furniture. There is a comprehensive display of greeting cards and gifts, a tea room, and Uncle Peter's Fudge Kitchen where you can try the superbly tasty fudge. Incidentally, the name New Russia Hall has nothing to do with Muscovy or the "Evil Empire" but comes from a corruption of "rushes" which once grew abundantly in the marshy ground nearby

STUART'S TABLE AT THE FARMER'S ARMS

Huxley Lane, Huxley, Cheshire CH3 9BG
Tel: 01829 781342 Fax: 01829 781794

The pretty little village of Huxley is hidden away in a maze of country lanes but for those who appreciate quality cuisine it's well worth seeking out for **Stuart's Table at the Farmer's Arms**. Stuart Turner used to work at this charming old inn close to the Shropshire Union Canal as the professional Chef and created the very popular restaurant area within the bar which he christened Stuart's Table. In July 2002 he took over as the licensee but happily he has continued to prepare his outstanding meals for the cosy, traditional (and non-smoking) restaurant.

Stuart's specialities are steaks, fish and chicken dishes and all meals are accompanied by olive oil baked potato served with crème fraiche, ratatouille, coleslaw, green salad, a mixed vinaigrette dressed salad and assorted breads. The breads are all home-baked and the delicious ice cream served in the desserts is also made on the premises. Food is served every lunchtime (noon until 3pm) and evening (6.30pm to 9.30pm) except for Sunday evening. On Saturdays everything is cooked on charcoal while at Sunday lunchtime a superb roast lunch is available. Stuart imports his own wines from 5 different countries so the wine list is extensive – and also very reasonably priced. If you prefer beer, there's a choice of 2 real ales along with a wide selection of popular brews. Children are welcome if eating; credit cards are accepted.

THE CALVELEY ARMS

Handley, nr Tattenhall, Chester CH3 9DT
Tel/Fax: 01829 770619
website: www.calveleyarms.co.uk

Runner-up in the *Cheshire Life* "Dining Pub of the Year, 2000-2001" and a constant presence in the *Good Pub Guide* for the last 7 years, **The Calveley Arms** has become one of the region's most popular eating places. It stands in the pleasant village of Handley, just off the A41 that links Chester and Whitchurch, only a 15-minute drive from Chester. First licensed in 1638 and still

retaining all its historic charm, the inn's smart black and white frontage promises much and the interior is as traditional as could be with a mass of wall and ceiling timbers, and a collection of jugs and pots, pictures, prints and ornaments. It all provides an atmospheric setting in which to enjoy the outstanding cooking prepared by and under the supervision of hosts Grant and Chrissy.

The food is a mega-attraction here, served every lunchtime and evening, and the 45 covers are soon taken so booking is always a good idea. The daily-changing specials board supplements a printed menu of unusual range and interest with fresh fish dishes something of a speciality of the house. Typical items on the main menu include hot avocado and Stilton (one of the best-selling dishes), Creole-style crab cakes, tarte flambée like they make it in Alsace, Madras-style curry, a classic moules à la crème and Breton chicken – grilled

chicken breast with a sauce of bacon, mushrooms and Cheddar cheese, then finished with cream. Sandwiches, baguettes and special salads are among the lighter options. Business clients can phone or fax their lunch order in advance and speedy service is guaranteed.

Four real ales – Boddington's and three guest brews – are popular orders at the bar and can be enjoyed in front of the open fire while taking part in a game of cribbage, dominoes or bar skittles. In fine weather, customers can enjoy their pint while watching or playing a game of boules in the rustic beer garden at the rear of the inn. Barbecues also take place here and also occasional al fresco music. Happy hour is 6-7pm, Monday to Friday, and on Sunday night a fun quiz begins at 9 o'clock. Mastercard and Visa credit cards are welcome; and the inn has its own car park.

Among the attractions in the vicinity are two famous castles: Beeston, built in the 13th century and partially destroyed by Cromwell; and 19th century Cholmondeley, a mock-medieval construction in a 30-acre garden.

and provided the basic materials for local basketmakers.

Tattenhall
8 miles SE of Chester off the A41

Tattenhall is a fine old village within sight of the twin castles of Beeston and Peckforton perched atop the Peckforton Hills. There are some attractive old houses and a Victorian church with a graveyard which gained notoriety during the 19th century because of the activities of a gang of grave-robbers. They lived in caves in the hills nearby and, once they had disposed of the bodies to medical gentlemen, used the empty coffins to store their booty from more conventional thieving. At that time Tattenhall was a busy little place. The Shropshire Union Canal passes close by and the village was served by two railway stations on different lines. Today, only one railway line survives (and no stations), the canal is used solely by pleasure craft, but the village is enjoying a new lease of life as a desirable community for people commuting to

Chester, a short drive away.

Small though it is, Tattenhall has entertained some distinguished visitors. No less a personage than King James I once stayed at The Bear & Ragged Staff. This attractive hostelry was then a modest one-storey building with a thatched roof but later became an important coaching inn, (the old mounting steps still stand outside). The pub's unusual name suggests some connection with the Earls of Warwick whose crest it is. (The first Earl supposedly strangled a bear, the second Earl clubbed a giant to death).

Saltney
2 miles SW of Chester off the A5104

For centuries, the ferry boat from Saltney on the south side of the River Dee provided a vital link for travellers from north Wales making their way to the great city of Chester. Modern roads put the ferrymen out of business a long time ago but their memory is honoured at the Saltney Ferry public house.

THE BELL PEPPER

21 Chester Street, Saltney, Chester, Cheshire CH4 8BL
Tel: 01244 683708

The little village of Saltney is well worth seeking out to sample Bob Teasdale's excellent cooking at **The Bell Pepper**. During the day it's a café/tea room offering home-made scones, cakes, soup, All Day Breakfasts, Light Bites, sandwiches and daily specials. On Thursday, Friday and Saturday evenings the Bell Pepper becomes a bistro serving an à la carte international cuisine – Tuscan-style roasted peppers as your starter perhaps, with a main course of Griddled Chicken Breast with a warm Chinese "millionaire" sauce, and finishing with one of Bob's famous fresh desserts. Feel free to bring your own wine – and there's no corkage charge! Bob is also happy to open on other nights for groups of 10 people or more.

GROSVENOR GARDEN CENTRE

Wrexham Road, Belgrave,
Chester CH4 9EB
Tel: 01244 625200 Fax: 01244 625210
e-mail: info@grosvenorgardencentre.co.uk
website:
www.grosvenorgardencentre.co.uk

Voted UK Garden Centre of the Year 2002 by the Garden Centre Association, Grosvenor Garden Centre was already well-known as Chester's premier garden centre. Established more than 20 years ago, the centre extends over fourteen acres, all of them bursting with ideas for your garden and house. There is a wonderful display of plants, trees, shrubs, herbaceous, alpines and bedding. The five-

year no quibble guarantee on hardy container-grown plants is a clear indication of Grosvenor's confidence in the quality of their plants. They also offer a free potting-up service · just choose your plants and the pots and they do the work for you. Not only will they plant up your pots for you "Grosvenor Gardening Solutions" provides a full Garden Maintenance and Landscaping service designed to solve all your gardening problems in a professional and efficient way.

Garden accessories on display include garden lighting and furniture, water fountains, stoneware and wind chimes and Grosvenor offers what is probably the largest range of containers to be found in the area. Tubs, pots, troughs, made of terracotta, stone, wood, ceramics and plastic

(including some Ali Baba-sized terracotta pots) · customers are really spoilt for choice. The centre also has a superior and stylish giftware department with the latest designs from the continent, a wonderful floristry area and a books and crafts department.

Other facilities include aquatic fish and plants, Canadian spas, log cabins, antique garden shop, conservatories, sheds and greenhouses, and the best selection of tents and camping equipment to be found for miles.

A popular amenity is the licensed Blue Café which offers breakfast, lunches and teas and the delicious locally-made Snugberry range of Jersey milk ice creams. Customers can enjoy their meals in the outdoor seating area overlooking the new planteria with its stunning array of planted containers.

Grosvenor has its own potter-in-residence, Ed Williams, whose beautiful pieces are perfect for birthday presents, anniversaries or just to spoil yourself! He will also accept commissions so that you can get exactly what you want · and at very affordable prices. The pottery also offers lessons · an ideal way to keep your kids amused while you explore the Centre at leisure.

Belgrave

4 miles S of Chester on the B5445

Belgrave is hardly large enough to qualify as a hamlet but it has given its name to the London area known as Belgravia. Both are owned by the Duke of Westminster, Britain's richest landowner, whose family home, Eaton Hall, stands beside the River Dee a couple of miles west of the village. The Duke's family, the Grosvenors, were well established in Cheshire by the 1300s but it was acquisition by marriage of a large estate to the west of London that brought them huge riches. As London expanded westwards during the 18th and 19th century, their once rural estate was developed into elegant squares and broad boulevards, many with names reflecting the Duke's Cheshire connections – Eaton Square, Eccleston Square, Grosvenor Place and Chester Row.

The Grosvenor's monstrous Victorian mansion suffered badly when it was occupied by the military during the Second World War. In the 1970s it was demolished and replaced by a more modest, concrete structure which has divided architectural opinion as to its merits – one writer described it "as modern as a 1970s airline terminal". The house is not open to the public but its gardens occasionally are.

The Wirral

Two Old English words meaning heathland covered with bog myrtle gave The Wirral its name and well into modern times it was a byword for a desolate place. The 14th century author of "Sir Gawayne and the Green Knight" writes of

"The wilderness of Wirral:
few lived there
Who loved with a good heart
either God or man".

The Wirral's inhabitants were infamous for preying on the shipwrecks tossed on to its marshy coastline by gales sweeping off the Irish Sea. The 19th century development of shipbuilding at

BIRKENHEAD PARK

Birkenhead, The Wirral
Tel: 0151 652 5197

Designed by Joseph Paxton, **Birkenhead Park** opened in 1847. It was the first publicly fimded park in the world and was the model for Central Park in New York.

There are two large ornamental lakes and many interesting architectural features including a magnificent Grand Entrance Arch, a swiss Bridge, a Romanesque Boathouse and six impressive period lodges.

The Park is undergoing a 1.5 million pound restoration programme, that over the next five

years will see it transformed back to its former glory. Situated in Birkenhead off the A553, or Merseyrail to Park Station.

Birkenhead brought industry on a large scale to the Mersey shore but also an influx of prosperous Liverpool commuters who colonised the villages of the Caldy and Grange Hills and transformed the former wilderness into a leafy suburbia. The 1974 Local Government changes handed two thirds of The Wirral to Merseyside leaving Cheshire with by far the most attractive third, the southern and western parts alongside the River Dee. Tourism officials now refer to The Wirral as the "Leisure Peninsula", a fair description of this appealing and comparatively little-known area. One of its major attractions is **Ness Gardens,** a 64-acre tract of superbly landscaped gardens on the banks of the River Dee. The gardens are run by the University of Liverpool as an Environmental and Horticultural Research Station and are planned to provide magnificent displays all year round. There are children's play and picnic areas, well-marked interest trails, and licensed refreshment rooms.

Neston

11 miles NW of Chester off the A540

Right up until the early 19th century, Neston was the most significant town in The Wirral, one of a string of small ports along the River Dee. In Tudor times, Neston had been one of the main embarkation points for travellers to Ireland but the silting up of the river was so swift and inexorable that by the time the New Quay, begun in 1545, was completed, it had became useless. Visiting Neston in the late 1700s, Anna Seward described the little town set on a hill overlooking the Dee Estuary as "a nest from the storm of the ocean".

Parkgate

12 miles NW of Chester via the A540 and B5134

After Neston port became unusable, maritime traffic moved along the Dee Estuary to Parkgate which, as the new gateway to Ireland, saw some notable

THE ROYAL OAK

23 Town Lane, Little Neston, South Wirral, Cheshire CH64 4DE
Tel: 0151 336 2364 Fax: 0151 336 5974
e-mail: donnataylor110@msn.co
website: www.theroyaloak@hscali.com

The **Royal Oak** is a homely and inviting place where landlords Barry and Donna offer warm and genuine hospitality. The bars have a very traditional look, with polished wood and brass, and the ales on offer include Cain's real ale. The food is excellent with plenty of choice from a main menu and a range of snacks. On Monday evenings authentic Mexican cuisine is served and Thai curry on Thursday. Booking is strongly recommended. Children have their own Little Oaks menu and an outside play area with a bouncy castle in summer. There's also a pool table, beer garden, live performers on Friday and a quiz on Sunday.

THE MARSH CAT RESTAURANT

1 Mostyn Square, Parkgate,
South Wirral CH64 6SL
Tel: 0151 336 1963 Fax: 0151 336 4998
e-mail: info@Marshcat.com
website: www.Marshcat.com

The superb views across the Dee estuary would in themselves make a visit to **The Marsh Cat** worthwhile but it is the outstanding cuisine served here that has attracted rave reviews. Chef Phil, his wife Jenny and business partner Andy, offer regularly changing menus that include a wide variety of dishes – Smoked Haddock Tagliatelle, perhaps, as a starter; Teriyaki Duck or Lemon Sole Crème Pois amongst the main dishes; while the vegetarian choices might include a tasty Vienamese Vegetable Curry. The Marsh Cat is open for lunch and dinner every day and such is its popularity bookings are advisable

visitors. John Wesley, who made regular trips to Ireland, preached here while waiting for a favourable wind, and George Frederick Handel returned via Parkgate after conducting the very first performance of "*The Messiah*" in Dublin. J.M.W. Turner came to sketch the lovely view across to the Flintshire hills. A little later, Parkgate enjoyed a brief spell as a fashionable spa. Lord Nelson's mistress, Lady Hamilton (who was born at nearby Ness where you can still see the family home, Swan Cottage) took the waters here in an effort to cure an unfortunate skin disease. Another visitor was Mrs Fitzherbert, already secretly

THE FOX & HOUNDS

Barnston Village, Wirral CH61 1BW
Tel: 0151 648 7685 / 1323
Fax: 0151 648 0872
website: www.the-fox-hounds.co.uk

Offering a wide choice of well kept real ales, which change regularly, **The Fox & Hounds** is a charming traditional hostelry with lots of character and a welcoming atmosphere. The three separate rooms, lounge, old bar and snug, have flagstone or wooden floors, and the walls are hung with interesting old prints of the area and memorabilia.

The inn is well known for its superb home-style pub food which is always freshly cooked, delicious and provides good value for money. There's always a selection of delicious desserts and on Sundays traditional roasts are served.

Food is available at lunchtime only from noon until 2pm and, such is the popularity of the cuisine, booking ahead is strongly advised. The licensee of the Fox & Hounds, Ralph Leech, can offer facilities for corporate lunches and parties of every kind. Ralph also has the Ship Hotel in Parkgate, an informal hotel with magnificent views, open fires and flagstone floors. The restaurant has an excellent reputation for its good food and fine wine and bar snacks are available lunchtimes and evenings. There are 26 letting rooms, all with private bathroom and every amenity. The Jug & Bottle in nearby Heswall also offers accommodation and has a very popular Tapas restaurant, called La Casa Montana.

At all three properties customers can be assured of a warm welcome, well-tended ales and top quality food.

THE SHIPPONS

8a Thingwall Road, Irby, Wirral CH61 3UA
Tel: 0151 648 0449 Fax: 0151 648 0736
e-mail: maggiemayhem@aol.co.uk

In 1994, where **The Shippons** now stands, the site was occupied by a group of cowhouses. The owner, Mr S. D. Thompson, completely demolished them and used the

desserts of the day. To accompany your meal there's a carefully chosen selection of wines from around the world.

If you're visiting on a Wednesday evening, there's a quiz that starts at 9.30pm and Shirley occasionally arranges a themed "Dress up night". The Shippons has a pleasant patio area at the rear and ample off road parking space. Credit cards are welcome, apart from American Express and Diners.

weathered old bricks to construct the present building, a delightful hostelry with oodles of character and charm. His joint licensee Shirley Arnold, has wide experience in the hospitality business, and has been running The Shippons since the day it opened. The pub is open all day, every day, with at least four real ales on tap – Thwaites, Bomber, Thoroughbred and a rotating guest ale as well as a wide range of all the popular pub beverages.

The pub enjoys a good reputation for its food which is available every lunchtime from noon until 2.30pm. The regular menu offers an appetising choice of light meals such as jacket potatoes, toastie sandwiches, and baguettes which are freshly baked to order. Main courses include old favourites such as Braised Steak & Onions, Liver & Onions, and Battered Haddock, with Steak & Kidney Pie and a really spicy Chilli con Carne as specialities of the house. There are vegetarian options such as Mushroom and Stilton Bake as well as a selection of healthy salads. The choice is extended by daily specials listed on the blackboard along with

JUG & BOTTLE

Mount Avenue, Heswall, Wirral,
Cheshire CH60 4RH
Tel: 0151 342 5535 Fax: 0151 342 4327
Restaurant: 0151 342 8578
website: www.the-jugandbottle.co.uk

One of the many attractions of the **Jug & Bottle** is the superb view it enjoys across the Dee Estuary to the skyline of Liverpool with its two soaring cathedrals. Ideally located for exploring the Wirral, the Jug & Bottle boasts an outstanding tapas restaurant, La Casa Montana, which offers an extensive choice of authentic Spanish dishes, including some wonderful paellas. Fine wines and excellent service add to the pleasure of eating here. There's also a friendly bar which serves hot and cold food at lunchtime. Recently completely refurbished, the hotel has 5 attractively furnished guest bedrooms, all with private bathrooms, colour Sky TV, and hospitality tray.

married to the Prince Regent, later George IV. When Holyhead developed into the main gateway to Ireland, Parkgate's days as a port and watering-place were numbered. But with fine Georgian houses lining the promenade, this attractive little place still retains the atmosphere of a gracious spa town.

Heswall
14 miles NW of Chester on the A540

Set on a steep hillside, Heswall was an important port before the silting up of the River Dee. After decades of decline, the town flourished again as a choice

THE COUNTRY MOUSE RESTAURANT

Brimstage Hall, Brimstage, The Wirral,
CH63 6JA
Tel: 0151 342 5382

The Country Mouse Restaurant is located in the courtyard of Brimstage Hall, a medieval pele that dates back to the 12 th century and has connections with Oliver Cromwell.

The restaurant occupies a former barn and is a delightful place, full of charm and character. It's owned and run by Val and Joe, with Val in charge of the cooking. Val was taught to bake by her father and can trace her baking ancestors back five generations. The delicious aroma of freshly-baked scones drifts pleasantly around the room and everything on the menu is prepared on the premises.

Val's superb cakes, some made to old family recipes, and wonderful feather-light meringues are particularly popular as are her home-made soups and hot lunches served with fresh country vegetables. In summer, there's a good choice of salads and on Sundays a light menu is available as an alternative to the superb traditional Sunday lunch for which booking is strongly recommended. The non-smoking restaurant is licensed and has an excellent wine list. Children are welcome and have their own menu.

In good weather, customers can enjoy their refreshments on the lawns surrounding the medieval tower and then wander around the fascinating craft and speciality shops occupying other buildings around the courtyard.

SEVEN STARS

Church Road, Thornton Hough, Wirral,
Cheshire CH63 1JW
Tel/Fax: 0151 336 4574
e-mail: tina.hignett@talk21.com
website: www.sevenstarsinn.net

The huge village green at Thornton Hough, covering some 14 acres and surrounded by half-timbered black and white houses, is one of the most picturesque spots in Cheshire. Overlooking this lovely green is the **Seven Stars** inn, built in the 1850s to provide light refreshment for travellers using the toll bridge nearby and still offering traditional hospitality more than a century and a quarter later. With its decorative beams, inglenook fireplace, its collection of antique water jugs

and absence of juke boxes or fruit machines, the Seven Stars is the epitome of the traditional English pub – except that the food is much better here! So much better in fact that booking ahead is advisable at all times.

At lunchtime customers can choose either from the regular menu or the specials board; in the evenings from the à la carte menu or from a different selection of specials. The appetising cuisine includes both traditional English and international dishes. Amongst the starters, for example, you might find a Prawn Risotto topped with deep fried cabbage edged by a lemon grass dressing or the Chef's Black Pudding set upon a smoked bacon bubble and squeak masked by an apricot and thyme jus. Main courses might offer a chargrilled salmon and sea bass ratatouille of vegetables edged by a red pepper coulis or a breast of

chicken stuffed with haggis wrapped in bacon served with glava sauce. Vegetarians and pasta lovers are well-catered for – spinach and red pepper lasagne or a cheese porcini ravioli perhaps. The delicious desserts include a contemporary style Cranachan – toasted oats, whiskey and raspberries folded into a light parfait – and a traditional egg custard served with cinnamon ice cream. To accompany your meal there's a good selection of wines by the bottle or glass, 5 real ales and a wide choice of other popular beverages. The non-smoking restaurant is open for lunch between noon and 2pm, Monday to Saturday; evenings between 6pm and 9.30pm, Tuesday to Saturday; and from noon until 6pm on Sunday. Children are welcome and all major credit cards accepted.

Mine host at the Seven Stars is Christina Hignett who used to work here as a waitress before taking over in January 2000. She has carried out a comprehensive overhaul of the décor while retaining the welcoming traditional atmosphere of this charming old inn. If you are anywhere in the neighbourhood of Thornton Hough, the Seven Stars provides an eating experience that should definitely not be missed.

retreat for Liverpool commuters following the opening of the railway tunnel under the Mersey in 1888. If you take the road down to the beach from the town centre there are outstanding views across the Dee estuary to the hills of Wales.

Brimstage
14 miles NW of Chester via M53 and A5137

The most striking building in this tiny hamlet is **Brimstage Hall,** a medieval pele, or fortified tower. It's not known why such a tower, more appropriate to the lawless border regions, should have been built in peaceful Cheshire. Another mystery is the date of its construction – estimates range from 1175 to 1350 and a raft of human bones found at the bottom of a long-forgotten well in 1957 failed to resolve any of these questions. There is another puzzle too: could the stone carving of a smirking domestic cat in the old chapel (now a gift shop) be the original of Lewis Carroll's "Cheshire Cat" which had a notorious habit of disappearing leaving only its smile behind? Today, the old courtyard is home to a cluster of craft and speciality shops, and an excellent tea room and restaurant, The Country Mouse (see entry page 233).

Thornton Hough
14 miles NW of Chester via the A540 and B5136

The huge village green at Thornton Hough, covering some 14 acres and surrounded by half-timbered black and white houses, was one of the most picturesque spots in Cheshire until it was relocated to Merseyside in 1974. Much of the village was built by Lord Leverhulme after he established his soap factory at Port Sunlight a few miles to the north and his grandson lives at Thornton Manor (private). The village boasts two churches, one of which has no fewer than 5 clocks – the fifth was installed by Joseph Hirst, a Yorkshire mill owner who also built houses here and wished to see a church clock from his bedroom window.

West Kirby
20 miles NW of Chester on the A540

Set beside the Dee estuary and looking across to the Welsh mountains, West Kirby was just a small fishing village until the railway link with Liverpool was established in the 1880s. Today, it's a bustling seaside town with some 28,000 inhabitants. A big attraction here is the **West Kirby Marine Lake**, a 52-acre man-made saltwater lake. With a maximum depth of 5 feet it offers a degree of safety unobtainable on the open sea. Courses in sailing, windsurfing and canoeing are available at the Wirral Sailing Centre.

West Kirby is well-known to birdwatchers and naturalists because of the **Hilbre Islands,** part-time islands that can be reached at low tide across Dee Sands. Permits (free) from the Wirral Borough Council are required to

The Farmers Arms

Hillbark Road, Frankby, Wirral CH48 1NJ
Tel: 0151 641 0159 Fax: 0151 641 0182
e-mail: charlie-farmer@tiscali.co.uk

Not many British inns have had a book written about their history but **The Farmers Arms** in Frankby certainly has. The book records the building of the inn in 1866 and how the cellar, which could contain nine barrels, was cut out of the solid rock. It had just two rooms, one on each side of the porch, which were known respectively as the Front Parlour and the Spit and Sawdust. Here, customers could enjoy their Birkenhead Brewery's "Peerless" bottled ales and stout – "Exquisite on the palate, elegant on the table" – with the most expensive

brews retailing at 2d (0.83p) a pint. The book also lists all the tenants and managers, one of whom was landlord here for 35 years.

Today's hosts at the Farmers Arms, Charlie and Jackie, have some way to go to beat that record (they took over in 1997) but Charlie has many years experience in the hospitality business and together they have made the inn one of the most popular in the Wirral. It has a spacious and very attractive beer garden where on summer weekends all day barbecues are held – weather permitting. Inside, the bars are full of charm and character, with lots of old beams and vintage memorabilia. Charlie and Jackie keep their

customers well entertained with a Folk Night on Monday, a quiz on Tuesday, a duo or solo artist on Wednesday, a DJ or singer on Saturday, and live entertainment on Sunday. Two big television screens are available for major sporting events.

The well-maintained ales on tap at the Farmers include 3 real ales – Old Speckled Hen, Flowers IPA and Cains – along with Whitbread Mild, Heineken and Heineken Export, Stella, cider and stouts. A major attraction here is the wholesome food on offer every lunchtime between noon and 2.30pm. All the meals are freshly prepared and range from light bites like potato wedges, jacket potatoes, hot filled baguettes and sandwiches to hearty meals such as sirloin steak, curries and fish dishes. Specialities of the house include Pork Curry and a tasty Lamb Stew served with red cabbage and bread and butter. Children are welcome if eating (they have their own choice of "Kids Stuff"); credit cards are accepted apart from American Express and Diners.

The inn is open all day, every day, and Charlie and Jackie are happy to cater for parties and functions of every kind and can offer full buffet facilities to suit all tastes.

Oyster Catchers, Hilbre Islands

booking office still has a pile of pre-decimal change at the ready, including silver sixpences, half-crowns and eight-sided threepenny pieces.

Birkenhead

20 miles NW of Chester off the M53

visit the main island where there is a resident warden. Two smaller islands, Middle Eye and the tiny Little Eye, do not require permits. The latter is notable for its impressive number of wader roosts.

West Kirby is also the starting point for the **Wirral Way**, a 12 mile long linear nature reserve and country park created mostly from the trackbed of the old West Kirby to Hooton railway. When it was opened in 1973 it was one of the first Country Parks in Britain. The local council has also produced a series of circular walks based around the former stations along the line. One of these, **Hadlow Road Station**, a short distance from the centre of Willaston, is especially interesting. The station hasn't seen a train since 1962 but everything here is spick and span, the signal box and ticket office apparently ready for action, a trolley laden with milk churns waiting on the platform. Restored to appear as it would have been on a typical day in 1952, the station's

If you were asked "Where is the largest group of Grade I listed buildings in England?", Birkenhead would probably not be your first guess. But you can find these buildings in Hamilton Square where you'll also find the **Old Town Hall**, although that only merits a Grade II rating. It now houses an exhibition telling the story of the famous Cammell Laird shipyard, a model of the Woodside area in 1934 when King George V opened the Queensway road tunnel under the Mersey, and a collection of delightful Della Robbia pottery. Also within the Town Hall are an art gallery, theatre, cinema and concert hall.

The **Birkenhead Heritage Trail** guides visitors around the town's various attractions and includes trips on a genuine Hong Kong tram and a beautifully restored Birkenhead tram of 1901. The trail takes in the Shore Road Pumping Station with its "Giant Grasshopper" steam pump. It was one of several used to extract water from the Mersey railway tunnel – Europe's very

THE QUEENS ARMS

Storeton Road, Oxton Village,
Birkenhead CH43 5TL
Tel: 0151 652 2053 Fax: 0151 652 2133
e-mail: d5cjh@aol.com

It was way back in 1728 that **The Queens Arms** began life as a coaching inn and more than two and a half centuries later it is still flourishing. As we go to press, landlords Christopher and Julie Hughes are completing a comprehensive refurbishment of the old inn which retains its traditional character. A major attraction at the Queens Arms is Christine's cooking – appetizing, honest to

goodness mostly traditional fare at value for money prices. The regular menu offers starters such as soup of the day served with warmed ciabatta bread, crispy chicken goujons with a barbecue sauce or a Combo for Two of onion rings, chicken strips, mushrooms, potato wedges and garlic bread.

Amongst the main courses are old favourites such as fish & chips or steak & mushroom pudding, as well as more recent arrivals like chicken tikka masala and home made lasagne. An All Day Breakfast is available and grills include rump or gammon steaks and a Mighty Mix Grill designed to satisfy a Desperate Dan size appetite. For those with lighter appetites there's a choice of sandwiches served deep filled on warm ciabatta bread. In addition to the printed menu, Christine also offers a selection of daily specials and some delicious desserts such as deepfilled apple pie or hot sponge &

custard. On Sundays, a beautiful Sunday lunch is served all day with a choice of lamb, beef or pork roast – booking ahead is strongly recommended. Food is available every day from noon until 7pm; children are welcome, and there are non-smoking areas. There are regular special offers on meals (just call for details) and all major credit cards except American Express and Diners are welcome.

The Queens Arms is open all day, every day for ale with Bass as the permanent real ale on tap along with another rotating guest ale. Other beverages on offer include Boddingtons, Tetley Smooth, Heineken, Heineken Export, Stella, Labatts, Strongbow, regular and extra cold Guinness. In good weather, customers can enjoy their drinks in the secure and well-tended beer garden at the rear of the inn. Two off road parking areas provide plenty of parking space.

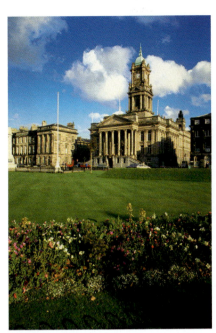
Hamilton Square, Birkenhead

Birkenhead Park, to the east of the town centre, is a remarkable example of an early Victorian urban park with 2 lakes, rockery, Swiss bridge and formal gardens. This vast parkland was designed by Sir Joseph Paxton, architect of London's Crystal Palace, who also designed the spectacular main entrance which is modelled on the Temple of Illysus in Athens. Interestingly, it became the model for an even more famous park – Central Park in New York.

Just out of town is the purpose-built **Williamson Art Gallery & Museum** which exhibits a wealth of local and maritime history, a permanent display of Victorian oil paintings, tapestries by Lee and English watercolours, and also hosts a full programme of temporary exhibitions.

first underwater rail tunnel. Other attractions along the trail include an Edwardian Street scene display, a unique historic transport collection and a visit to the Pacific Road Arts and Exhibition Centre. Just along from Pacific Road is Egerton Bridge which offers a bird's eye view over the docklands. Moored alongside East Float Dock Road are two historic warships, now museums. Both the frigate HMS Plymouth and the submarine HMS Onyx served during the Falklands War and are now preserved as they were in the 1980s. Also on display is a German U-boat, U534, whose sinking marked the end of the Battle of the Atlantic in May 1945. The submarine was recovered after lying 50 years on the seabed.

Bebington
12 miles NW of Chester off the A41

Much of the Wirral's Merseyside is heavily industrialised but a dramatic exception is **Port Sunlight** near Bebington. This model village was created in 1888 by William Hesketh Lever, later 1st Viscount Leverhulme, to house the workers in his soap factory and was named after his most famous product, Sunlight Soap. Leverhulme wanted to provide "a new Arcadia, ventilated and drained on the most scientific principles". Some thirty architects were employed to create the individually designed rows of rustic

Lady Lever Art Gallery, Port Sunlight

cottages and the whole village is now a Conservation Area. The history of the village and its community is explored at the Port Sunlight Heritage Centre where there are scale models of the village, a Victorian port and Sunlight House, original plans for the building and displays of period advertising and soap packaging. A major attraction is the **Lady Lever Art Gallery** which houses a magnificent collection of pre-Raphaelite paintings by Millais and Rosetti, portraits by Gainsborough and Reynolds, dramatic landscapes by Turner and Constable, an impressive Wedgwood collection and some superb pieces of 18th century furniture. The gallery also has a gift shop and a popular tea room, the Lady Lever Café.

Eastham

10 miles NW of Chester off the A41

Eastham Woods Country Park (also now in Merseyside) is a 76 acre oasis of countryside amidst industrial Merseyside

and enjoys considerable status amongst bird-watchers as one of few northern woodlands with all three species of native woodpecker in residence. Just a mile or so from the Park is Eastham village, another little oasis with a church and old houses grouped around the village green. The venerable yew tree in the churchyard is reputed to be the oldest in England.

The Welsh Borders

Awake or asleep, the medieval Lords of the Marches made sure their swords were close at hand. At any time, a band of wild-haired Welshmen might rush down from the hills to attack the hated Normans who had dispossessed them of their land. A thousand years earlier their enemies had been the Romans and the centuries-old struggle along the Marches would only end when one of their own people, Henry Tudor, defeated Richard III in 1485 and ascended the throne as Henry VII.

Conflict was to flare up again during the Civil War when the Welsh supported the Royalist forces against mainly Parliamentary Cheshire but nowadays the valley of the Dee is a peaceful and picturesque area, and nowhere more so than around Farndon on the Denbighshire border.

Farndon

7 miles S of Chester off the B5130

Built on a hillside overlooking the River
Dee, Farndon is literally a stone's throw
from Wales. Most travellers agree that
the best approach to the principality is
by way of this little town and its ancient
bridge. Records show that building of
the bridge began in 1345 and it is one of
only two surviving medieval bridges in
the county, the other being in Chester.
From Farndon's bridge, riverside walks
by the Dee extend almost up to its
partner in Chester. During the Civil
War, Farndon's strategic position
between Royalist North Wales and
parliamentarian Cheshire led to many
skirmishes here. Those stirring events
are colourfully depicted in a stained
glass window in the church, although
only the Royalist heroes are included.

One Farndon man who deserves a
memorial of some kind but doesn't have
one is John Speed, the famous
cartographer, who was born here in
1542. He followed his father's trade as a
tailor, married and had 18 children, and
was nearly 50 before he was able to
devote himself full time to researching
and producing his beautifully drawn
maps. Fortunately, he lived to the age of
87 and his fifty-four Maps of England
and Wales were the first really accurate
ones to be published.

THE FARNDON ARMS

High Street, Farndon, Cheshire CH3 7PU
Tel: 01829 270570 Fax: 01829 271428
e-mail: beerseller.farndonarms.virgin.net
website: www.farndonarms.com

The Farndon Arms is a ravishing black and
white building, decked in summer with huge
hanging baskets of colourful flowers. Parts of
this lovely old building date back to the
1700s when it was a coaching inn on the
London to Anglesey route.

Travellers would pause here for
refreshment before their coach
resumed its journey along the High
Street, crossed the ancient bridge
over the River Dee and found itself
in Wales. Today, this outstanding
inn is owned and run by Keith and
Beryl and their son Martin who is
the 5th generation of his family to
be licensees.

Martin is the chef and his menus
offer a remarkable range of old
favourites along with innovative
newcomers: steaks of "I'll never

manage this" proportions, or simple bangers
and mash; an authentic black pudding, or
melted goat's cheese on a bed of French leaf
under a tomato fondue. Food is available
every day from opening time until 10pm and
the inn is a member of Hi-Life Diners Club
whose members enjoy a "Two meals for the
price of one" deal.

The Farndon Arms is a great place to eat,
but also a great place to stay. There are 7
comfortable en suite guest bedrooms, all
with a 3 diamond rating from the English
Tourist Board.

THE ROYAL OAK

Higher Kinnerton, Flintshire CH4 9BE
Tel: 01244 660871 Fax: 01244 661395

Lying just over the Welsh border in the village of Higher Kinnerton, **The Royal Oak** is one of the oldest and most picturesque coaching inns in north Wales. Dating back to around 1630, the inn boasts a resident ghost and stands where one of the most famous trees in the country once towered. Here in September 1644 King Charles I, fleeing from Cromwell's troops after his defeat at Chester, evaded his pursuers by hiding amidst the branches of the Kinnerton Oak. Derek Thompson, an accomplished artist who has run the Royal Oak for more than ten years,

together with his wife Lee, has inscribed this romantic tale around the walls of the old beamed snug. It's just one of the many charming features here, along with the inglenook crackling with log fires and the fascinating collection of old water jugs, plates and potties.

The inn is also renowned for its restaurant, a distinctive 1993 building where, it's generally agreed, you'll find the best food in the area. A team of top chefs create superb dishes using top quality ingredients such as salmon from the nearby River Dee, trout, local game and selected steak. And if you are just looking for a light meal, then the bar menu offers an excellent choice of filled baguettes or jacket potatoes, ploughmans and sandwiches.

To accompany your meal, there's a wide selection of beers, including 5 real ales, an outstanding wine list and one of the best selections of Irish malts in the country. Food is available every lunchtime (noon to 2.30pm) and evening (6.30pm to 9.30pm; from 5.30pm on Saturday); and from noon to 9.30pm on Sunday. The restaurant is open lunchtimes and evenings 7 days a week - booking is strongly recommended.

With its wonderfully traditional atmosphere, friendly staff and outstanding fare, the Royal Oak is a truly exceptional hidden place, although only a mere six miles from the centre of Chester.

Higher Kinnerton

8 miles SW of Chester off the A55/A5104

One of the oldest and most picturesque coaching inns in north Wales, the Royal Oak also boasts a resident ghost and stands where one of the most famous trees in the country once towered. Here in September 1644 King Charles I, fleeing Cromwell's troops after his defeat at Chester, evaded his pursuers by hiding amidst the branches of the Kinnerton Oak. Derek Thompson, an accomplished artist who runs the Royal Oak together with his wife Lee, has inscribed this romantic tale around the walls of the old beamed snug. It's just one of the many charming features here, along with the inglenook crackling with log fires and the fascinating collection of old pots and water jugs.

Malpas

14 miles S of Chester on the B5069

With its charming black and white cottages and elegant Georgian houses Malpas is one of the most delightful old villages in Cheshire though its Norman-French name implies that it once lay in difficult terrain – "mal passage". Of the Norman castle that once protected this hill-top border town only a grassy mound behind the red sandstone church survives. Approached through 18th century gates attributed to Vanbrugh, **St Oswald's Church** is lavishly decorated with a striking array of gargoyles but is most notable for the splendour of its interior. The nave roof is brilliant with gilded bosses and winged angels, all created around 1480, and there are two magnificent chapels separated from the nave by delicately carved screens. The Brereton chapel dates from 1522 and contains an alabaster effigy of Sir Randal Brereton, in the armour of a medieval knight, together with his lady. Across the aisle, the Cholmondeley chapel commemorates Sir Hugh Cholmondeley who died in 1605.

The Cholmondeley family owned huge estates around Malpas and it was they

FOX & HOUNDS

Malpas Road, Tilston, Malpas,
Cheshire SY14 7HH
Tel: 01829 250967

The peaceful and picturesque little village of Tilston is fortunate in having a fine old hostelry in the **Fox & Hounds.** The pub had been closed for 2 years before Jan and Mark Parry arrived here in March 2002. In a short time they have attracted a loyal clientele and prove popular with visitors. Jan is an accomplished cook and offers an inviting menu of Pub Grub – and one night a week the inn hosts a themed evening. Food is available every evening from 5pm until 9pm, and at

lunchtimes Wednesday, Sunday and Bank Holidays between noon and 2.30pm. There's a large beer garden at the rear where barbecues are held in summer. Children are welcome; credit cards are not accepted.

who built the town's attractive old almshouses and a school in the 18th century. They lived at Cholmondeley Castle, a few miles to the north-east. The Gothic-style castle is not open to the public but the 800 acres of **Cholmondeley Castle Garden** are. The gardens are planted with a variety of acid-loving plants including rhododendrons, hydrangeas, magnolias, camellias, dogwoods, mahonias and viburnums. There's a lovely Temple Garden with a rockery, lake and islands, and a Silver Garden planted with distinctive silver-leafed plants as a commemoration of Elizabeth II's Silver Jubilee.

Rossett
6 miles S of Chester off the A483

In Rossett, a pleasant village beside the River Alyn, and about a mile across the border into north Wales, is The Golden Grove inn. Here, history strikes as an almost tangible force when you enter the inn's portals for the first time. The entrance and reception area of what is now the bar, (including a tiny snug bar) was the original 13th century inn in its entirety. The low oak beams and ornate carved dark wood bar were additions during the 1600s. There are three dates carved into the intricate workings of the bar, but they are well hidden unless you know where to look. Naturally, such an ancient establishment has its own ghost, one James Clarke who actually expired at the inn on April 21st, 1880. James was generally believed to be the landlady's lover; certainly, she had him buried in the courtyard and erected a headstone to his memory.

TOURIST INFORMATION CENTRES

CHESHIRE

ALTRINCHAM

20 Stamford New Road
Altrincham
Cheshire
WA14 1EJ
Tel: 0161 912 5931
Fax: 0161 941 7089
e-mail: tic@trafford.gov.uk

CHESTER (NORTHGATE STREET)

Town Hall
Northgate Street
Chester
Cheshire
CH1 2HJ
Tel: 01244 402111
Fax: 01244 400420
e-mail: tis@chestercc.gov.uk
website: www.chestercc.gov.uk

CHESTER (VICARS LANE)

Chester Visitor Centre
Vicars Lane
Chester
Cheshire
CH1 1QX
Tel: 01244 402111
Fax: 01244 403188
e-mail: tis@chestercc.gov.uk

CONGLETON

Town Hall
High Street
Congleton
Cheshire
CW12 1BN
Tel: 01260 271095
Fax: 01260 298243
e-mail: tourism@congleton.gov.uk
website: www.congletonasea.com

KNUTSFORD

Council Offices
Toft Road
Knutsford
Cheshire
WA16 6TA
Tel: 01565 632611
Fax: 01565 652367
e-mail: whats_on@macclesfield.gov.uk
website: www.macclesfield.gov.uk

MACCLESFIELD

Macclesfield
Town Hall
Macclesfield
Cheshire
SK10 1DX
Tel: 01625 504114
Fax: 01625 504116
e-mail: Informationcentre@macclesfield.gov.uk
website: www.macclesfield.gov.uk

NANTWICH

Church House
Church Walk
Nantwich
Cheshire
CW5 5RG
Tel: 01270 610983
Fax: 01270 610880
e-mail: touristi@netcentral.co.uk

NORTHWICH

1 The Arcade
Northwich
Cheshire
CW9 5AS
Tel: 01606 353534
Fax: 01606 353516
e-mail: cberesford@valeroyal.gov.uk

RUNCORN

6 Church Street
Runcorn
Cheshire
WA7 1LT
Tel: 01928 576776
Fax: 01928 569656
e-mail: tourist.info@halton-borough.gov.uk
website: www.halton.gov.uk

STOCKPORT

Graylaw House
Chestergate
Stockport
Cheshire
SK1 1NH
Tel: 0161 474 4444
Fax: 0161 429 6348
e-mail: tourist.information@stockport.gov.uk
website: www.stockport.gov.uk

WARRINGTON

The Market Hall
Academy Way
Warrington
Cheshire
WA1 2EN
Tel: 01925 632571
Fax: 01925 574735
e-mail: informationcentre@warrington.gov.uk

GREATER MANCHESTER

BOLTON

Town Hall
Victoria Square
Bolton
Greater Manchester
BL1 1RU
Tel: 01204 334400
Fax: 01204 398101
e-mail: touristinfo@bolton.gov.uk

BURY

The Met Arts Centre
Market Street
Bury
Greater Manchester
BL9 0BN
Tel: 0161 253 5111
Fax: 0161 253 5919
e-mail: touristinformation@bury.gov.uk

ENGLAND'S NORTH WEST VISITOR CENTRE

Tourist Information Centre
Portland Street
Manchester
Greater Manchester
Tel: 0845 600 6040

MANCHESTER (TOWN HALL)

Manchester Visitor Centre
Town Hall Extension
Lloyd St
Manchester
Greater Manchester
M60 2LA
Tel: 0161 234 3157 (0161 234 3158)
Fax: 0161 236 9900
e-mail: manchester-visitor-centre@notes.manchester.gov.uk

MANCHESTER AIRPORT (TRM 2)

International Arrivals Hall
Terminal 2
Manchester Airport
Manchester

Greater Manchester
M90 4TU
Tel: 0161 489 6412
Fax: 0161 489 6413
e-mail: miat2@nwtb2.u-net.com

MANCHESTER AIRPORT (TRM 1)

International Arrivals Hall
Terminal 1
Manchester Airport
Manchester
Greater Manchester
M90 3NY
Tel: 0161 436 3344
Fax: 0161 489 8831
e-mail: miat1@nwtb2.u-net.com

SADDLEWORTH

Saddleworth Museum
High Street
Uppermill
Saddleworth
Oldham
Greater Manchester
OL3 6HS
Tel: 01457 870336
Fax: 01457 870336
e-mail: ecs.saddleworthtic@oldham.gov.uk

SALFORD

1 The Quays
Salford
Greater Manchester
M5 2SQ
Tel: 0161 848 8601
Fax: 0161 872 3848
e-mail: christine.ellis@salford.gov.uk

WIGAN

Trencherfield Mill
Wallgate
Wigan
Greater Manchester
WN3 4EL
Tel: 01942 825677
Fax: 01942 825677
e-mail: infounit@wiganmbc.gov.uk

LANCASHIRE

ACCRINGTON

Town Hall
Blackburn Road
Accrington
Lancashire
BB5 1LA
Tel: 01254 872595
Fax: 01254 380291
e-mail: infopoint@acc11.fsnet.co.uk

ASHTON-UNDER-LYNE
32 Market Street
Ashton-Under-Lyne
Lancashire
OL6 6ER
Tel: 0161 343 4343
Fax: 0161 343 7225
e-mail:
tourist.information@mail.tameside.gov.uk

BARNOLDSWICK
The Council Shop
Fernlea Avenue
Barnoldswick
Lancashire
BB18 5DL
Tel: 01282 666704
Fax: 01282 666704

BENTHAM
26 Main St
High Bentham
Via Lancaster
Lancashire
LA2 7HL
Tel : 015242 62549
Fax : 015242 61030
e-mail: post@benthamdt.demon.co.uk

BLACKBURN
Tourist Information Centre
15-17 Railway Road
Blackburn
Lancashire
BB1 5AX
Tel (01254 53277)
Fax: 01254 683536
e-mail: paulin.whittaker@blackburn.gov.uk
www.blackburn.gov.uk

BLACKPOOL (CLIFTON STREET)
1 Clifton Street
Blackpool
Lancashire
FY1 1LY
Tel: 01253 478222
Fax: 01253 478210
e-mail: tic@blackpool.gov.uk

BLACKPOOL (PLEASURE BEACH)
Blackpool Pleasure Beach
Unit 25
Ocean Boulevard
Blackpool
Lancashire
FY4 1PL
Tel: 01253 403223
Fax: 01253 408718
e-mail: andrew.carruthers@bpbltd.com

BURNLEY
Tourist Information Centre
Burnley Mechanics
Manchester Road
Burnley
Lancashire
BB11 1JA
Tel. (01282 664421)
Fax: 01282 664431
e-mail: tic@burnley.gov.uk
website: www.burnley.gov.uk

CLEVELEYS
Victoria Square
Thornton
Cleveleys
Lancashire
FY5 1AU
Tel: 01253 853378
Fax: 01253 866124

CLITHEROE
12-14 Market Place
Clitheroe
Lancashire
BB7 2DA
Tel: 01200 425566
Fax: 01200 414488
e-mail: tourism@ribblevalley-gov.uk

FLEETWOOD
Old Ferry Office
The Esplanade
Fleetwood
Lancashire
FY7 6DL
Tel: 01253 773953
Fax: 01253 876656

GARSTANG
Discovery Centre
High Street
Garstang
Lancashire
PR3 1FU
Tel: 01995 602125
Fax: 01253 604325

LANCASTER (CUMBRIA GATEWAY)
Lancaster Services
M6 North
White Carr Lane,
Bay Horse
Lancaster
Lancashire
LA2 9DU
Tel: 01524 792181
Fax: 01524 792676

LANCASTER

29 Castle Hill
Lancaster
Lancashire
LA1 1YN
Tel: 01524 32878
Fax: 01524 847472
e-mail: athomas@lancaster.gov.uk

LYTHAM ST ANNES

67 St Annes Road West
Lytham St Annes
Lancashire
FY8 1SH
Tel: 0906 680 0033
Fax: 01253 640708
e-mail: touristinformation@fylde.gov.uk

MORECAMBE

Old Station Buildings
Marine Road Central
Morecambe
Lancashire
LA4 4DB
Tel: 01524 582808
Fax: 01524 832549
e-mail: tourism@lancaster.gov.uk

OLDHAM

12 Albion Street
Oldham
Lancashire
OL1 3BD
Tel: 0161 627 1024
Fax: 0161 911 3064
e-mail: els.tourist@oldham.gov.uk

PENDLE HERITAGE CENTRE

Park Hill
Barrowford
Nelson
Lancashire
BB9 6JQ
Tel: 01282 661701
Fax: 01282 661701
e-mail: tic@htnw.co.uk

PRESTON

The Guildhall
Lancaster Road
Preston
Lancashire
PR1 1HT
Tel: 01772 253731
Fax: 01772 563850
e-mail: tourism@preston.gov.uk

RAWTENSTALL

41-45 Kay Street
Rawtenstall
Rossendale
Lancashire
BB4 7LS
Tel: 01706 226590 (01706 244678)
Fax: 01706 226590
e-mail: rossendale_leisure@compuserve.com

ROCHDALE

The Clock Tower
Town Hall
Rochdale
Lancashire
OL16 1AB
Tel: 01706 356592
Fax: 01706 864215
e-mail: tic@rochdale.gov.uk

MERSEYSIDE

BIRKENHEAD

Tourist Information Centre
Woodside Ferry Terminal
Birkenhead
Merseyside
CH41 6DU
Tel (01516 476780)
website: www.wirral.gov.uk

LIVERPOOL

Tourist Information Centre
Queen Square Building
Roe Street
Liverpool
Merseyside
L1 1RG
Tel (09066 806886)
e-mail: askme@visitliverpool.com
website: www.visitliverpool.com

LIVERPOOL

Tourist Information Centre
Unit 4
Atlantic Pavilion
Albert Dock
Liverpool
Merseyside
L3 4AE
Tel (09066 806886)
e-mail: askme@visitliverpool.com
website: www.visitliverpool.com

SOUTHPORT

Tourist Information Centre
112 Lord Street
Southport
Merseyside
PR8 1NY
Tel (01704 533333)
e-mail: sue@visitsouthport.org.uk
website: www.visitsouthport.com

INDEX OF TOWNS, VILLAGES AND PLACES OF INTEREST

LIST OF ADVERTISERS

HIDDEN PLACES ORDER FORM

To order any of our publications just fill in the payment details below and complete the order form **overleaf**. For orders of less than 4 copies please add £1 per book for postage and packing. Orders over 4 copies are P & P free.

NAME: ....

ADDRESS: ....

....

....

POSTCODE: ....

TEL NO: ....

Please Complete Either:

I enclose a cheque for £ .... made payable to Travel Publishing Ltd

Or Visa/Mastercard Details

Card No: ....

Expiry Date: ....

Signature: ....

Please either send, telephone or e-mail your order to:

Travel Publishing Ltd, 7a Apollo House, Calleva Park,
Aldermaston, Berkshire RG7 8TN
Tel : 0118 981 7777   Fax: 0118 982 0077
e-mail: karen@travelpublishing.co.uk
website: www.travelpublishing.co.uk

	Price	Quantity	Value

Hidden Places Regional Titles

	Price	Quantity	Value
Cambs & Lincolnshire	£7.99	_____	_____
Chilterns	£8.99	_____	_____
Cornwall	£8.99	_____	_____
Derbyshire	£8.99	_____	_____
Devon	£8.99	_____	_____
Dorset, Hants & Isle of Wight	£8.99	_____	_____
East Anglia	£8.99	_____	_____
Gloucs, Wiltshire & Somerset	£8.99	_____	_____
Heart of England	£7.99	_____	_____
Hereford, Worcs & Shropshire	£7.99	_____	_____
Highlands & Islands	£7.99	_____	_____
Kent	£8.99	_____	_____
Lake District & Cumbria	£8.99	_____	_____
Lancashire & Cheshire	£8.99	_____	_____
Lincolnshire & Nottinghamshire	£8.99	_____	_____
Northumberland & Durham	£8.99	_____	_____
Sussex	£7.99	_____	_____
Thames Valley	£7.99	_____	_____
Yorkshire	£8.99	_____	_____

Hidden Places National Titles

	Price	Quantity	Value
England	£9.99	_____	_____
Ireland	£9.99	_____	_____
Scotland	£9.99	_____	_____
Wales	£9.99	_____	_____

Hidden Inns Titles

	Price	Quantity	Value
East Anglia	£5.99	_____	_____
Heart of England	£5.99	_____	_____
Lancashire & Cheshire	£5.99	_____	_____
South	£5.99	_____	_____
South East	£5.99	_____	_____
South and Central Scotland	£5.99	_____	_____
North of England	£5.99	_____	_____
Wales	£5.99	_____	_____
Welsh Borders	£5.99	_____	_____
West Country	£5.99	_____	_____
Yorkshire	£5.99	_____	_____
	Postage	_____	_____
	TOTAL	_____	_____

For orders of less than 4 copies please add £1 per book for postage & packing. Orders over 4 copies P & P free.

HIDDEN PLACES ORDER FORM

To order any of our publications just fill in the payment details below and complete the order form **overleaf**. For orders of less than 4 copies please add £1 per book for postage and packing. Orders over 4 copies are P & P free.

NAME: ....

ADDRESS: ....

....

....

POSTCODE: ....

TEL NO: ....

Please Complete Either:

I enclose a cheque for £ .... made payable to Travel Publishing Ltd

Or Visa/Mastercard Details

Card No: ....

Expiry Date: ....

Signature: ....

Please either send, telephone or e-mail your order to:

Travel Publishing Ltd, 7a Apollo House, Calleva Park,
Aldermaston, Berkshire RG7 8TN
Tel : 0118 981 7777   Fax: 0118 982 0077
e-mail: karen@travelpublishing.co.uk
website: www.travelpublishing.co.uk

Comment or Reason for Recommendation:

_____

_____

_____

_____

_____

_____

_____

_____

_____

_____

_____

_____

_____

_____

_____

_____

_____

Signed: _____

Date: _____